International Journal on Advances in Telecommunications

2017 vol. 10 nr. 1&2

Printed from e-media with permission by:

Curran Associates, Inc.
57 Morehouse Lane
Red Hook, NY 12571

Some format issues inherent in the e-media version may also appear in this print version.

Printed by Curran Associates, Inc. (2018)

International Academy, Research, and Industry Association (IARIA)
412 Derby Way
Wilmington, DE 19810

Phone: (408) 893-6407
Fax: (408) 527-6351

petre@iaria.org

Additional copies of this publication are available from:

Curran Associates, Inc.
57 Morehouse Lane
Red Hook, NY 12571 USA
Phone: 845-758-0400
Fax: 845-758-2633
Email: curran@proceedings.com
Web: www.proceedings.com

The *International Journal on Advances in Telecommunications* is published by IARIA.
ISSN: 1942-2601
journals site: http://www.iariajournals.org
contact: petre@iaria.org

Sponsored by IARIA
www.iaria.org

International Journal on Advances in Telecommunications
Volume 10, Number 1 & 2, 2017

Miguel Arjona Ramirez, São Paulo University, Brasil
Radu Arsinte, Technical University of Cluj-Napoca, Romania
Tulin Atmaca, Institut Mines-Telecom/ Telecom SudParis, France
Mario Ezequiel Augusto, Santa Catarina State University, Brazil
Marco Aurelio Spohn, Federal University of Fronteira Sul (UFFS), Brazil
Philip L. Balcaen, University of British Columbia Okanagan - Kelowna, Canada
Marco Baldi, Università Politecnica delle Marche, Italy
Ilija Basicevic, University of Novi Sad, Serbia
Carlos Becker Westphall, Federal University of Santa Catarina, Brazil
Mark Bentum, University of Twente, The Netherlands
David Bernstein, Huawei Technologies, Ltd., USA
Eugen Borcoci, University "Politehnica"of Bucharest (UPB), Romania
Fernando Boronat Seguí, Universidad Politecnica de Valencia, Spain
Christos Bouras, University of Patras, Greece
Martin Brandl, Danube University Krems, Austria
Julien Broisin, IRIT, France
Dumitru Burdescu, University of Craiova, Romania
Andi Buzo, University "Politehnica" of Bucharest (UPB), Romania
Shkelzen Cakaj, Telecom of Kosovo / Prishtina University, Kosovo
Enzo Alberto Candreva, DEIS-University of Bologna, Italy
Rodrigo Capobianco Guido, São Paulo State University, Brazil
Hakima Chaouchi, Telecom SudParis, France
Silviu Ciochina, Universitatea Politehnica din Bucuresti, Romania
José Coimbra, Universidade do Algarve, Portugal
Hugo Coll Ferri, Polytechnic University of Valencia, Spain
Noel Crespi, Institut TELECOM SudParis-Evry, France
Leonardo Dagui de Oliveira, Escola Politécnica da Universidade de São Paulo, Brazil
Kevin Daimi, University of Detroit Mercy, USA
Gerard Damm, Alcatel Lucent, USA
Francescantonio Della Rosa, Tampere University of Technology, Finland
Chérif Diallo, Consultant Sécurité des Systèmes d'Information, France
Klaus Drechsler, Fraunhofer Institute for Computer Graphics Research IGD, Germany
Jawad Drissi, Cameron University , USA
António Manuel Duarte Nogueira, University of Aveiro / Institute of Telecommunications, Portugal
Alban Duverdier, CNES (French Space Agency) Paris, France
Nicholas Evans, EURECOM, France
Fabrizio Falchi, ISTI - CNR, Italy
Mário F. S. Ferreira, University of Aveiro, Portugal
Bruno Filipe Marques, Polytechnic Institute of Viseu, Portugal
Robert Forster, Edgemount Solutions, USA
John-Austen Francisco, Rutgers, the State University of New Jersey, USA
Kaori Fujinami, Tokyo University of Agriculture and Technology, Japan
Shauneen Furlong , University of Ottawa, Canada / Liverpool John Moores University, UK
Ana-Belén García-Hernando, Universidad Politécnica de Madrid, Spain
Bezalel Gavish, Southern Methodist University, USA
Christos K. Georgiadis, University of Macedonia, Greece

International Journal on Advances in Telecommunications
Volume 10, Numbers 1 & 2, 2017

CONTENTS

Interference Suppression and Signal Detection for LTE and WLAN Signals in Cognitive Radio Applications

Johanna Vartiainen
and Risto Vuohtoniemi

Centre for Wireless
Communications
University of Oulu
Oulu, Finland
Email: johanna.vartiainen@oulu.fi
Email: risto.vuohtoniemi@oulu.fi

Attaphongse Taparugssanagorn
and Natthanan Promsuk

School of Engineering and Technology
ICT Department, Telecommunications
Asian Institute of Technology (AIT)
Pathum Thani, Thailand
Email: attaphongset@ait.asia
Email: st117805@ait.asia

***Abstract*—Cognitive radio spectrum is traditionally divided into two spaces. Black space is reserved to primary users transmissions and secondary users are able to transmit in white space. To get more capacity, black space has been divided into black and grey spaces. Grey space includes interfering signals coming from primary and other secondary users, so the need for interference suppression has grown. Novel applications like Internet of Things generate narrowband interfering signals. In this paper, the performance of the forward consecutive mean excision algorithm (FCME) method is studied in the presence of narrowband interfering signals. In addition, the extension of the FCME method called the localization algorithm based on double-thresholding (LAD) method that uses three thresholds is proposed to be used for both narrowband interference suppression and intended signal detection. Both Long Term Evolution (LTE) signal simulations and real-world LTE and Wireless Local Area Network (WLAN) signal measurements were used to verify the usability of the methods in future cognitive radio applications.**

***Keywords*–interference suppression; signal detection; grey zone; cognitive radio; measurements.**

I. INTRODUCTION

Heavily used spectrum calls for new technologies and innovations. Novel applications and signals like Long Term Evolution (LTE) generate novel interfering environments like discussed in COCORA 2016 [1]. Cognitive radio (CR) [2][3][4] [5][6][7] offers possibility to effective spectrum usage allowing secondary users (SU) to transmit at unreserved frequencies if they guarantee that primary users (PU) transmissions are not disturbed. Earlier, spectrum was divided into two zones (spaces): black and white zone. As black zone was fully reserved to PUs and off limits to secondary users, their transmission was allowed in white zones where there were no PU transmissions. The problem in this classification is that if the spectrum is not totally unused, secondary users are not able to transmit. Thus, the spectrum usage is not as efficient as it could be. Instead, spectra can be divided into three zones: white, grey (or gray) and black zone [8]. In this model, the SU transmission is allowed in white and grey spaces, as black spaces are reserved for PUs.

Cognitive radio has several novel applications. Long Term Evolution Advanced (LTE-A) is a 4G mobile communication technology [9]. LTE for M2M communication (LTE-M) exploits cognitive radio technology and utilizes flexible and intelligent spectrum usage. Its focus is on high capacity. LTE-A enables one of the newest topics called Wide Area Internet of Things (IoT) [10], where sensors, systems and other smart devices are connected to Internet. Therein, long-range communication, long battery life and minimal amount of data, as well as narrow bandwidth are key issues. IoT (or, widely thinking, Network of Things, NoT [11]) is already here. However, there are several problems and challenges. Many IoT devices use already overcrowded unlicensed bands. Another possibility is to use operated mobile communication networks but it wastes financial/frequency resources and technologies like 3G and LTE do not support IoT directly. Secondly, radio networks come more and more complex. Self-organized networks (SON) [12] form a key to manage complex IoT networks. One of the existing SON solutions is LTE standard. However, SON has no intelligent learning aka cognitivity. Cognitive IoT (CIoT) term has been proposed to highlight required intelligence [13][14]. CIoT can be considered to be a technological revolution that brings a new era of communication, connectivity and computing. It has been predicted that by 2020, there are billions of connected devices in the world [15]. Thus, cognitivity is really needed.

As cognitive radio technology offers more efficient spectrum use, there are many challenges. One of those is that the cognitive world is an interference-intensive environment. Especially in-band interfering signals cause problems. There are three main types of interference in CR: from SU to PU (SU-PU interference), from PU to SU (PU-SU interference), and interference among SUs (SU-SU interference) [16][17]. The basic idea in CR is that SU must not interfere PUs, so there should not be SU-PU interference. Instead, SU may be interfered by PUs or other SUs. When there are multiple PUs and SUs with different applications and technologies, cumulative interference is a problematic task [18]. In grey spaces, there is interference from PU (and possible other SU) transmissions. It is efficient to mitigate unknown interference in order to achieve higher capacity. Therefore, interference suppression (IS) methods are needed.

It is crystal clear that when operating in real-world with mobile devices and varying environment, computational complexity is one of the key issues. Fast and reliable as well as cost-effective, powersave and adaptive methods are needed. Thus, it is beneficial if one method does several operations. In this paper, a transform domain IS method called the forward consecutive mean excision (FCME) algorithm [19][20] is used for interfering signal suppression (IS) in cognitive radio applications [1]. Its extension called the localization algorithm based on double-thresholding (LAD) method [21][22] can be used for intended signal detection. Both the methods detect all kind of signals regardless of their modulation types. The difference is that the LAD method is more accurate and, thus, suitable for detection. Thus, the extended LAD method that uses three thresholds is proposed to be used for both interference suppression and intended signal detection. The FCME algorithm and the LAD method are blind constant false alarm rate (CFAR) -type methods that are able to find all kind of relatively narrowband (RNB) signals in all kind of environments and in all kind of frequency areas. Here, RNB means that the suppressed signal is narrowband with respect to the studied bandwidth. The wider the studied band is the wider the suppressed signal can be.

First, future cognitive radio applications and interference environment in cognitive radios are considered. Focus is on IS in SU receiver interfered by PUs and other SUs. A scenario that clarifies the interference environment is presented and IS methods are discussed. The FCME algorithm and LAD methods are presented and those feasibilities are considered. Simulations for LTE-signals are used to verify the performance of the extended LAD method that uses three thresholds. Measurement results for LTE and Wireless Local Area Network (WLAN) signals are used to verify the performance of the FCME IS method.

This paper is organized as follows. The state of art is discussed in Section II. Section III focuses on interference environment in cognitive radios as Section IV considers interference suppression. The FCME algorithm and the LAD method are presented and their feasibility is considered in Section V. Simulation and measurement results are presented in Section VI. Conclusions are drawn in Section VII.

II. State of the Art

Future applications that use cognitive approach include, for example, LTE-A and cognitive IoT [23][24]. LTE-A is an advanced version of LTE. Therein, orthogonal Frequency Division Multiplex (OFDM) signal is used. In OFDM systems, data is divided between several closely spaced carriers. LTE downlink uses OFDM signal as uplink uses Single Carrier Frequency Division Multiple Access (SC-FDMA). Downlink signal has more power than uplink signal. Thus, its interference distance is larger than uplink signals. OFDM offers high data bandwidths and tolerance to interference. As LTE uses 6 bandwidths up to 20 MHz, LTE-A may offer even 100 MHz bandwidth. LTE-A offers about three times greater spectrum efficiency when compared to LTE. In addition, some kind of cognitive characteristics are expected [25][26][27]. RNB interfering signals exist especially at grey zones. This calls for IS.

In the network ecosystem, it is expected that cognitive IoT [28][29] will be the next 'big' thing to focus on. Wide-area IoT is a network of nodes like sensors and it offers connections between/to/from systems and smart devices (i.e., objects) [10][30]. Cognitive IoT enables objects to learn, think and understand both the physical and social world. Connected objects are intelligent and autonomous and they are able to interact with environment and networks so that the amount of human intervention is minimized. Basically, a human cognition process is integrated into IoT system design. Technically, CIoT operates as a transparent bridge between the social and physical world. The radio platform in CIoT devices should be efficient, simple, agile and have low power. CIoT has several advantages, including time, money and effort saving while resource efficiency is increased. It offers adaptable and simple automated systems. CIoT will consist of numerous heterogeneous, interconnected, embedded and intelligent devices that will generate a huge amount of data. The long-range (even tens of kilometers) connection of nodes via cellular connections is expected. Data sent by nodes is minimal and transmissions may seldom occur. Thus, there is no need to use wide bandwidths for a transmission. This saves power consumption but also spectrum resources.

Proposed technologies include, e.g., LoRa ('long range') [31], Neul ('cloud' in English) [32], Global System for Mobile (GSM), SigFox [33], and LTE-M [34]. As Neul is able to operate in bands below 1 GHz and LoRa as well as SigFox operate in ISM band, LTE-M operates in LTE frequencies. In SigFox, messages are 100 Hz wide. In Neul, 180 kHz band is needed. A common thing is that the ultra-narrowband (UNB) signals are proposed to be used. For example, LTE-M (BW 1.4 MHz) and narrowband IoT (NB-IoT) in LTE bands (BW 200 kHz) are studied. In LTE-M, maximum transmit power is of the order of 20 dBm. In the Third-Generation Partnership Project's (3GPP) Radio Access Network Plenary Meeting 69, it was decided to standardize narrowband IoT [35][36]. Most of those technologies are on the phase of development. In any case, it is expected that the amount of narrowband signals is growing. Thus, IS is required, especially when it is operated in mobile bands.

III. Interference Environment in CR

The received discrete-time signal is assumed to be of form

$$r(n) = \sum_{i=1}^{m} s_i(n) + \sum_{j=1}^{p} i_j(n) + \eta, n \in \mathbb{Z}, \quad (1)$$

where $s_i(n)$ is the ith intended (relatively) narrowband signal, $i_j(n)$ is the jth unknown (relatively) narrowband interfering signal, m is the number of intended signals, p is the number of interfering signals, and η is a complex additive white Gaussian noise (AWGN) with variance σ_η^2. Here, relatively narrowband signal means that the joint bandwidth of the intended and interfering signal(s) is less than 80% of the total bandwidth, so the FCME method is able to operate [19].

In modern CR, the spectrum is divided into three zones - white, grey and black. In Figure 1, zone classification is presented. It is assumed that PU-SU distance is >y km in the white zone, <x km in the black zone, and in the grey zone it holds that x km <PU-SU-distance <y km [37]. It means that if SU is more than y km from the PU, SU is allowed to transmit. If SU is closer than y km but further than x km from the PU, SU may be able to transmit with low power. Spectrum sensing

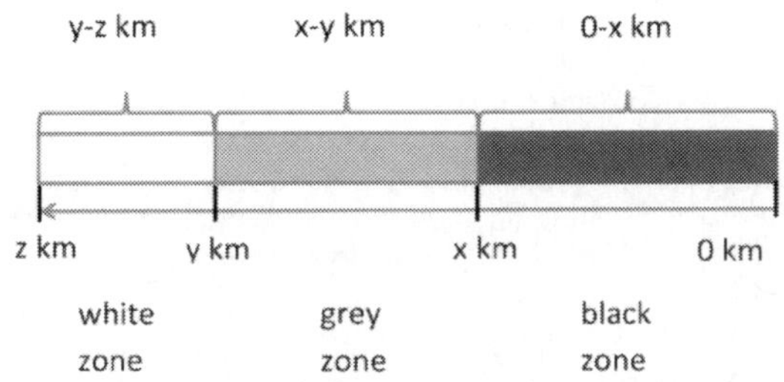

Figure 1: White, grey and black zones.

is required before transmission and there are interfering signals so IS is needed to ensure SU transmissions. If PU-SU distance is less than x km, SU transmission is not allowed.

Interference environment differs between the zones. White space contains only noise. Therein, the noise is most commonly additive white Gaussian (AWGN) noise at the receiver's front-end, and man-made noise. This is related to the used frequency band. Grey space contains interfering signals within the noise, which causes challenges. Grey space is occupied by PU (and possible other SU) signals with low to medium power that means interference with low to medium power. IS is required especially is this zone. Black space includes communications signals, possible interfering signals, and noise. In black space, there are PU signals with high power and SUs have no access.

There must be some rules that enable SUs to transmit in grey zone without causing any harm to PUs. According to [38], SU can transmit at the same time as PU if the limit of interference temperature at the desired receiver is not reached. In [3], it is considered the maximum amount of interference that a receiver is able to tolerate, i.e., an interference temperature model. This can be used when studying interference from SU to PU network. In [39], primary radio network (PRN) defines some interference margin. This can be done based on channel conditions and target performance metric. Interference margin is broadcasted to the cognitive radio network. In any case, the maximum transmit power of SUs is limited.

In our scenario presented in Figure 2, it is assumed that we have one PU base station (BS), several PU mobile stations and several SUs. SU terminals form microcells. Part or all of SUs are mobile and part of SUs may be intelligent devices or sensors (i.e., IoT). Between SUs, weak signal powers are needed for a transmission. One microcell can consist of, for example, devices in an office room. They can use the same or different signal types than PU. For example, in the office room case, WLAN can be used. Between the intelligent devices (IoT), UNB signals are used. It is assumed that SUs operate at grey zone, so IS is required to ensure the quality of SU transmissions.

SUs measure signals transmitted by PU base stations and estimate relative distance to them. Using this information, SUs know whether their short range communication will cause harmful interference to the PU base station. To enable secondary transmissions under continuous interference caused by the PU base station this interference is attenuated by IS.

The secondary access point knows the locations of PU terminals or SUs measure the power levels of the signals

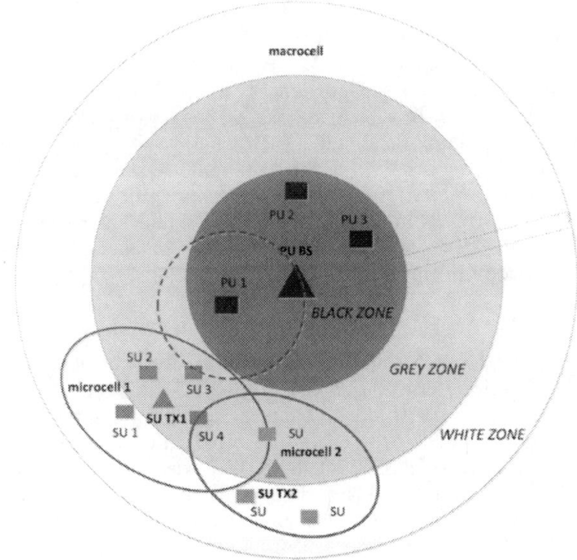

Figure 2: Scenario with one macrocell and two microcells.

coming from PU mobile terminals in the uplink. If it is assumed that SUs know the locations of PUs, SUs do not interfere with PUs. If SUs do not know PUs locations, their transmission is allowed when received PU signal power is below some predetermined threshold. If the level of the power coming from a certain primary terminal is small, it is assumed that secondary transmission generates negligible interference towards primary terminal. However, it may happen that SUs don't sense closely spaced silent PUs.

Let us consider microcell 1 in Figure 2. There are one SU transmitter SU TX1 and four terminals SU $i, i = 1, \cdots, 4$. In addition to the intended signal from SU TX1, SU 1 receives the noise η, SU 2 receives PU downlink (PU BS) signal and the noise η, SU 3 receives PU downlink (PU BS) and PU uplink (PU 1) signals and the noise η, and SU 4 receives PU downlink (PU BS) signal, signal from other microcell's SU, and the noise η. That is, we get from (1) that

$$r_1(n) = s(n) + \eta, \tag{2}$$

$$r_2(n) = s(n) + i_2(n) + \eta, \tag{3}$$

$$r_3(n) = s(n) + \sum_{j=1}^{2} i_j(n) + \eta, \tag{4}$$

$$r_4(n) = s(n) + \sum_{j=2}^{3} i_j(n) + \eta, \tag{5}$$

where $i_1(n)$ is PU 1, $i_2(n)$ is PU BS and $i_3(n)$ is other SU. For example, if it is assumed that PUs are in the LTE-A network and SUs use WLAN signals, receiver SU 2 has to suppress OFDM signal, receiver SU 3 has to suppress OFDM and SC-FDMA signals, and receiver SU 4 has to suppress OFDM and WLAN signals.

In addition, interfering and communication (intended) signals have to be separated from each other. The receiver has to know what signals are interfering signals to be suppressed and what signals are of interest. In an ideal situation, detected and interfering signals have distinct characteristics. However, this is not always the situation. An easy way to separate an interfering signal from the intended signal is to use different bandwidths. For example, in LTE networks, it is known that there are 6 different signal bandwidths between 1.4 and 20 MHz that are used [9]. Especially if a different signal type is used, it is easy to separate interfering signals from our information signal. It can also be assumed that interfering signal has higher power than the desired signal. However, this consideration is out of the scope of this paper.

IV. Interference Suppression

Interference suppression exploits the characteristics of desired/interfering signal by filtering the received signal [40]. After 1970, IS techniques have been widely studied. IS techniques include, for example, filters, cyclostationarity, transform-domain methods like wavelets and short-time Fourier transform (STFT), high order statistics, spatial processing like beamforming and joint detection/multiuser detection [41]. Filter-based IS is performed in the time domain. Those can be further divided into linear and nonlinear methods. Optimal filter (Wiener filter) can be defined only if the interference and signal of interest are known by their Power Spectral Densities (PSDs), which is only possible when they are stationary. Usually, the signal, the interference or both are nonstationary, so adaptive filtering is the alternative capable of tracking their characteristics. Linear predictive filters can be made adaptive using, for example, the least mean square (LMS) algorithm. In filter-based IS, both computational complexity and hardware costs are low but co-channel interference cannot be suppressed, and no interference with similar waveforms to signals can be suppressed. Cyclostationarity based IS has low hardware complexity but medium computational complexity. This may cause challenges in real-time low-power applications.

In transform domain IS [42], signal is suppressed in frequency or in some other transform domain (like fractional Fourier transform). Usually, frequency domain is used, so signal is transformed using the Fourier transform. Computational complexity is medium, but transform domain IS cannot be used when interference and signal-of-interest have the same kind of waveforms and spectral power concentration. However, waveform design may be used. Transform domain IS has low hardware complexity. High-order statistics based IS is computationally complex, and multiple antennas/samplers are needed, so its hardware cost is high and computational complexity too. In beamforming, co-channel interference as well as interference with similar waveforms to the signal of interest can be suppressed, but because of multiple antennas, the hardware cost is high. Its computational complexity is medium.

The less about the interfering signal characteristics is known, the more demanding the IS task will be. As most of the IS methods need some information about the suppressed signals and/or noise, there are some methods that are able to operate blindly [19]. Blind IS methods do not need any *a priori* information about the interfering signals, their modulations or other characteristics. Also, the noise level can be unknown, so it has to be estimated. Blind IS methods are well suited for demanding and varying environments.

V. The FCME and the LAD methods

The adaptively operating FCME method [19] was originally proposed for impulsive IS in the time domain. It was noticed later that the method is practical also in the frequency domain [20]. Earlier, the FCME method has mainly been studied against sinusoidal and impulsive signals that are narrowband ones. The computational complexity of the FCME method is $N\log_2(N)$ due to the sorting [20]. Analysis of the FCME method has been presented in [20].

The FCME method adapts according to the noise level, so no information about the noise level is required. Because the noise is used as a basis of calculation, there is no need for information about the suppressed signals. Even though it is assumed in the calculation that the noise is Gaussian, the FCME method operates even if the noise is not purely Gaussian [20]. In fact, it is sufficient that the noise differs from the signal. When it is assumed that the noise is Gaussian, x^2 (=the energy of samples) has a chi-squared distribution with two degrees of freedom. Thus, the used IS threshold is calculated using [19]

$$T_h = -\ln(P_{FA,DES})\overline{x^2} = T_{CME}\overline{x^2}, \qquad (6)$$

where $T_{CME} = -\ln(P_{FA,DES})$ is the used pre-determined threshold parameter [20], $P_{FA,DES}$ is the desired false alarm rate used in constant false alarm rate (CFAR) methods,

$$\overline{x^2} = \frac{1}{Q}\sum_{i=1}^{Q}|x_i|^2 \qquad (7)$$

denotes the average sample mean, and Q is the size of the set. For example, when it is selected that $P_{FA,DES} = 0.1$ (=10% of the samples are above the threshold in the noise-only case), the threshold parameter $T_{CME} = -\ln(0.1) = 2.3$. In cognitive radio related applications, controlling $P_{FA,DES}$ is important, because $P_{FA,DES}$ is directly related to the loss of spectral opportunities and caused interference [20]. Selection of proper $P_{FA,DES}$ values is discussed more detailed in [20]. The FCME method rearranges the frequency-domain samples in an ascending order according to the sample energy, selects 10% of the smallest samples to form the set Q, and calculates the mean of Q. After that, (6) is used to calculate the first threshold. Then, Q is updated to include all the samples below the threshold, a new mean is calculated, and a new threshold is computed. This is continued until there are no new samples below the threshold. Finally, samples above the threshold are from interfering signal(s) and suppressed.

The FCME algorithm is blind and it is independent of modulation methods, signal types and amounts of signals. It can be used in all frequency areas, from kHz to GHz. The only requirements are that (1) the signal(s) can not cover the whole bandwidth under consideration, and (2) the signal(s) are above the noise level. The first requirement means that the FCME method can be used against RNB signals. For example, 10 MHz signal is wideband when the studied bandwidth is that 10 MHz, but RNB when the studied bandwidth is, e.g., 100 MHz. In fact, it is enough that the interfering signal does not cover more than 80% of the studied bandwidth. However, the narrower the interference is, the better the FCME method operates [43].

The LAD method [21] uses two FCME-thresholds in order to enhance the detection capability of the FCME method

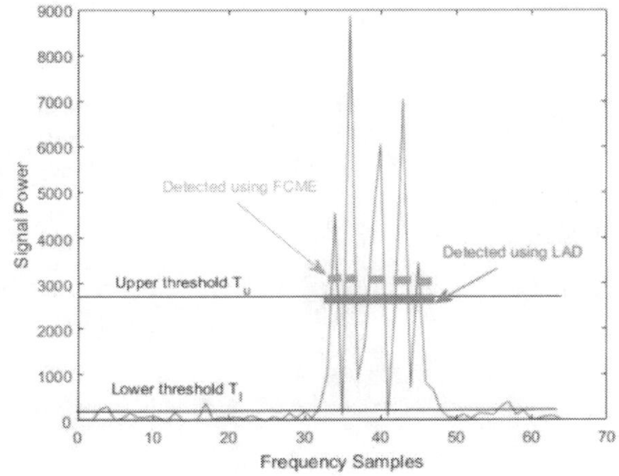

Figure 3: Detection difference between the FCME and LAD methods. The LAD method finds one signal, as FCME finds five.

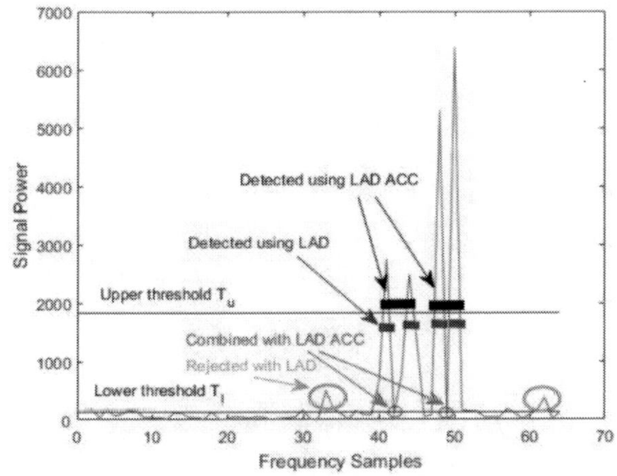

Figure 4: The LAD and LAD ACC methods.

[20]. One threshold is enough for interference suppressing, but causes problems in intended signal detection. If the threshold is too low, too much are detected. Instead, if the threshold is too high, not all the intended signals are detected. In the LAD method, the FCME algorithm is run twice with two different threshold parameters

$$T_{CME1} = -\ln(P_{FA,DES1}) \tag{8}$$

and

$$T_{CME2} = -\ln(P_{FA,DES2}) \tag{9}$$

in order to get two thresholds,

$$T_u = T_{CME1}\overline{x_j^2} \tag{10}$$

and

$$T_l = T_{CME2}\overline{x_l^2}. \tag{11}$$

Selection of proper values of $P_{FA,DES1}$ and $P_{FA,DES2}$ is presented in [20] and in references therein. Usually, $T_{CME1} = 13.81$ ($P_{FA,DES1} = 10^{-4}$) and $T_{CME2} = 2.66$ ($P_{FA,DES2} = 0.07$) are used [20].

After having two thresholds, a clustering is performed. Therein, adjacent samples above the lower threshold are grouped to form a cluster. If the largest element of that cluster exceeds the upper threshold, the cluster is accepted and decided to correspond a signal. Otherwise the cluster is rejected and decided to contain only noise samples. The detection difference between the FCME and LAD methods is illustrated in Figure 3. There is one raised cosine binary phase shift keying (RC-BPSK) signal whose bandwidth is 20% of the total bandwidth and signal-to-noise ratio (SNR) is 10 dB. The LAD method is able to find one signal. Instead, the FCME algorithm finds 5 signals if the upper threshold is used. If the FCME algorithm uses some other lower threshold, it still finds at least 5 signals because of the fluctuation of the signal.

The LAD method with adjacent cluster combining (ACC) [44] enhances the performance of the LAD method. Therein, if two or more accepted clusters are separated by at most p samples below the lower threshold, the accepted clusters are combined together to form one signal. The value of p is, for example, 1, 2 or 3 [20]. This enhances the correctly detected number of signals as well as bandwidth estimation accuracy of the LAD method [22]. In Figure 4, there are two RC-BPSK signals whose bandwidths are 5 and 8% of the total bandwidth. SNRs are 5 and 4 dB. The LAD method finds four signals, as the LAD ACC method finds two signals.

When considering IS, the LAD lower threshold may be too low thus suppressing too much. In addition, the LAD upper threshold may be too high thus suppressing too less. This problem can be solved when extending the LAD method include three thresholds instead of two. Then, the FCME algorithm is run three times with three values of $P_{FA,DES}$ to get three thresholds: the lowest one is the LAD lower threshold T_l, the highest one is the LAD upper threshold T_u, and the threshold in the middle T_m is the threshold used in the IS. Note, that the LAD method corresponds the FCME algorithm when $P_{FA,DES1} = P_{FA,DES2} (= P_{FA,DES3})$.

When both IS and detection are performed, it is possible to perform
(a) both IS and detection at the same time,
(b) first IS and then detection, or
(c) use IS only for detecting interfering signal(s).
Case (a) saves some time because the algorithm is run only once. IS part can be done using only one (T_u, T_m or T_l) or both the thresholds (T_u and T_l). In case (b), IS uses only one threshold (T_u, T_m or T_l) as detection uses both the thresholds (T_u and T_l). Case (c) can be used when the interference situation is mapped, so only one (T_u, T_m or T_l) or both the thresholds (T_u or T_l) can be used. In the latter case, interfering signal characteristics can also be estimated.

VI. Simulations and Measurements

In this paper, both simulations and real-life measurements are considered.

A. Simulations

The IS and signal detection ability of the extended LAD method that uses three thresholds was studied using MATLAB

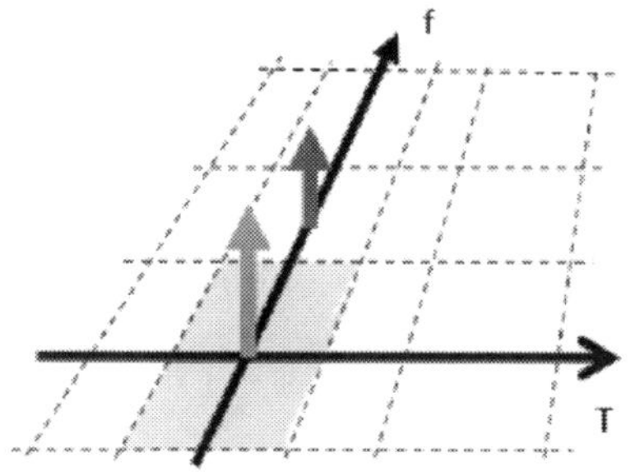

Figure 5: Received signals at receiver. Intended signal and PU-SU interference, T=time and f=frequency.

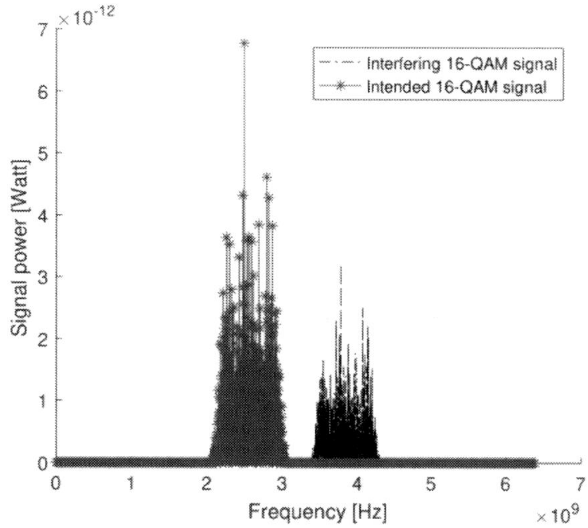

Figure 6: One intended 16-QAM signal and one interfering 16-QAM signal. SNR=15 dB, SIR=12 dB.

simulations. In the simulations the focus was on the last 100 meters at IoT network. There was a total of N devices, which were uniformly and independently deployed in a 2-dimensional circular plane with plane radius R. This deployment results in a 2-D Poisson point distribution of devices. After the network was formed the devices were assumed to be static. The noise was additive white Gaussian noise (AWGN). The signals and the noise were assumed to be uncorrelated. Here, 16-quadrature amplitude modulation (QAM) signal that transmits 4 bits per symbol was used. It is one of the modulation types used in LTE. There were 1024 samples and fast Fourier transformation (FFT) was used. In the simulations, IS and detection were performed at the same time. IS was performed using one threshold $T_m = 6.9$, as detection was performed using two LAD thresholds $T_u = 9.21$ and $T_l = 2.3$. SNR is the ratio of intended signal energy to noise power, as signal-to-interference ratio (SIR) is the ratio of intended signal energy to interfering signal energy.

The first situation is like (3), i.e., there is PU-SU interference (Figure 5). Thus, the received signal is of form $r_2(n) = s(n) + i_2(n) + \eta$, where $s(n)$ and $i_2(n)$ are both 16-QAM signals. Now, $s(n)$ is intended signal (red arrow) as $i_2(n)$ is interfering signal from PU (blue arrow). Their bandwidth covers about 30% of the total bandwidth. In Figure 6, SNR=15 dB and SIR=12 dB, so intended signal is stronger than interfering signal. Figure 7 shows the situation after interference suppression and signal detection. In Figure 8, SNR=12 dB and SIR=15 dB more, so intended signal is weaker than interfering signal. The situation after signal detection and IS is illustrated in Figure 9. It can be said that both the methods perform well.

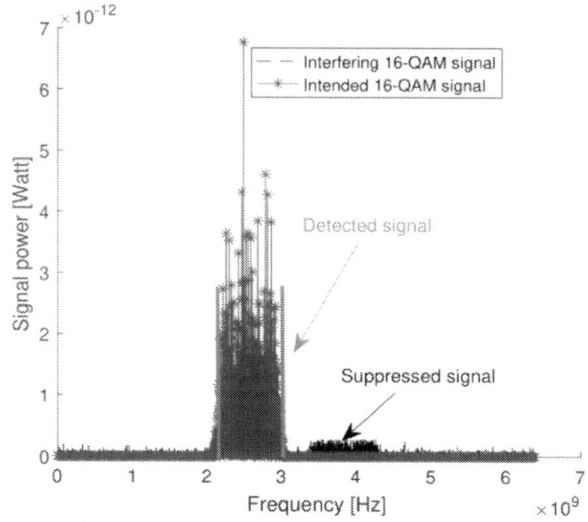

Figure 7: One intended 16-QAM signal and one interfering 16-QAM signal. After interference suppression and detection. SNR=15 dB, SIR=12 dB.

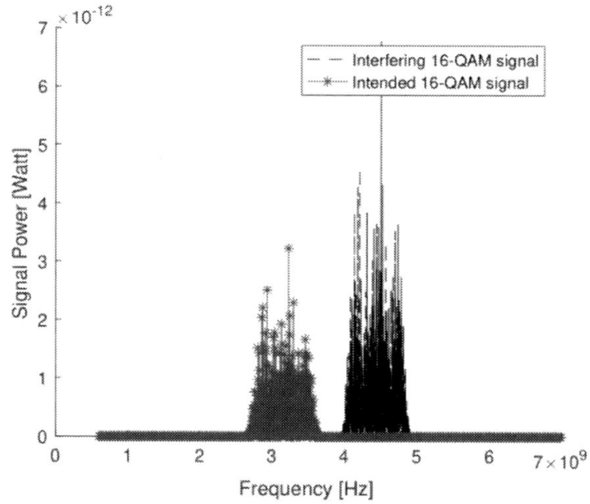

Figure 8: One intended 16-QAM signal and one interfering 16-QAM signal. SNR=12 dB, SIR=15 dB.

Next, $r_4(n) = s(n) + \sum_{j=2}^{3} i_j(n) + \eta$ like in (5). Now

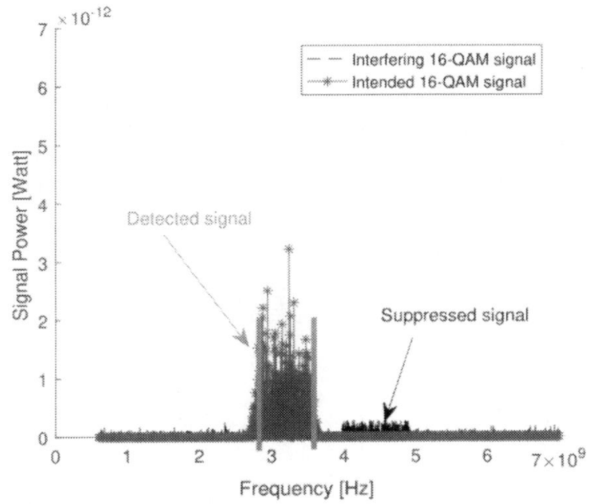

Figure 9: One intended 16-QAM signal and one interfering 16-QAM signal. After interference suppression and detection. SNR=12 dB, SIR=15 dB.

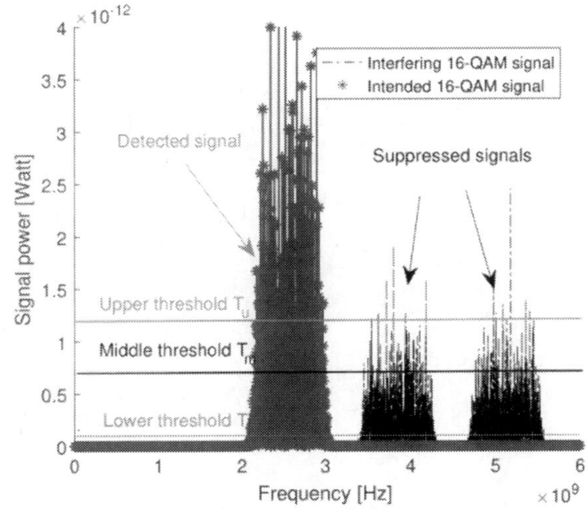

Figure 11: One intended 16-QAM signal and two interfering 16-QAM signals. Interference suppression (T_m) and detection (T_u and T_l) thresholds. SNR=15 dB, SIR=12 dB.

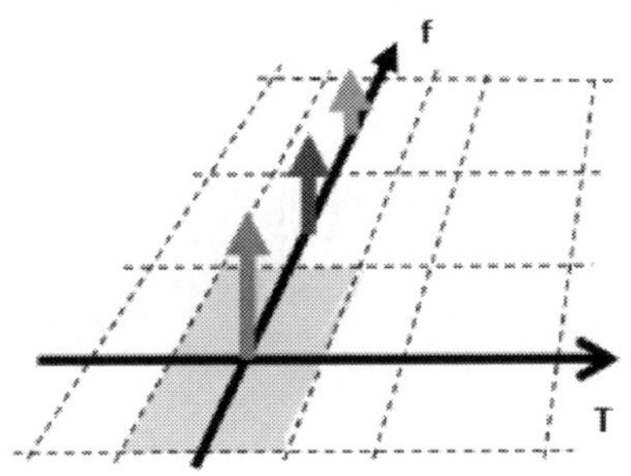

Figure 10: Received signals at receiver. Intended signal, PU-SU and SU-SU interference, T=time and f=frequency.

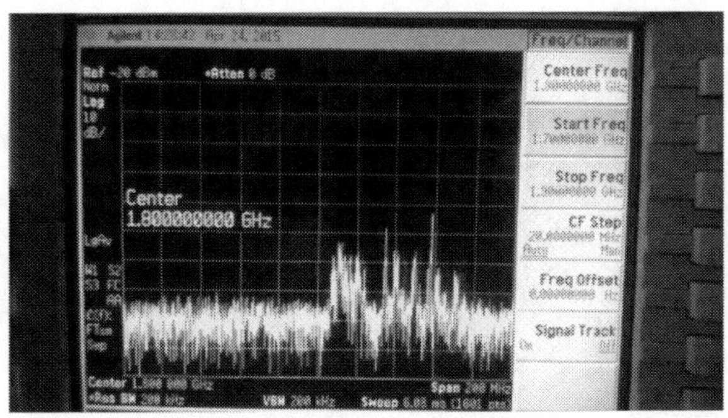

Figure 12: Agilent E4446. LTE1800 network downlink signals.

there are two suppressed signals: one is from PU and one is from other SU so there is both PU-SU and SU-SU interference (Figure 10). Now, $s(n)$ is intended signal (red arrow), $i_2(n)$ is interfering signal from PU (blue arrow), and $i_3(n)$ is interfering signal from other SU (green arrow). Their bandwidth covers about 45% of the total bandwidth. In Figure 11, all the thresholds T_u, T_l and T_m are presented. As the intended signal is detected using theresholds T_u and T_l, the IS is performed using threshold T_m. As can be seen, all the signals are found and both the interfering signals are suppressed.

B. Measurements

The IS performance of the FCME method against RNB signals was studied using real-world wireless data. The results are based on real-life measurements. Measurements were performed using spectrum analyzer Agilent E4446 [45] (Figure 12). Three types of signals were studied, namely the LTE uplink, LTE downlink, and WLAN signals. All those signals are commonly used wireless signals. Both LTE1800 network frequencies and WLAN signals were measured at the University of Oulu, Finland. IS was performed using the FCME method with threshold parameter 4.6, i.e., desired false alarm rate $P_{FA,DES} = 1\% = 0.01$ [20].

LTE1800 network operates at 2×75 MHz band so that uplink is on $1.710 - 1.785$ GHz and downlink is on $1.805 - 1.880$ GHz [46]. LTE downlink uses OFDM signal as uplink uses SC-FDMA. LTE assumes a small nominal guard band (10% of the band, excluding 1.4 MHz case).

One measurement at $1.7 - 1.9$ GHz containing 1000 time domain sweeps and 1601 frequency domain points is seen in Figure 13. Therein, yellow means strong signal power (=signal) as green means weaker signal power (=noise). Therein, only downlink signaling is present. Downlink signals have larger interference distance than uplink signals. Interfering signals cover about 30% of the studied bandwidth. In Figure 14, situation after the FCME IS is presented. Therein, yellow means strong signal power as white means no signal power. It can be seen that the signals (white) have been suppressed and the noise is now dominant (yellow). On uplink signal frequencies where no signals are present (600 first frequency

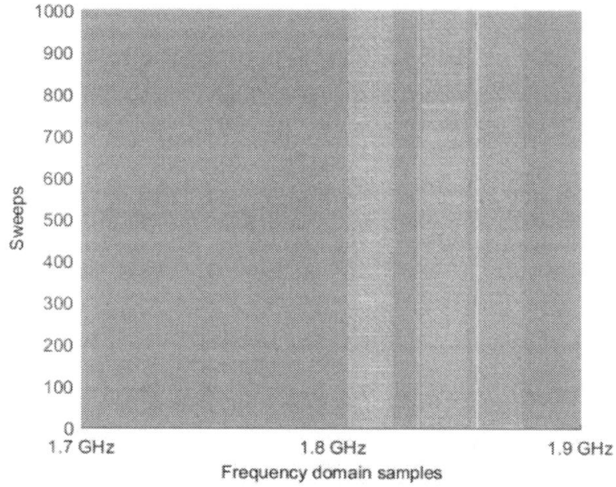

Figure 13: LTE1800 network frequencies. Spectrogram of downlink signals present.

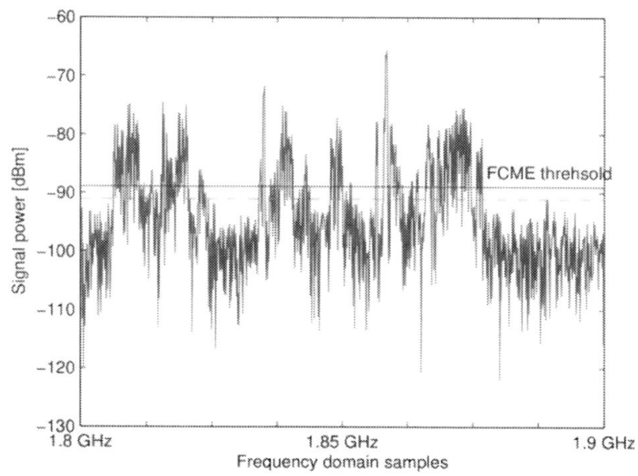

Figure 15: IS using the FCME method for LTE downlink signals. Upper threshold when the FCME calculated on 1.8 – 1.9 GHz, lower threshold (dashed line) when the FCME calculated on 1.7 – 1.9 GHz.

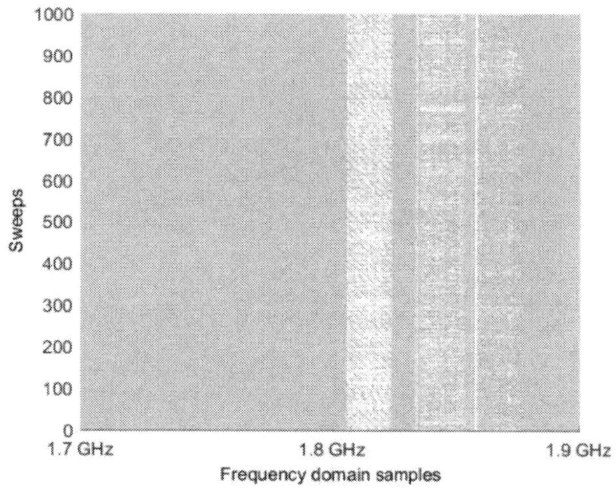

Figure 14: LTE1800 network frequencies. Spectrogram of suppressed downlink signals. The FCME method was used.

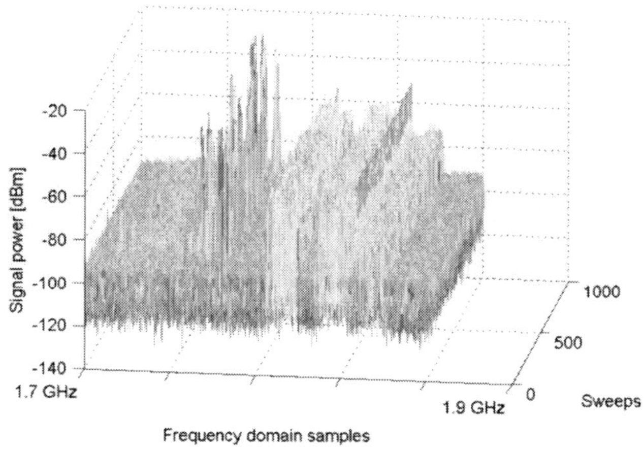

Figure 16: LTE1800 network frequencies. Uplink and downlink signals present.

domain samples), average noise value is −99 dBm before and after IS.

In Figure 15, first line (sweep) of the previous case is presented more closely. The FCME thresholds after two cases are presented. In the first case, the FCME is calculated using frequencies 1.8 – 1.9 GHz (downlink). Interfering signals cover about 60% of the studied bandwidth. The threshold is −89 dBm (upper line). In the second case, the threshold is calculated using both uplink and downlink frequencies 1.7−1.9 GHz when there is no uplink signals (like case in Figure 13), i.e., SU is so far away from PU that only downlink signals are present. Interfering signals cover about 30% of the studied bandwidth. In that case, the threshold is −91 dBm (lower dashed threshold). It can be noticed that when the studied bandwidth is doubled and this extra band contains only noise, we get 2 dB gain.

Next, both uplink and downlink signals are present. There were 2001 frequency domain points and 1000 time sweeps. Figure 16 presents one measurement at 1.7 – 1.9 GHz. Both uplink and downlink signals are present. In Figure 17, one snapshot when both uplink and downlink signals are present is presented. Therein, both signals are suppressed.

In the WLAN measurements, 2.4−2.5 GHz frequency area was used. There were 1000 sweeps and 1201 frequency domain data points. In Figure 18, one snapshot is presented when there is a WLAN signal present and the FCME algorithm is used to perform IS. As can be seen, the WLAN signal is found.

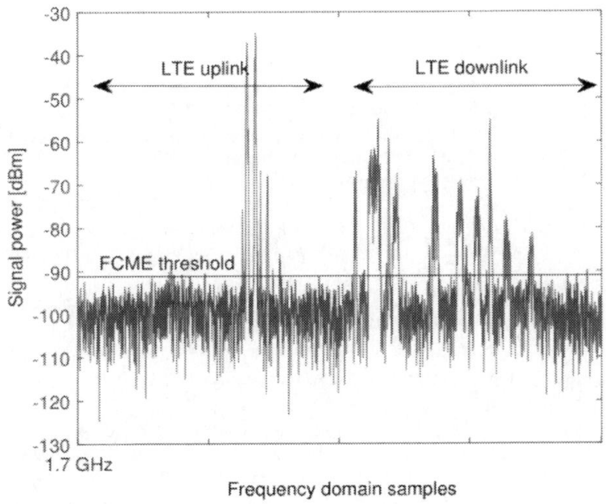

Figure 17: LTE1800 network frequencies. Uplink and downlink signals present. IS using the FCME method.

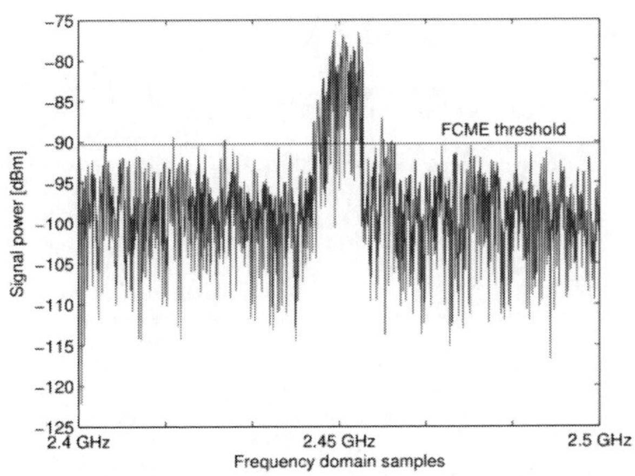

Figure 18: IS using the FCME method at frequencies $2.4-2.5$ GHz where WLAN signals exist. Threshold is -90 dBm.

Next, the desired false alarm rate ($P_{FA,DES}$) values are compared to the achieved false alarm rate (P_{FA}) values in the noise-only case. Figure 19 presents one situation when there is only noise present. According to the definition of the FCME method, threshold parameter 4.6 means that 1% of the samples is above the threshold when there is only noise present. Here, there are 1201 samples so $P_{FA,DES} = 1\% = 12$ samples. In Figure 19, 12 samples are over the threshold, so $P_{FA,DES} = P_{FA}$. We had 896 measurement sweeps in the noise-only case at WLAN frequencies. Therein, minimum 1 sample and maximum 19 samples were over the threshold as the mean was 10 samples and median value was 9 samples. Those were close of required 12 samples. Note that the definition has been made for pure AWGN noise.

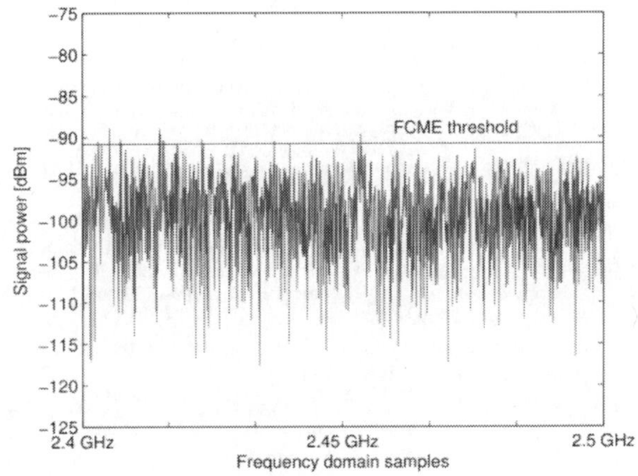

Figure 19: IS using the FCME method at frequencies $2.4-2.5$ GHz where are no signals present. Threshold is -91 dBm. $1\% = 12$ samples are above the threshold, as expected.

VII. Conclusion

In this paper, the performance of the forward consecutive mean excision (FCME) interference suppression method was studied against relatively narrowband interfering signals existing in the novel cognitive radio networks. The focus was on interference suppression in secondary user receiver suffering interfering signals caused by primary and other secondary users. In addition, the extension of the FCME method called the localization algorithm based on double-thresholding (LAD) method that uses three thresholds was proposed to be used for both interference suppression and intended signal detection. LTE simulations confirmed the performance of the extended LAD method that uses three thresholds. Real-world LTE and WLAN measurements were performed in order to verify the performance of the FCME method. It was noted that the extended LAD method that uses three thresholds can be used for detecting and suppressing LTE signals, and the FCME method is able to suppress LTE OFDM and SC-FDMA signals as well as WLAN signals. Our future work includes statistical analysis, more detected and suppressed signals, as well as comparisons to other methods.

ACKNOWLEDGMENT

The research of Johanna Vartiainen was funded by the Academy of Finland.

References

[1] J. Vartiainen and R. Vuohtoniemi, "LTE and WLAN interference suppression in CR applications," in Proc. The Sixth International Conference on Advances in Cognitive Radio (COCORA), Lisbon, Portugal, Feb. 2016, pp. 33–38.

[2] J. Mitola III and G. Q. M. Jr., "Cognitive radio: making software radios more personal," IEEE Pers. Commun., vol. 6, no. 4, 1999, pp. 13–18.

[3] S. Haykin, "Cognitive radio: Brain-empowered wireless communications," IEEE J. Select. Areas Commun., vol. 23, no. 2, Feb. 2005, pp. 201–220.

[4] V. Chakravarthy, A. Shaw, M. Temple, and J. Stephens, "Cognitive radio - an adaptive waveform with spectral sharing capability," in IEEE Wireless Commun. and Networking Conf., New Orleans, LA, USA, Mar.13–17 2005, pp. 724–729.

[5] S. N. Shankar, C. Cordeiro, and K. Challapali, "Spectrum agile radios: Utilization and sensing architectures," in IEEE Int. Symposium on Dynamic Spectrum Access Networks (DySpAN) 2005, vol. 1, Baltimore, USA, Nov. 2005, pp. 160–169.

[6] T. Yucek and H. Arslan, "A survey of spectrum sensing algorithms for cognitive radio applications," IEEE Commun. Surveys and Tutorials, vol. 11, no. 1, 2009, pp. 116–130.

[7] J. Mitola III, "Cognitive radio architecture evolution," IEEE Proceedings, vol. 97, no. 4, 2009, pp. 626–641.

[8] S. Haykin, D. J. Thomson, and J. H. Reed, "Spectrum sensing for cognitive radio - the utility of the multitaper method and cyclostationarity for sensing the radio spectrum, including the digital tv spectrum, is studied theoretically and experimentally," Proc. of the IEEE, vol. 97, no. 5, May 2009, pp. 849–877.

[9] 3GPP, "The mobile broadband standard," (2013), http://www.3gpp.org [retrieved: May, 2017].

[10] K. Ashton, "That 'internet of things' thing," RFID Journal, June 2009, http://www.rfidjournal.com/articles/view?4986 [retrieved: May, 2017].

[11] J. Voas, "Networks of 'things'," NIST Special Publication 800-183, July 2016. http://dx.doi.org/10.6028/NIST. SP.800-183 [retrieved: May, 2017].

[12] O.-C. Iacoboaiea, B. Sayrac, S. B. Jemaa, and P. Bianchi, "SON coordination in heterogenous networks: A reinforcement learning framework," IEEE Trans. Wirel. Commun., vol. 15, no. 9, 2016, pp. 5835–5847.

[13] R. F. Shigueta, M. Fonseca, A. C. Viana, A. Ziviani, and A. Munaretto, "A strategy for opportunistic cognitive channel allocation in wireless internet of things," in IFIP Wireless Days, Rio de Janeiro, Brazil, Nov 2014.

[14] A. Alja and A. H. Aghvami, "Cognitive machine-to-machine communications for internet-of-things: A protocol stack perspective," IEEE IoT Journal, vol. 2, no. 2, 2016, pp. 103–112.

[15] A. Nordrum, "Popular internet of things forecast of 50 billion devices by 2020 is outdated," in IEEE Spectrum, Aug. 2016, http://spectrum.ieee.org/tech-talk/telecom/internet/popular-internet-of-things-forecast-of-50-billion-devices-by-2020-is-outdated [retrieved: May, 2017].

[16] Z. Chen, "Interference modelling and management for cognitive radio networks," Ph.D. dissertation, Doctoral Thesis (submitted), Apr. 2011, http://www.ros.hw.ac.uk/bitstream/10399/2421/1/ChenZ_0511_eps.pdf [retrieved: May, 2017].

[17] K. Nishimori, H. Yomo, and P. Popovski, "Distributed interference cancellation for cognitive radios using periodic signals of the primary system," IEEE Trans. Wirel. Commun., vol. 10, no. 9, 2011, pp. 2971 – 2981.

[18] J. Peha, "Spectrum sharing in the gray space," Telecommunications Policy Journal, vol. 37, no. 2-3, 2013, pp. 167–177.

[19] H. Saarnisaari, P. Henttu, and M. Juntti, "Iterative multidimensional impulse detectors for communications based on the classical diagnostic methods," IEEE Trans. Commun., vol. 53, no. 3, Mar. 2005, pp. 395–398.

[20] J. Vartiainen, "Concentrated signal extraction using consecutive mean excision algorithms," Ph.D. dissertation, Acta Univ Oul Technica C 368. Faculty of Technology, University of Oulu, Finland, Nov. 2010, http://jultika.oulu.fi/Record/isbn978-951-42-6349-1 [retrieved: May, 2017].

[21] J. Vartiainen, J. J. Lehtomäki, and H. Saarnisaari, "Double-threshold based narrowband signal extraction," in Proc. IEEE Veh. Technol. Conf. (VTC) 2005, Stockholm, Sweden, May/June 2005, pp. 1288–1292.

[22] J. Vartiainen, J. J. Lehtomäki, H. Saarnisaari, and M. Juntti, "Two-dimensional signal localization algorithm for spectrum sensing," IEICE Trans. Commun., vol. E93-B, no. 11, Nov. 2010, pp. 3129–3136.

[23] J. A. Stankovic, "Research directions for the internet of things," IEEE Int. of Things Journal, vol. 1, no. 1, Feb. 2014, pp. 3–9.

[24] A. H. Ngu, M. Gutierrez, V. Metsis, S. Nepal, and Q. Z. Sheng, "IoT middleware: A survey on issues and enabling technologies," IEEE Int. of Things Journal, vol. 4, no. 1, Feb. 2017, pp. 1–20.

[25] P. Karunakaran, T. Wagner, A. Scherb, and W. Gerstacker, "Sensing for spectrum sharing in cognitive LTE-A cellular networks," cornell University Library. http://arxiv.org/abs/1401.8226 [retrieved: May, 2017].

[26] L. Zhang, L. Yang, and T. Yang, "Cognitive interference management for LTE-A femtocells with distributed carrier selection," in Proc. IEEE Veh. Technol. Conf. (VTC) Fall, 2010, pp. 1–5.

[27] V. Osa, C. Hearranz, J. F. Monserrat, and X. Gelabert, "Implementing opportunistic spectrum access in LTE-advanced," EURASIP Journal on Wireless Communications and Networking, vol. 99, 2012, pp. 1–17.

[28] Q. Wu et al., "Cognitive internet of things: A new paradigm beyond connection," IEEE Journal of Internet of Things, vol. 1, no. 2, 2014, pp. 1–15, [retrieved: May, 2017].

[29] J. Tervonen, K.Mikhaylov, S. Pieska, J. Jamsa, and M.Heikkila, "Cognitive internet-of-things solutions enabled by wireless sensor and actuator networks," in IEEE Conf. on Cognitive Infocommun. (CogInfoCom), 2014, pp. 97–102.

[30] F. Xia, L. T. Yang, L. Wang, and A. Vine, "Internet of things," Int. Journal of Commun. Systems, vol. 25, 2012, pp. 1101–1102.

[31] LoRa, http://lora-alliance.org/ [retrieved: May, 2017].

[32] Neul, www.neul.com [retrieved: May, 2017].

[33] SigFox, www.sigfox.com [retrieved: May, 2017].

[34] Nokia, "LTE M2M - optimizing LTE for the internet of things," in White paper, 2014, http://networks.nokia.com/file/34496/lte-m-optimizing-lte-for-the-internet-of-things [retrieved: May, 2017].

[35] J. Gozalvez, "New 3GPP standarf for IoT," IEEE Vehicular Technology Magazine, vol. 11, no. 1, Mar. 2016, pp. 14–20.

[36] 3GPP16, "Standardization of NB-IOT completed," (2016), http://www.3gpp.org/news-events/3gpp-news [retrieved: May, 2017].

[37] Z. Feng and Y. Xu, "Cognitive TD-LTE system operating in TV white space in china," ITU-R WP 5A, Geneva, Switzerland, (2013), http://studylib.net/doc/13258156/cognitive-td-lte-system-operating-in-tv-white-space-in-china [retrieved: May, 2017].

[38] J. Mitra and L. Lampe, "Sensing and suppression of impulsive interference," in Canadian Conference on Electrical and Computer Engineering (CCECE), Canada, May 2009, pp. 219–224.

[39] Y. Ma, D. I. Kim, and Z. Wu, "Optimization of OFDMA-based cellular cognitive radio networks," IEEE Trans. on Commun., vol. 58, no. 8, 2010, pp. 2265–2276.

[40] J. Andrews, "Interference cancelation for cellular systems: a contemporary overview," IEEE Wireless Comm., vol. 12, no. 2, Apr. 2005, pp. 19–29.

[41] X. Hong, Z. Chen, C.-X. Wang, S. A. Vorobyov, and J. S. Thompson, "Cognitive radio networks - interference cancelation and management techniques," IEEE Veh. Technol. Magazine, Dec. 2009, pp. 76–84.

[42] L. B. Milstein and P. K. Das, "An analysis of a real-time transform domain filtering digital communication system - part I: Narrowband interference rejection using eral-time Fourier transforms," IEEE Trans. Commun., vol. 28, 1980, pp. 816–824.

[43] J. Vartiainen, J. J. Lehtomäki, H. Saarnisaari, and M. Juntti, "Analysis of the consecutive mean excision algorithms," J. Elect. Comp. Eng., 2011, pp. 1–13.

[44] J. Vartiainen, H. Sarvanko, J. Lehtomäki, M. Juntti, and M. Latva-aho, "Spectrum sensing with LAD based methods," in Proc. IEEE Int. Symp. Pers., Indoor, Mobile Radio Commun. (PIMRC), Athens, Greece, Aug. 2007, pp. 1–5.

[45] Agilent, http://www.agilent.com [retrieved: May, 2017].

[46] Nokia Siemens Networks, "Introducing LTE with maximum reuse of GSM assets," in White paper, 2011, http://www.gsma.com/spectrum/introducing-lte-with-maximum-reuse-of-gsm-asset/ [retrieved: May, 2017].

International Journal on Advances in Telecommunications, vol 10 no 1 & 2, year 2017, http://www.iariajournals.org/telecommunications/

Impact of Analytics and Meta-learning on Estimating Geomagnetic Storms
A Two-stage Framework for Prediction

Taylor K. Larkin[1] and Denise J. McManus[2]
Information Systems, Statistics, and Management Science
Culverhouse College of Commerce
The University of Alabama
Tuscaloosa, AL 35487-0226
Email: tklarkin@crimson.ua.edu[1], dmcmanus@cba.ua.edu[2]

***Abstract*—Cataclysmic damage to telecommunication infrastructures, from power grids to satellites, is a global concern. Natural disasters, such as hurricanes, tsunamis, floods, mud slides, and tornadoes have impacted telecommunication services while costing millions of dollars in damages and loss of business. Geomagnetic storms, specifically coronal mass ejections, have the same risk of imposing catastrophic devastation as other natural disasters. With increases in data availability, accurate predictions can be made using sophisticated ensemble modeling schemes. In this work, one such scheme, referred to as stacked generalization, is used to predict a geomagnetic storm index value associated with 2,811 coronal mass ejection events that occurred between 1996 and 2014. To increase lead time, two rounds (stages) of stacked generalization using data relevant to a coronal mass ejection's life span are executed. Results show that for this dataset, stacked generalization performs significantly better than using a single model in both stages for the most important error metrics. In addition, overall variable importance scores for each predictor variable can be calculated from this ensemble strategy. Utilizing these importance scores can help aid telecommunication researchers in studying the significant drivers of geomagnetic storms while also maintaining predictive accuracy.**

Keywords–ensemble modeling; space weather; quantile regression; stacked generalization; telecommunications.

I. Introduction

Predicting geomagnetic storms is an ever-present problem in today's society, given the increased emphasis on advanced technologies [1]. These storms are fueled by coronal mass ejections (CMEs), which are colossal bursts of magnetic field and plasma from the Sun as displayed in Figure 1. Typically, a CME travels at speeds between 400 and 1,000 kilometers per second [2] resulting in an arrival time of approximately one to four days [3]; however, they can move as slowly as 100 kilometers per second or as quickly as 3,000 kilometers per second (or around 6.7 million miles per hour) [4]. These phenomena can contain a mass of solar material exceeding 10^{13} kilograms (or approximately 22 trillion pounds) [5] and can explode with the force of a billion hydrogen bombs [6]. Naturally, CME events are often associated with solar activity such as sunspots [4]. During the solar minimum of the 11 year solar cycle (the period of time where the Sun has fewer sunspots and, hence, weaker magnetic fields), CME events occur about once a day. During a solar maximum, this daily estimate increases to four or five. One plausible theory for these incidents taking place involves the Sun needing to release energy. As more sunspots develop, more coronal magnetic field structures become entangled; therefore, more energy is required to control the volatility and convolution. Once the energy surpasses a certain level, it becomes beneficial for the Sun to release these complex magnetic structures [2].

When this force approaches Earth, it collides with the magnetosphere. The magnetosphere is the area encompassing Earth's magnetic field and serves as the line of defense against solar winds. The National Oceanic and Atmospheric Administration (NOAA) describes this event as "the appearance of water flowing around a rock in a stream" [7] as shown in Figure 2.

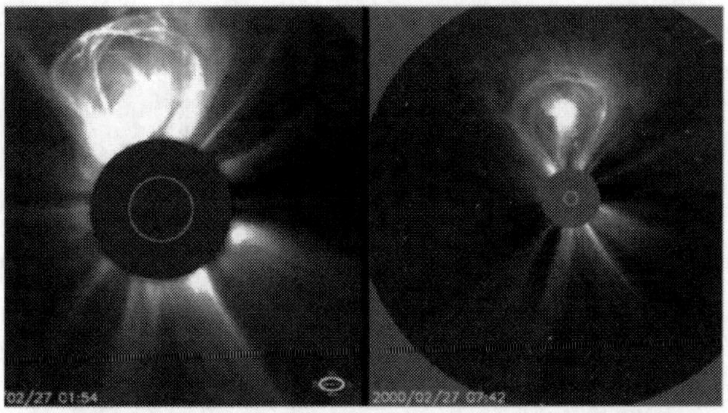

Figure 1. LASCO coronagraph images [4], courtesy of the NASA/ESA SOHO mission.

Figure 2. Rendering of Earth's magnetosphere interacting with the solar wind from the Sun [8], courtesy of the NASA.

After the solar winds compress Earth's magnetic field on the day side (the side facing the Sun), they travel along the elongated magnetosphere into Earth's dark side (the side opposite of the Sun). The electrons are accelerated and energized in the tails of the magnetosphere, filtering down to the Polar Regions and clashing with atmospheric gases causing geomagnetic storms. This energy transfer emits the brilliance known as the *Aurora Borealis*, or Northern Lights, and the *Aurora Australis*, or Southern Lights, which can be seen near the respective poles.

While mainly responsible for the illustrious Northern Lights, geomagnetic storms have the potential to cause cataclysmic damage to Earth. Normally, the magnetic field is able to deflect most of the incoming plasma particles from the Sun. However, when a CME contains a strong southward-directed magnetic field component (B_z), energy is transferred from the CME's magnetic field to Earth's through a process called magnetic reconnection [9][10][11] (as cited in [12]). Magnetic reconnection leads to an injection of plasma particles in Earth's geomagnetic field and a reduction of the magnetosphere towards the equator [2]. Consequently, more energy is amassed in the upper atmosphere, particularly at the poles. Moreover, this energy is impressed upon power transformers causing an acute over-saturation and inducing black-outs via geomagnetically induced currents (GICs) [13]. Some other residuals of this over-accumulation of energy include the corrosion of pipelines, deteriorations of radio and GPS communications, radiation hazards in higher latitudes, damages to spacecrafts, and deficiencies in solar arrays [14]. These ramifications pose a significant threat to global telecommunications and electrical power infrastructures as CMEs continue to be launched towards Earth [15] and remain the primary source of major geomagnetic disturbances [16][17][18] (as cited in [19]). From a business perspective, risk factor mitigation is an absolute necessity within the global business environment [20]. This can be accomplished using advanced analytical techniques on data collected about these phenomena.

The subsequent sections of this work read as follows. Section II introduces previous studies on predicting geomagnetic storms. Section III provides detail about the basics of the methodology used, the dataset studied, and the experimental strategy. Section IV displays and discusses the results as well as postulates areas for future work. Section V concludes with a summary.

II. Literature Review

A. Predicting Dangerous CMEs

CMEs present an ever-increasing threat to Earth as society becomes more dependent on technology, such as satellites and telecommunication operations. Nevertheless, because of this increase in technology, more data has been collected about these acts and the solar wind condition in general. This, in turn, has allowed for empirical models to be developed. Burton, McPherron, and Russell [21] presented an algorithm to predict the disturbance storm time index (DST) value [22] based on solar wind and interplanetary magnetic field parameters. The DST value is a popular metric to assess geomagnetic activity. Expressed in nanoteslas (nT) and recorded every hour from observatories around the world, it measures the depression of the equatorial geomagnetic field, or horizontal component of the magnetic field; thus, the smaller the value of the DST, the more significant the disturbance of the magnetic field [2]. Many researchers have used this information for building forecasting models to predict geomagnetic storms [23][24].

However, many of these systems only use *in-situ* data, or data that can only be measured close to Earth. To improve prediction, studies have included data gathered at the onset of a CME and the near-Earth interplanetary information (IPI) regarding the solar wind condition as the CME approaches Earth [25][26][27]. These have ranged from using logistic regression [26] to neural networks [28] to make predictions based on this combination of data. Further improvements have been made by using multi-step frameworks. To narrow the scope, this work will focus on reviewing two recent two-step procedures that predict geomagnetic storms using both near-Earth IPI and CME properties taken near the Sun.

Valach, Bochníček, Hejda, and Revallo [29] reinforced one of the primary issues facing geomagnetic storm prediction: the inability to estimate the orientation of the interplanetary magnetic field from an incoming CME more than a few hours out. It is well-known that one of the largest predictor variables is the magnitude of the aforementioned magnetic field component B_z [21][26][2]; however, this is difficult to predict prior to reaching the L1 Lagrangian point (the position close to Earth where much of the IPI is collected) due to complexities in a CME's magnetic topology [30]. Hence, under the assumption that the direction of the magnetic field component is unpredictable, the authors first study the behavior of B_z for 2,882 days between 1997 to 2007 before implementing any predictive construct. Based on their analysis, they determined that for the majority of the days with a high-level of geomagnetic activity, B_z was negative for at least 16 hours during the course of the day (behavior exhibited by roughly 31% of the days studied). Then, after building a neural network using these observations, they forecasted the daily level of geomagnetic activity with initial CME and solar X-ray information. The benefits to their approach are that the predictions are timely (absence of IPI in the second step enable forecasts at least a day out) and are well-suited for the strongest of storms (since the training observations are composed of days where B_z is negative for more than 16 hours). However, as noted by the authors, it does not do as well differentiating moderate and weak geomagnetic storms. In addition, the time scale of the prediction is in days, which is not as granular as hours.

Kim, Moon, Gopalswamy, Park, and Kim [27] argued that only using information based on urgent warning IPI for prediction does not provide a practical lead time for preparations to be made on Earth, even though the forecasts are more accurate. At the same time, strictly employing initial CME data becomes frivolous as each CME experiences changes in composition as they propagate through the interplanetary medium, thereby, making prediction difficult. Therefore, the authors constructed a two-step forecasting system using both urgent warning IPI and initial CME data. At the first stage, they applied multiple linear regression models to predict the strength of geomagnetic activity for northward and southward events at the onset of a CME using its location, speed, and direction parameter (estimated from the magnetic orientation angle of the related active region on the Sun). The estimation of the direction (north or south) is based on the assumption that these rarely deviate from that of the associated active region [31]. Next, they administered a set of rules based on the IPI to update the forecast and classify the impending CME as causing a moderate or intense storm. This method contributes a medium-term to short-term forecast from the first observance of a CME to its approach to Earth. While this method yields accurate and interpretable results, only 55 CMEs from 1997-2003 were studied. Moreover, the absence of using a validation scheme when creating the rules can lead to over-fitting when predicting on future data [32].

Interestingly enough, the former work assumes the direction of the magnetic field component in a CME is unpredictable while the latter estimates this in their step one models. In this work, the direction is not considered in any of the steps. Instead, the dataset captures values of B_z prior to the climax of a given geomagnetic storm [33]. Thus, if this value is high in magnitude, then this reflects the southward behavior.

Aside from the work by Dryer et al. [25], which used an ensemble of four physics-based models to predict shock arrival times, the idea of using ensembles of models has not been very prevalent in the literature. Stacked generalization [34] is a type of ensemble that uses the individual predictions from a set of base models as inputs for another model to make a final prediction. This strategy has been the backbone of successful schemes in areas such as predicting financial fraud [35], bankruptcy [36], and user ratings in the famous Netflix Prize competition [37]. Therefore, leveraging more advanced ensemble frameworks for predictive modeling has the opportunity to increase accuracy in this field.

B. Stacked Generalization

The idea of stacked generalization can be simplified in the following way:

- Construct a dataset consisting of predictions from a set of level 0 (or base) learners using a training and a test set. Refer to this as the metadata.
- Generate a level 1 (or meta) learner that utilizes the predictions made at the previous level as inputs. That is, train the meta-learner on the metadata as opposed to the original training data.

Often times, the predictions from the base learners are determined via k-fold cross-validation [38]. Define the dataset $S = \{(y_i, \boldsymbol{x}_i), i = 1, ..., n\}$ where $\boldsymbol{x}_i$ is a vector of predictor variables and y_i is the corresponding response value for the ith observation. Specifically, split the dataset S into k near equal and disjoint sets such that $S_1, S_2, ..., S_k$. Let $S^{-k} = S - S_k$ and S_k be the training and test sets, respectively. Execute the base-learner on the first S^{-k} parts and produce a prediction for the held-out part S_k. Repeat this procedure until each subset of S has been used as a test set exactly once. Extract all the hold-out predictions to create the metadata. Because generating the metadata is an independent process across each base-learner, it can be parallelized for faster computation. That is, each base-learner can be trained at the same time. This is key as time plays a pivotal role in geomagnetic storm prediction [27].

The meta-learner's purpose is to gain information about the generalization behavior of each learner trained at the base-level. Popular choices for meta-learners have been linear models [39]. While this ensemble strategy leverages the strengths and weaknesses of the base-learners, it can be prone to over-fitting [40]. Therefore, in order to combat this issue, employing regularized linear methods can perform better than their non-regularized counterparts [41][38][42]. Reid and Grudic [42] experimented with three regularization penalties: ridge [43], lasso [44], and the elastic net [45]. The authors showed that imposing these penalties perform well on multi-class datasets. They commented that using the lasso and elastic net penalties can promote sparse solutions that can reduce the size of the ensemble at the meta-level. Pruning the size of an ensemble model has been explored in other works [46][47][48]. It can lead to better generalization and promote the necessary diversity in the base-learner predictions [34].

Based upon the results in previous studies, it seems advantageous to implement a regularized meta-learner to have the best potential for success in stacked generalization. By using various types of penalty functions, a learning system can effectively make predictions and provide sparse solutions, even in situations with severe multicollinearity since all of the base-learners are trying to predict the same outcome [38]. However, none of the studies mentioned above discuss how to choose a meta-learner when the outlier values are important for regression tasks. Specifically for predicting geomagnetic storms, outliers are important because strong CMEs do not occur often; hence, a meta-learner cannot downplay the effect of these for prediction. If anything, the meta-learner should treat these values with more emphasis. In addition, subsetting the data to only include these outliers for model construction inhibits meta-knowledge to be gained for all CME events. Therefore, for this study, a regularized quantile regression model is chosen for the meta-learner in order to more adequately deal with outliers, improve accuracy, and promote sparse solutions.

C. Regularized Quantile Regression

Recall the ordinary least squares (OLS) solution for the coefficients in linear regression:

$$\hat{\beta}^{ols} = (\boldsymbol{X}'\boldsymbol{X})^{-1}\boldsymbol{X}'\boldsymbol{Y} \tag{1}$$

where $\boldsymbol{X}$ is the predictor matrix of dimension $n \times (p+1)$ and $\boldsymbol{Y}$ is the vector of outcomes of dimension $n \times 1$ for n observations and p predictor variables. Specifically,

$$\boldsymbol{X} = \begin{pmatrix} 1 & x_{11} & x_{12} & \dots & x_{1p} \\ 1 & x_{21} & x_{22} & \dots & x_{2p} \\ 1 & \vdots & \vdots & \ddots & \vdots \\ 1 & x_{n1} & x_{n2} & \dots & x_{np} \end{pmatrix} \quad \boldsymbol{Y} = \begin{pmatrix} y_1 \\ y_2 \\ \vdots \\ y_n \end{pmatrix}$$

Alternatively, Eq. (1) can be written as the following optimization problem:

$$\underset{\boldsymbol{\beta}}{\text{argmin}} \quad \frac{1}{n}\sum_{i=1}^{n}(y_i - \boldsymbol{x}_i'\boldsymbol{\beta})^2 \tag{2}$$

To apply regularization to the estimated coefficients, a penalty term can be added such that [49]

$$\underset{\boldsymbol{\beta}}{\text{argmin}} \quad \frac{1}{n}\sum_{i=1}^{n}(y_i - \boldsymbol{x}_i'\boldsymbol{\beta})^2 + \sum_{j=1}^{p} p_\lambda(|\beta_j|) \tag{3}$$

where $p_\lambda(\cdot)$ dictates the type of penalty function with a non-negative constant λ to determine the amount of regularization. Utilizing constrained regression approaches enables the ability to perform variable selection or improve prediction in particular environments. However, the main goal in these methods is to estimate the conditional mean of some response given a set of predictor variables. Situations may arise where it is more advantageous to investigate a certain part of the conditional distribution [50][51]; hence, quantile regression was developed [52]. The goal of quantile regression is to offer "a comprehensive strategy for completing the regression picture" (pg. 20) [53]. In general, this involves minimizing the sum of asymmetrically weighted absolute residuals [52]

$$\underset{\beta}{\operatorname{argmin}} \; \frac{1}{n}\left[\sum_{i\in\{i:y_i\geq \boldsymbol{x}_i'\boldsymbol{\beta}\}} \tau|y_i - \boldsymbol{x}_i'\boldsymbol{\beta}| + \sum_{i\in\{i:y_i< \boldsymbol{x}_i'\boldsymbol{\beta}\}} (1-\tau)|y_i - \boldsymbol{x}_i'\boldsymbol{\beta}| \right] \quad (4)$$

for some given quantile level τ. In this way, different weights are placed on positive (under-prediction) and negative (over-prediction) errors corresponding to the desired quantile. Note that when $\tau = 0.5$, this simply reduces to median regression. As with the linear case, the coefficients in quantile regression can be penalized the same way. Using lasso has been a popular choice due to its sparse nature [54][55]. However, it has been shown that lasso has some limitations in high-dimensional situations or ones with severe multicollinearity [45]. In addition, it lacks oracle properties [56][57]. That is, lasso does not select the correct subset of predictor variables while also efficiently estimating the non-zero coefficients as if only the truly influential predictor variables are included in the model, asymptotically [58]. Thus other penalties, such as the smoothly clipped absolute deviation (SCAD) [56], have been developed. This has been shown to retain oracle properties for penalized quantile regression models [59]. It can be defined as a quadratic spline function with knots at λ and $a\lambda$ to make the following objective function:

$$\underset{\beta}{\operatorname{argmin}} \; \frac{1}{n}\left[\sum_{i\in\{i:y_i\geq \boldsymbol{x}_i'\boldsymbol{\beta}\}} \tau|y_i - \boldsymbol{x}_i'\boldsymbol{\beta}| + \sum_{i\in\{i:y_i< \boldsymbol{x}_i'\boldsymbol{\beta}\}} (1-\tau)|y_i - \boldsymbol{x}_i'\boldsymbol{\beta}| \right] + \sum_{j=1}^{p} p_\lambda(|\beta_j|) \quad (5)$$

where

$$p_\lambda(|\beta|) = \begin{cases} \lambda|\beta| & 0 \leq |\beta| < \lambda \\ \dfrac{a\lambda|\beta| - (\beta^2+\lambda^2)/2}{a-1} & \lambda \leq |\beta| \leq a\lambda \\ \dfrac{(a+1)\lambda^2}{2} & |\beta| > a\lambda \end{cases}$$

for some $a > 2$ and $\lambda > 0$. By assigning different weights depending on $|\beta|$, SCAD avoids over-penalizing large coefficients, as is a common problem in lasso [56][59][49]. Traditionally, solving Eq. (5) is difficult due to its non-convex nature. Fortunately, efficient algorithms have been developed to increase the computational speed for solving these non-differentiable and non-convex optimization problems [49]. Because of the advantages of using the SCAD penalty, this work employs this type of regularization on a quantile regression model at the meta-level. Note that subsequent uses of SCAD refer to the quantile regression model in Eq. (5).

D. A Two-stage Approach

Given the success of multi-step approaches, this work executes two rounds of stacked generalization using two data sources:

1) Initial CME properties taken at the time of ejection
2) Initial CME properties taken at the time of ejection plus the IPI

The execution of stacked generalization on the first data source, noted as stage one, can provide a preliminary estimate as to how strong a CME will be. Then, after adding the important IPI in stage two, the forecast can be updated to more accurately reflect the potential danger from the respective CME. This two-stage meta-learning approach seeks to emulate Kim et al.'s [27] medium-term to short-term forecast for predicting geomagnetic storms. To increase in the interpretation of the framework, the variable importance strategy for stacked generalization described by Larkin [33] is instituted. This involves calculating model-specific variable importance scores for each base-learner and then weighting these scores based on the coefficients from SCAD to produce a final aggregated variable importance score for each predictor variable.

III. Methodology

A. Data

Four sources are considered to construct the experimental dataset: near-Earth CME information provided by Richardson and Cane [60][61], OMNI hourly averaged solar wind data at one AU (astronomical unit) from the Coordinated Data Analysis (Workshop) Web [62], CME measurements given by the Large Angle and Spectrometric Coronagraph (LASCO) located on the Solar and Heliospheric Observatory (SOHO) satellite [63], and some Sun characteristics recorded by NOAA [64]. These data are combined so that each CME has been assigned IPI values (such as B_z) prior to the DST minimum during a predicted area of effect on Earth. Establishing these values before the DST minimum gives a lead time prior to the climax of the geomagnetic storms and allows for a more realistic prediction scenario, especially since B_z typically minimizes prior to the minimization of the DST value [65]. Also included are the initial measurements about the speed and angle of a CME at the time of ejection from the Sun and daily Sun characteristics on the day of ejection. After filtering out missing values and some unnecessary rows, a dataset composed of 2,811 CME events from 1996 to 2014 with 28 predictor variables is ready for analysis [33]. Note only 16 of the 28 predictor variables will be be used in the first stage. Approximately 5% of the observations in the dataset are deemed as strongly geoeffective (i.e. produce a geomagnetic storm with a DST ≤ -100nT). The list of predictor variables is divided into initial CME and solar characteristics in Table I and the subsequent IPI in Table II. Predictor variables types are denoted as continuous (C), discrete (D), or binary (B).

B. Experimental Set-up

The analysis is performed in the R environment version 3.3.2 [66] using the **caret** (Classification And REgression Training) package [67]. This package allows for a streamlined user interface for applying a diverse set of predictive models from different packages with options to perform various pre-processing, post-processing, resampling, and visualization

TABLE I. LIST OF INITIAL CME PROPERTIES AND SUN CHARACTERISTICS

Variable	Type	Description
MPA	C	Measurement position angle of CME at the height-time measurements (degrees)
AW	C	Sky-plane width of CME (degrees)
LS	C	Linear speed of CME (km/s)
SOI	C	Quadratic speed of CME at initial height measurement (km/s)
SOF	C	Quadratic speed of CME at final height measurement (km/s)
SOR	C	Quadratic speed of CME at height of 20 solar radii (km/s)
Acc	C	Acceleration of CME in (m/s^2)
$Poor$	B	Noted as a poor event in the comments
Very_Poor	B	Noted as a very poor event in the comments
$RFlux$	C	Daily average 10.7cm flux values of solar radio emissions on CME ejection day in 10^{-22}J/s/m^2/Hz
SSN	D	Number of sunspots recorded on CME ejection day
SSA	C	Sum of the corrected area of all observed sunspots on CME ejection day in millionths of the solar hemisphere
NR	D	Number of new sunspot regions on CME ejection day
$XrayC$	D	Number of C-class solar flares on CME ejection day
$XrayM$	D	Number of M-class solar flares on CME ejection day
$XrayX$	D	Number of X-class solar flares on CME ejection day

TABLE II. LIST OF IPI

Variable	Type	Description
E_y	C	Interplanetary electric field in millivolts per meter (mV/m)
B_x	C	X-component magnetic field component (nT)
B_y	C	Y-component magnetic field component (nT)
B_z	C	Southward magnetic field component (nT)
V_{sw}	C	Plasma flow speed (km/s)
Phi	C	Plasma flow direction longitude (degrees)
$Theta$	C	Plasma flow direction latitude (degrees)
D_p	C	Proton density in Newtons per cubic centimeter (N/cm^3)
Na_Np	C	Alpha to proton ratio
T_p	C	Proton temperature in degrees Kelvin (K)
P	C	Flow pressure in nanopascals (nPa)
$Beta$	C	Plasma beta

techniques. In addition, for those models that can perform variable importance estimation, the **caret** package can automatically extract these measures for a practitioner's use. Due to the large number of models available, a rich series of machine learning algorithms and statistical models may be realized to construct the foundation of base-learners. Care is taken to ensure a diverse collection of 50 models and algorithms is used [46]. Unfortunately, in an effort to include a larger number of base-learners, not every model is able to provide model-specific variable importance scores. That is, they either do not have a way to calculate variable importance or **caret** does not implement one. For this study, less than half (42%) of base-learners have model-specific importance scores. For those that do not, the R^2 statistic is calculated using a loess smoother which is fit between the outcome and each predictor variable, as done by default within the package [68]. A summary of the 50 chosen base-learners is listed in Table III. Asterisks "*" indicate those methods that can provide model-specific variable importance scores.

Another advantage to using **caret** is the option to easily tune the parameters for a given learner by simply specifying a number for $tuneLength$ in the $train$ function. Each model has a predefined range of tuning values to search over proportional the $tuneLength$. The higher the $tuneLength$, the more tuning executed. The number of tuning parameters range for each model. In this experimental set-up, $tuneLength$ is left at the default value of three.

For the SCAD implementation, the **rqPen** R package is chosen [69]. This package offers estimation for SCAD as well as other penalized quantile regression models including lasso. In addition, it can utilize the recently proposed and efficient iterative coordinate descent algorithm [49] to compute SCAD solutions using the *QICD* function. Because this function is not offered in **caret**, it is incorporated within the **caret** framework by creating a custom model. It is important to implement this within **caret** to be sure SCAD is trained across the same folds as the base-learners for a fair comparison. To tune SCAD, only two parameters are adjusted: the regularization value λ and the quantile level τ. The parameter a in Eq. (5) is left at the suggested default value of 3.7. The value of λ controls how much to penalize the coefficients and works similarly as λ in the popular **glmnet** package [70]. A diverse range of values are investigated: $\lambda = \{1000, 1, 0.001\}$. For many applications of quantile regression, the selection of the quantile level τ is determined by the user to best suit the research goal. In this work, τ is treated as a tuning parameter to best find a balanced between accurately predicting the much rarer dangerous geomagnetic storms and the more common weaker counterpart. Quantile levels $\tau = \{0.1, 0.2, 0.3\}$ are selected since the 20th percentile of the DST value in this dataset is -49nT, which is approximately the threshold (-50nT) between weak and moderate storms for other works (e.g., [71]). For comparison, τ in the *rqlasso* and *rqnc* methods is set to 0.2. Since the default amount of tuning is instituted, nine different parameter combinations for SCAD are tested. To benchmark the performance of using SCAD as the meta-learner, linear regression is also execute by calling the **caret** method *lm* at the meta-level.

C. Estimating Predictive Performance

For many of the previous studies in predicting geomagnetic storms, the main performance metric utilized has been unweighted error criterion (e.g. root mean square error (RMSE) [23]). While RMSE does penalize larger errors more via the

TABLE III. LIST OF BASE-LEARNERS

Model/Algorithm/Learner	**caret** Method	Model/Algorithm/Learner	**caret** Method
Bagged Regression Trees*	*treebag*	Neural Network*	*nnet*
Bayesian Lasso	*blasso*	Neural Network with Feature Extraction	*pcaNNet*
Bayesian Lasso (Model Averaged)	*blassoAveraged*	Non-convex Penalized Quantile Regression	*rqnc*
Bayesian Regularized Neural Network	*brnn*	Non-negative Least Squares*	*nnls*
Bayesian Ridge Regression	*bridge*	Partial Least Squares*	*pls*
Boosted Linear Model*	*glmboost*	Partitioning Using Deletion, Substitution, and Addition Moves*	*partDSA*
Boosted Tree	*bstTree*	Principal Component Regression	*pcr*
Conditional Inference Random Forest*	*cforest*	Projection Pursuit Regression	*ppr*
Conditional Inference Tree	*ctree*	Quantile Random Forest	*qrf*
Cubist*	*cubist*	Quantile Regression with Lasso Penalty	*rqlasso*
Extreme Gradient Boosting with Linear Booster*	*xgbLinear*	Random Forest*	*ranger*
Extreme Gradient Boosting with Tree Booster*	*xgbTree*	Regression Tree with One Standard Error Rule*	*rpart1SE*
Extreme Learning Machine	*elm*	Regularized Random Forest*	*RRFglobal*
Generalized Additive Model using Loess*	*gamLoess*	Relaxed Lasso	*relaxo*
Generalized Additive Model using Splines*	*gamSpline*	Ridge Regression with Variable Selection	*foba*
Independent Component Regression	*icr*	Robust Linear Model	*rlm*
k-Nearest Neighbors Regression	*kknn*	Self-organizing Map	*bdk*
Lasso and Elastic Net Regression*	*glmnet*	Spike and Slab Regression	*spikeslab*
Least Angle Regression	*lars2*	Stacked AutoEncoder Deep Neural Network	*dnn*
Linear Regression*	*lm*	Stochastic Gradient Boosting*	*gbm*
Linear Regression with Stepwise Selection	*leapSeq*	Supervised Principal Component Analysis	*superpc*
Multi-layer Perceptron	*mlp*	Support Vector Machine with Linear Kernel	*svmLinear*
Multi-layer Perceptron Network by Stochastic Gradient Descent*	*mlpSGD*	Support Vector Machine with Polynomial Kernel	*svmPoly*
Multivariate Adaptive Regression Splines*	*earth*	Support Vector Machine with Radial Basis Function Kernel	*svmRadialSigma*
Multivariate Adaptive Regression Splines (Bagged with Generalized Cross-validation Pruning)*	*bagEarthGCV*	Weighted k-Nearest Neighbors	*knn*

squaring operator, it treats each observation the same. In the context of predicting geomagnetic storms, it is more important for a model to accurately forecast the DST value associated for the strongest of storms. At the same time, focusing strictly on these observations can severely bias a model. Hence, the central metric used in this work for comparison as well as optimizing each learner's parameters is weighted mean absolute error (WMAE), which can be defined as

$$\text{WMAE} = \frac{1}{\sum w_i} \sum_{i=1}^{n} w_i |y_i - \hat{y}_i| \tag{6}$$

such that $\hat{y}_i$ is the predicted response value and w_i is the weight associated with the ith observation. This is implemented within **caret** by creating a custom metric. Adopting WMAE allows for the opportunity to penalize models for inaccuracies when forecasting the more important observations. Given the potential impact that dangerous storms can have, strong CMEs are weighted as 10 times more important than the others (DST > -100nT). Using this 10:1 ratio seems to be a conservative balance since strong geomangetic storms can result in economic losses in trillions of U.S. dollars [72]. In addition to WMAE, the overall RMSE and RMSE for the strong CME events will also be reported.

Each of these error metrics are calculated from an average of ten repeats of 10-fold (10×10) nested cross-validation to ensure a good estimation of error in the presence of parameter tuning [73]. Furthermore, significance tests between the SCAD meta-learner and each individual learner are conducted on the population of error metrics (100 estimates for each from the 10×10 nested cross-validation) using the corrected repeated k-fold cross-validation test [74]. It is important to test for significant differences to investigate if the extra computation of stacked generalization is worth the effort compared to simply using the best performing model [75]. All base-learners and meta-learners are trained over the same folds with the only difference being that the meta-learners use the metadata as its inputs instead of the CME predictor variables. The metadata is generated using 10-fold nested cross-validation. Note that this cross-validation is separate from the nested cross-validation used to estimate the error. Finally, after all of the error testing is complete, each learner is trained on all of the data with the parameters optimized via 10-fold cross-validation. The purpose of this is to enable the variable importance scores extracted from SCAD and the base-learners to be based on all of the data.

IV. RESULTS AND DISCUSSION

Table IV reflects the results of the performance in both stages. The first column lists both meta-learners and the ten most accurate base-learners ranked in ascending order by the average WMAE from the second stage. The subsequent columns represent the averaged error metrics for all CME events (WMAE and RMSE) and only those which triggered a strong geomagnetic disturbance (RMSE). Bold and italics indicate the best performing method. The dagger symbol "†" denotes instances where a significant difference between SCAD and the other learners is *not* found at the conventional

0.05 significance level.

Not surprisingly, accuracy greatly increases in the second stage, a direct consequence of including the IPI. In addition, the majority of the best performing base-learners are all bagging or boosting ensemble models. It is natural for these types of techniques to achieve good predictions. Regardless, SCAD yields the lowest WMAE and RMSE on strong CMEs compared to these in either stage. In addition, SCAD performs statistically better than the most accurate base-learners by themselves for these two metrics in stage two and better than the majority in stage one. This provides evidence that the implementation of stacked generalization here has more predictive power than using just one model. Ting and Witten [39] indicated in their analysis that stacked generalization delivers substantial improvements in accuracy for larger datasets. This is likely due to a more accurate estimation from the cross-validation process when generating the metadata. Hence, it is probable that with more data, stacked generalization can continue to enhance geomagnetic storm prediction over using only one technique.

Notably, the dominance of SCAD falters when evaluating RMSE for all events. This is expected since the majority of the other methods are estimating the conditional mean, rather than a particular part of the DST value's distribution. It is important to reinforce that analyzing the overall RMSE alone can be misleading in this context. For instance, the best performing base-learner in stage one, the regularized random forest, achieves a statistically lower error (RMSE = 27.96) compared to SCAD (RMSE = 34.90). However, looking at the strong CME RMSE reveals a much higher value (87.19 compared to 67.61). This occurs for the linear regression meta-learner as well. Hence, if a practitioner only considered this metric, a degradation in accuracy for the strong events will be realized. Therefore, for practical purposes in predicting geomagnetic storms, it is more appropriate to analyze error metrics such as the WMAE or subsets of RMSE, given the most costly and dangerous storms do not occur very often.

In addition to the arguments above against only considering RMSE on all CME events, additional benefits of using SCAD over linear regression at the meta-level exist, namely the sparsity property. Because linear regression does not perform variable selection, each base-learner prediction is given some weight to make a final estimate. However, with SCAD, certain subsets can be selected, depending on the tuning parameters. This, thereby, reduces the complexity of the problem. During these experiments, SCAD selects 48.31 and 18.71 base-learner predictions on average in stages one and two, respectively. Moreover, any attempt at making any inference at the meta-level using linear regression is frivolous due to the high amount of correlation, which will cause the coefficient estimates to become erratic [76]. Hence, SCAD should be preferred over linear regression for this dataset since it can produce sparser and more interpretable solutions with statistically better error in the important metrics. The quality of being able to dynamically select which base-learners are most useful for prediction at the meta-level may help improve on the fixed form bias issues of stacked generalization mentioned by Vilalta and Drissi [77].

The variable importance scores from stacked generalization can be found in Figure 3 for both stages. Note that these are min-max normalized to represent a score out of 100 where 100 signifies the most useful predictor variable. Note further that since stage one does not use all the predictor variables, not all are listed. The most significant predictor variable in stage one for predicting DST is the sunspot area (SSA). Its high ranking makes sense since sunspot activity can be closely tied with CME occurrences [2]. In stage two, the two most dominating are E_y (which is an interaction between B_z and V_{sw}) and B_z. Given the strong relationship between these predictor variables and the DST value throughout the literature, their contributions towards prediction makes sense. More importantly, the higher values placed on E_y and B_z and lower values on those such as D_p and T_p in determining geomagnetic storm intensity is consistent with other literature (see [26][78][79][80][27] and references therein). Note that when the IPI is introduced, the influence of the stage one predictor variables decreases. This is to be expected given the advantages of using IPI.

Though the study of stacked generalization is not a new concept, this idea has not been explored in the realm of forecasting geomagnetic storm strength from CMEs much if not at all. Given the importance of making forecasts, it becomes all the more important to leverage the best analytical tools for space weather prediction. As shown in other studies, it is necessary to incorporate IPI since these are the most useful for determining the DST value. However, as emphasized by Kim et al. [27], this leaves little time to prepare on Earth once the information is collected at the L1 Lagrangian point. Research in attaining IPI sooner is currently being done. Savani et al. [81] are working towards resolving this type of issue by predicting the magnetic structure of impending CMEs. More accurate forecasts of the IPI will lead to better predictions with more lead time. In addition, since time is such a factor, computationally efficient approaches must be used. Luckily, although stacked generalization requires extra computation, especially for large datasets, it can be easily parallelized across many clusters since creating the metadata is an independent process. This allows for scalability as new models and algorithms are constantly being developed. Incorporating a larger number of faster and smarter base-learners provides the opportunity to increase predictive power.

This study brings several future work opportunities. Firstly, as more data is collected on CMEs in more advanced ways, implementation on larger datasets is possible for both classification and regression tasks. With more data, stacked generalization is more probable to find predictive improvements [39]. Secondly, this work only includes 50 base-learners. Increasing this number by incorporating different models and algorithms could yield even better results. With regards to the respective variable importances, exploring ways to extract model-specific measures can be investigated, despite whether a model or algorithm inherently implements them or not. Additionally, analyzing the variable importance scores at different quantiles may reveal some new behaviors regarding the predictor variables, much like in quantile process regression [82]. Furthermore, introducing some type of cost matrix, as done for MetaFraud [35], or re-weighting WMAE can better optimize parameters at both the base and meta-levels.

V. Conclusion

In this work, a meta-learning framework is suggested to predict geomagnetic storms. This approach consists of two stages:

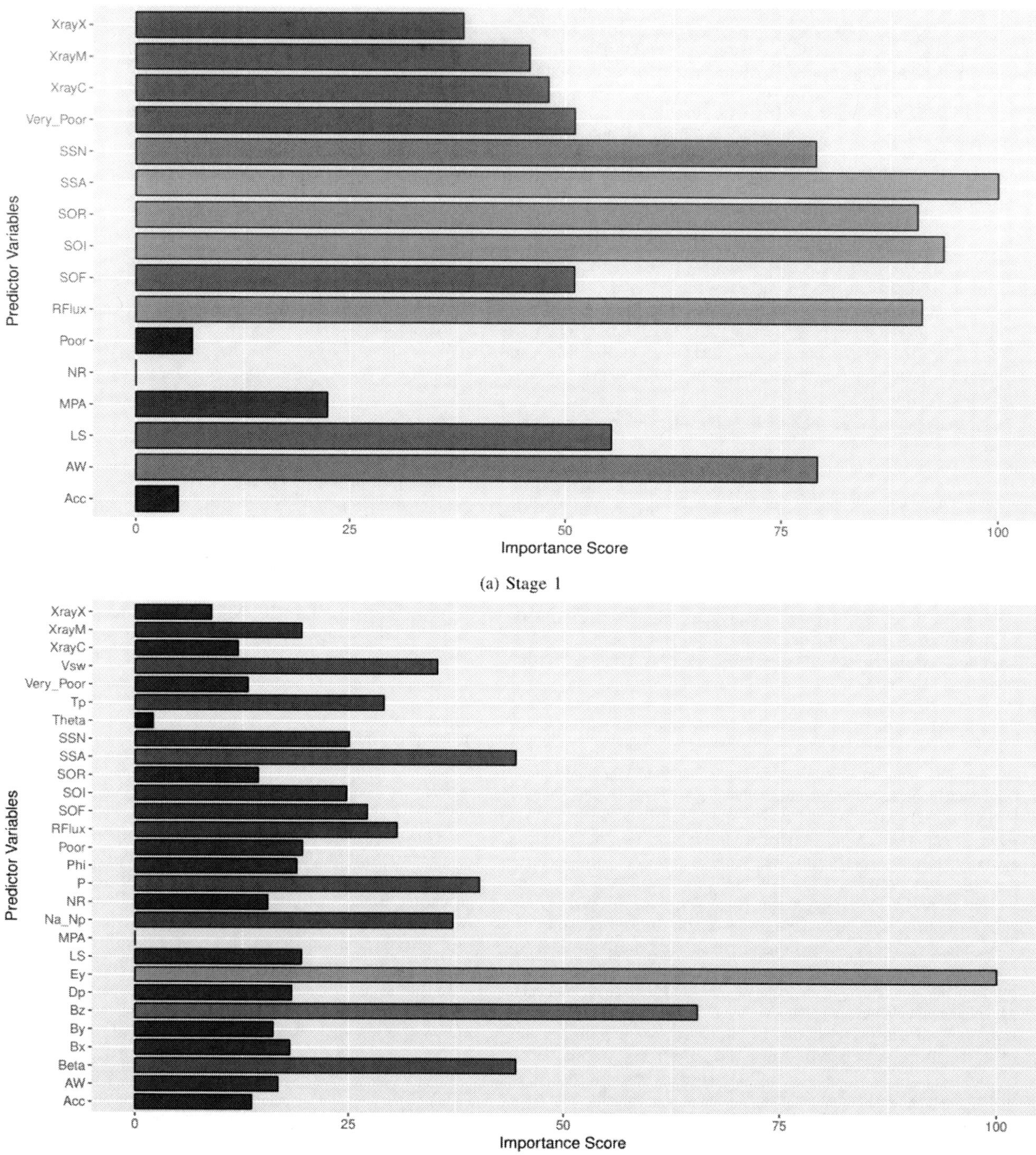

(a) Stage 1

(b) Stage 2

Figure 3. Variable importance scores from stacked generalization in both stages.

TABLE IV. PREDICTIVE PERFORMANCE

	Stage 1			Stage 2		
Learner	All CMEs		Strong CMEs	All CMEs		Strong CMEs
(Meta)	WMAE	RMSE	RMSE	WMAE	RMSE	RMSE
SCAD	***33.59***	34.90	***67.61***	***18.44***	18.76	***39.17***
Linear Regression	35.96	28.86	91.63	19.41†	***17.85***	46.09
(Base)	WMAE	RMSE	RMSE	WMAE	RMSE	RMSE
Cubist	38.35	30.98	96.44	20.04	18.20†	47.04
Extreme Gradient Boosting with Linear Booster	35.11†	29.41	85.28	20.41	19.32†	51.06
Extreme Gradient Boosting with Tree Booster	35.56†	28.80	85.84	20.68	19.25†	49.40
Random Forest	35.70†	28.21	87.98	20.74	18.32†	50.27
Regularized Random Forest	35.48†	***27.96***	87.19	20.88	18.39†	50.95
Boosted Tree	37.59	29.08	92.71	21.27	19.09†	51.86
Multivariate Adaptive Regression Splines (Bagged with Generalized Cross-Validation Pruning)	39.57	29.89	99.45	21.84	19.17†	51.70
Stochastic Gradient Boosting	38.48	29.78	95.03	21.95	19.44†	52.30
Conditional Inference Random Forest	39.70	29.92	101.74	22.07	19.00†	53.87

1) Execute stacked generalization with a SCAD penalized quantile meta-learner to make a preliminary estimate of DST based on initial CME and Sun data.
2) Update the prediction with another round of stacked generalization after collecting the vital IPI.

The general outline is similar to the process by Kim et al. [27]. However, instead of focusing on estimating the conditional mean for DST, quantile regression is implemented to find a better balance between predicting dangerous geomagnetic storms effectively without rendering estimation for the weaker ones useless. Using a regularized quantile regression model at the meta-level provides more adaptability since it can specify specific parts of the conditional distribution and choose the best number of base-learners for that particular region. The posited method is evaluated on an inclusive dataset consisting of various characteristics about the solar wind condition, CMEs, and the Sun. In addition, careful experimental methodology is utilized to estimate generalization error and statistical significance. Results show that this framework performs significantly better on the most informative error metrics than the best tuned model or algorithm at the base-level. Moreover, this approach provides an opportunity to study the critical space weather indicators at the beginning of a CME's life and right before its impact on Earth via the variable importance scores from stacked generalization.

Given our dependence on telecommunications and commercial satellites, any disruption in these services could cost millions of dollars for corporations and government agencies world-wide. At the same time, logistically, these entities cannot simply shut down power or telecommunication operations every time a CME approaches Earth. Therefore, it is imperative to make accurate classifications and forecasts as to which of these CMEs that approach Earth can have the potential to trigger devastating geomagnetic storms. Putting into action more sophisticated modeling techniques like stacked generalization have the opportunity to improve predictions. Instituting these in multi-step approaches can greatly benefit in preparation time for geomagnetic storms. Utilizing more complex systems enables the ability to make more accurate predictions, thereby, saving money and reducing the probability for severe geomagnetic storm events wreaking havoc on modern society.

ACKNOWLEDGMENT

We would like to thank NASA for their images and the creation of the CME catalog. This CME catalog is generated and maintained at the CDAW Data Center by NASA and The Catholic University of America in cooperation with the Naval Research Laboratory. SOHO is a project of international cooperation between ESA and NASA. In addition, we would like to thank the Goddard Space Flight Center/Space Physics Data Facility (GSFC/SPDF), OMNIWeb, and NOAA for their public use databases. An earlier version of this research was presented at Data Analytics 2016: The Fifth International Conference on Data Analytics.

REFERENCES

[1] T. Larkin and D. McManus, "Impact of analytics and meta-learning on predicting geomagnetic storms: Risk to global telecommunications," in Data Analytics 2016, The Fifth International Conference on Data Analytics, S. Bhulai and I. Semanjski, Eds. IARIA, October 2016, pp. 8–13.

[2] T. Howard, Coronal Mass Ejections: An Introduction. Springer Science & Business Media, 2011, vol. 376.

[3] N. Srivastava and P. Venkatakrishnan, "Solar and interplanetary sources of major geomagnetic storms during 1996–2002," Journal of Geophysical Research: Space Physics (1978–2012), vol. 109, no. A10, 2004, pp. 1–13.

[4] National Oceanic and Atmospheric Administration, "Coronal mass ejections," Available: http://www.swpc.noaa.gov/phenomena/coronal-mass-ejections [accessed: 2017-05-22].

[5] R. MacQueen, "Coronal transients: A summary," Philosophical Transactions of the Royal Society of London A: Mathematical, Physical and Engineering Sciences, vol. 297, no. 1433, 1980, pp. 605–620.

[6] National Aeronautics and Space Administration, "Coronal mass ejections," Available: http://helios.gsfc.nasa.gov/cme.html [accessed: 2017-05-22].

[7] National Oceanic and Atmospheric Administration, "Earth's magnetosphere," Available: http://www.swpc.noaa.gov/phenomena/earths-magnetosphere [accessed: 2017-05-22].

[8] National Aeronautics and Space Administration, "Magnetospheres," Available: https://science.nasa.gov/heliophysics/focus-areas/magnetosphere-ionosphere [accessed: 2017-05-22].

[9] J. W. Dungey, "Interplanetary magnetic field and the auroral zones," Physical Review Letters, vol. 6, no. 2, 1961, pp. 47–48.

[10] D. H. Fairfield and L. Cahill, "Transition region magnetic field and polar magnetic disturbances," Journal of Geophysical Research, vol. 71, no. 1, 1966, pp. 155–169.

[11] W. D. Gonzalez and B. T. Tsurutani, "Criteria of interplanetary parameters causing intense magnetic storms (DST <-100 nT)," Planetary and Space Science, vol. 35, no. 9, 1987, pp. 1101–1109.

[12] Y. Wang, P. Ye, S. Wang, G. Zhou, and J. Wang, "A statistical study on the geoeffectiveness of Earth-directed coronal mass ejections from March 1997 to December 2000," Journal of Geophysical Research: Space Physics (1978–2012), vol. 107, no. A11, 2002, pp. SSH 2–1–SSH 2–9.

[13] J. Kappernman and V. D. Albertson, "Bracing for the geomagnetic storms," Spectrum, IEEE, vol. 27, no. 3, 1990, pp. 27–33.

[14] Space Studies Board and others, Severe Space Weather Events: Understanding Societal and Economic Impacts: A Workshop Report. National Academies Press, 2008.

[15] D. Baker, X. Li, A. Pulkkinen, C. Ngwira, M. Mays, A. Galvin, and K. Simunac, "A major solar eruptive event in July 2012: Defining extreme space weather scenarios," Space Weather, vol. 11, no. 10, 2013, pp. 585–591.

[16] J. Gosling, S. Bame, D. McComas, and J. Phillips, "Coronal mass ejections and large geomagnetic storms," Geophysical Research Letters, vol. 17, no. 7, 1990, pp. 901–904.

[17] V. Bothmer and R. Schwenn, "The interplanetary and solar causes of major geomagnetic storms," Journal of Geomagnetism and Geoelectricity, vol. 47, no. 11, 1995, pp. 1127–1132.

[18] B. T. Tsurutani and W. D. Gonzalez, "The interplanetary causes of magnetic storms: A review," Washington DC American Geophysical Union Geophysical Monograph Series, vol. 98, 1997, pp. 77–89.

[19] J. Zhang, K. Dere, R. Howard, and V. Bothmer, "Identification of solar sources of major geomagnetic storms between 1996 and 2000," The Astrophysical Journal, vol. 582, no. 1, 2003, pp. 520–533.

[20] D. McManus, H. Carr, and B. Adams, "Wireless on the precipice: The 14th century revisited," Communications of the ACM, vol. 54, no. 6, 2011, pp. 138–143.

[21] R. K. Burton, R. McPherron, and C. Russell, "An empirical relationship between interplanetary conditions and DST," Journal of Geophysical Research, vol. 80, no. 31, 1975, pp. 4204–4214.

[22] M. Sugiura, "Hourly values of equatorial DST for the IGY," Ann. Int. Geophys. Yr., vol. 35, 1964, pp. 1–44.

[23] E.-Y. Ji, Y.-J. Moon, N. Gopalswamy, and D.-H. Lee, "Comparison of DST forecast models for intense geomagnetic storms," Journal of Geophysical Research: Space Physics, vol. 117, no. A3, 2012, pp. 1–9.

[24] T. Andriyas and S. Andriyas, "Relevance vector machines as a tool for forecasting geomagnetic storms during years 1996–2007," Journal of Atmospheric and Solar-Terrestrial Physics, vol. 125, 2015, pp. 10–20.

[25] M. Dryer, Z. Smith, C. Fry, W. Sun, C. Deehr, and S.-I. Akasofu, "Real-time shock arrival predictions during the halloween 2003 epoch," Space Weather, vol. 2, no. 9, 2004, pp. 1–10.

[26] N. Srivastava, "A logistic regression model for predicting the occurrence of intense geomagnetic storms," in Annales Geophysicae, vol. 23, no. 9, 2005, pp. 2969–2974.

[27] R.-S. Kim, Y.-J. Moon, N. Gopalswamy, Y.-D. Park, and Y.-H. Kim, "Two-step forecast of geomagnetic storm using coronal mass ejection and solar wind condition," Space Weather, vol. 12, no. 4, 2014, pp. 246–256.

[28] J. Uwamahoro, L. McKinnell, and J. Habarulema, "Estimating the geoeffectiveness of halo CMEs from associated solar and IP parameters using neural networks," Annales Geophysicae-Atmospheres Hydrospheresand Space Sciences, vol. 30, no. 6, 2012, pp. 963–972.

[29] F. Valach, J. Bochníček, P. Hejda, and M. Revallo, "Strong geomagnetic activity forecast by neural networks under dominant southern orientation of the interplanetary magnetic field," Advances in Space Research, vol. 53, no. 4, 2014, pp. 589–598.

[30] R. Schwenn, "Space weather: The solar perspective," Living Reviews in Solar Physics, vol. 3, no. 1, 2006, pp. 1–72.

[31] V. Yurchyshyn, V. Abramenko, and D. Tripathi, "Rotation of white-light coronal mass ejection structures as inferred from lasco coronagraph," The Astrophysical Journal, vol. 705, no. 1, 2009, p. 426.

[32] D. M. Hawkins, "The problem of overfitting," Journal of Chemical Information and Computer Sciences, vol. 44, no. 1, 2004, pp. 1–12.

[33] T. Larkin, "Advanced analytical tools for geomagnetic storm prediction: Ensembles and their insights," Ph.D. dissertation, The University of Alabama, 2017, unpublished thesis.

[34] D. H. Wolpert, "Stacked generalization," Neural Networks, vol. 5, no. 2, 1992, pp. 241–259.

[35] A. Abbasi, C. Albrecht, A. Vance, and J. Hansen, "Metafraud: A meta-learning framework for detecting financial fraud," MIS Quarterly, vol. 36, no. 4, 2012, pp. 1293–1327.

[36] C.-F. Tsai and Y.-F. Hsu, "A meta-learning framework for bankruptcy prediction," Journal of Forecasting, vol. 32, no. 2, 2013, pp. 167–179.

[37] J. Sill, G. Takács, L. Mackey, and D. Lin, "Feature-weighted linear stacking," arXiv preprint arXiv:0911.0460, 2009, pp. 1–17.

[38] L. Breiman, "Stacked regressions," Machine Learning, vol. 24, no. 1, 1996, pp. 49–64.

[39] K. M. Ting and I. H. Witten, "Issues in stacked generalization," J. Artif. Intell. Res.(JAIR), vol. 10, 1999, pp. 271–289.

[40] R. Caruana, A. Niculescu-Mizil, G. Crew, and A. Ksikes, "Ensemble selection from libraries of models," in Proceedings of the Twenty-first International Conference on Machine Learning. ACM, 2004, pp. 18–25.

[41] M. LeBlanc and R. Tibshirani, "Combining estimates in regression and classification," Journal of the American Statistical Association, vol. 91, no. 436, 1996, pp. 1641–1650.

[42] S. Reid and G. Grudic, "Regularized linear models in stacked generalization," in Multiple Classifier Systems. Springer, 2009, pp. 112–121.

[43] A. E. Hoerl and R. W. Kennard, "Ridge regression: Biased estimation for nonorthogonal problems," Technometrics, 1970, pp. 55–67.

[44] R. Tibshirani, "Regression shrinkage and selection via the lasso," Journal of the Royal Statistical Society. Series B (Methodological), 1996, pp. 267–288.

[45] H. Zou and T. Hastie, "Regularization and variable selection via the elastic net," Journal of the Royal Statistical Society: Series B (Statistical Methodology), vol. 67, no. 2, 2005, pp. 301–320.

[46] G. Zenobi and P. Cunningham, "Using diversity in preparing ensembles of classifiers based on different feature subsets to minimize generalization error," in Machine Learning: ECML 2001. Springer, 2001, pp. 576–587.

[47] Z.-H. Zhou, J. Wu, and W. Tang, "Ensembling neural networks: many could be better than all," Artificial Intelligence, vol. 137, no. 1, 2002, pp. 239–263.

[48] N. Rooney, D. Patterson, and C. Nugent, "Pruning extensions to stacking," Intelligent Data Analysis, vol. 10, no. 1, 2006, pp. 47–66.

[49] B. Peng and L. Wang, "An iterative coordinate descent algorithm for high-dimensional nonconvex penalized quantile regression," Journal of Computational and Graphical Statistics, vol. 24, no. 3, 2015, pp. 676–694.

[50] F. Mosteller and J. W. Tukey, "Data analysis and regression: A second course in statistics," Addison-Wesley Series in Behavioral Science: Quantitative Methods, 1977.

[51] B. S. Cade and B. R. Noon, "A gentle introduction to quantile regression for ecologists," Frontiers in Ecology and the Environment, vol. 1, no. 8, 2003, pp. 412–420.

[52] R. Koenker and G. Bassett Jr, "Regression quantiles," Econometrica: Journal of the Econometric Society, 1978, pp. 33–50.

[53] R. Koenker and K. Hallock, "Quantile regression: An introduction," Journal of Economic Perspectives, vol. 15, no. 4, 2001, pp. 43–56.

[54] R. Koenker, "Quantile regression for longitudinal data," Journal of Multivariate Analysis, vol. 91, no. 1, 2004, pp. 74–89.

[55] Y. Li and J. Zhu, "L1-norm quantile regression," Journal of Computational and Graphical Statistics, 2012.

[56] J. Fan and R. Li, "Variable selection via nonconcave penalized likelihood and its oracle properties," Journal of the American Statistical Association, vol. 96, no. 456, 2001, pp. 1348–1360.

[57] H. Zou, "The adaptive lasso and its oracle properties," Journal of the American Statistical Association, vol. 101, no. 476, 2006, pp. 1418–1429.

[58] F. Audrino and L. Camponovo, "Oracle properties and finite sample

inference of the adaptive lasso for time series regression models," arXiv preprint arXiv:1312.1473, 2013.

[59] Y. Wu and Y. Liu, "Variable selection in quantile regression," Statistica Sinica, 2009, pp. 801–817.

[60] H. Cane and I. Richardson, "Interplanetary coronal mass ejections in the near-earth solar wind during 1996–2002," Journal of Geophysical Research: Space Physics (1978–2012), vol. 108, no. A4, 2003, pp. SSH 6–1–SSH 6–13.

[61] I. Richardson and H. Cane, "Near-earth interplanetary coronal mass ejections during solar cycle 23 (1996–2009): Catalog and summary of properties," Solar Physics, vol. 264, no. 1, 2010, pp. 189–237.

[62] J. King and N. Papitashvili, "Solar wind spatial scales in and comparisons of hourly wind and ACE plasma and magnetic field data," Journal of Geophysical Research: Space Physics, vol. 110, no. A2, 2005, pp. 1–8.

[63] N. Gopalswamy, S. Yashiro, G. Michalek, G. Stenborg, A. Vourlidas, S. Freeland, and R. Howard, "The SOHO/LASCO CME catalog," Earth, Moon, and Planets, vol. 104, no. 1-4, 2009, pp. 295–313.

[64] National Oceanic and Atmospheric Administration, "Index of /pub/warehouse," Available: ftp://ftp.swpc.noaa.gov/pub/warehouse [accessed: 2017-05-22].

[65] G.-H. Moon, "Variation of Magnetic Field (By, Bz) Polarity and Statistical Analysis of Solar Wind Parameters during the Magnetic Storm Period," Journal of Astronomy and Space Sciences, vol. 28, no. 2, 2011, pp. 123–132.

[66] R Core Team, R: A Language and Environment for Statistical Computing, R Foundation for Statistical Computing, Vienna, Austria, 2017, Available: https://www.R-project.org/ [accessed: 2017-05-22].

[67] M. K. C. from Jed Wing, S. Weston, A. Williams, C. Keefer, A. Engelhardt, T. Cooper, Z. Mayer, B. Kenkel, the R Core Team, M. Benesty, R. Lescarbeau, A. Ziem, L. Scrucca, Y. Tang, C. Candan, and T. Hunt., caret: classification and regression training, 2016, R package version 6.0-70. Available: https://CRAN.R-project.org/package=caret [accessed: 2016-07-27].

[68] M. Kuhn, "Building predictive models in R using the caret package," Journal of Statistical Software, vol. 28, no. 5, 2008, pp. 1–26.

[69] B. Sherwood and A. Maidman, rqPen: Penalized Quantile Regression, 2016, R package version 1.4. Available: https://CRAN.R-project.org/package=rqPen [accessed: 2016-07-27].

[70] J. Friedman, T. Hastie, and R. Tibshirani, "Regularization paths for generalized linear models via coordinate descent," Journal of Statistical Software, vol. 33, no. 1, 2010, p. 1.

[71] C. Loewe and G. Prölss, "Classification and mean behavior of magnetic storms," Journal of Geophysical Research: Space Physics, vol. 102, no. A7, 1997, pp. 14 209–14 213.

[72] Lloyd's and the Atmospheric and Environmental Research Inc., "Solar storm risk to the north american electrical grid," 2013, Available: https://www.lloyds.com/~/media/lloyds/reports/emerging%20risk%20reports/solar%20storm%20risk%20to%20the%20north%20american%20electric%20grid.pdf [accessed: 2017-05-22].

[73] S. Varma and R. Simon, "Bias in error estimation when using cross-validation for model selection," BMC Bioinformatics, vol. 7, no. 1, 2006, p. 91.

[74] R. R. Bouckaert and E. Frank, "Evaluating the replicability of significance tests for comparing learning algorithms," in Advances in Knowledge Discovery and Data Mining. Springer, 2004, pp. 3–12.

[75] S. Džeroski and B. Ženko, "Is combining classifiers with stacking better than selecting the best one?" Machine Learning, vol. 54, no. 3, 2004, pp. 255–273.

[76] T. Hastie, R. Tibshirani, and J. Friedman, The Elements of Statistical Learning: Data Mining, Inference, and Prediction. New York: Springer, 2009.

[77] R. Vilalta and Y. Drissi, "A perspective view and survey of meta-learning," Artificial Intelligence Review, vol. 18, no. 2, 2002, pp. 77–95.

[78] E. Echer, W. Gonzalez, and B. Tsurutani, "Interplanetary conditions leading to superintense geomagnetic storms (DST <= -250 nT) during solar cycle 23," Geophysical Research Letters, vol. 35, no. 6, 2008.

[79] Y. I. Yermolaev, M. Y. Yermolaev, I. Lodkina, and N. Nikolaeva, "Statistical investigation of heliospheric conditions resulting in magnetic storms: 2," Cosmic Research, vol. 45, no. 6, 2007, pp. 461–470.

[80] E.-Y. Ji, Y.-J. Moon, K.-H. Kim, and D.-H. Lee, "Statistical comparison of interplanetary conditions causing intense geomagnetic storms (DST <= -100 nT)," Journal of Geophysical Research: Space Physics (1978–2012), vol. 115, no. A10, 2010.

[81] N. Savani, A. Vourlidas, A. Szabo, M. Mays, I. Richardson, B. Thompson, A. Pulkkinen, R. Evans, and T. Nieves-Chinchilla, "Predicting the magnetic vectors within coronal mass ejections arriving at earth: 1. initial architecture," Space Weather, 2015.

[82] R. Koenker and J. A. Machado, "Goodness of fit and related inference processes for quantile regression," Journal of the American Statistical Association, vol. 94, no. 448, 1999, pp. 1296–1310.

International Journal on Advances in Telecommunications, vol 10 no 1 & 2, year 2017, http://www.iariajournals.org/telecommunications/

Near Capacity Signaling over Fading Channels using Coherent Turbo Coded OFDM and Massive MIMO

K. Vasudevan

Dept. of EE
IIT Kanpur
India
Email: vasu@iitk.ac.in

***Abstract*—The minimum average signal-to-noise ratio (SNR) per bit required for error-free transmission over a fading channel is derived, and is shown to be equal to that of the additive white Gaussian noise (AWGN) channel, which is -1.6 dB. Discrete-time algorithms are presented for timing and carrier synchronization, as well as channel estimation, for turbo coded multiple input multiple output (MIMO) orthogonal frequency division multiplexed (OFDM) systems. Simulation results show that it is possible to achieve a bit error rate of 10^{-5} at an average SNR per bit of 5.5 dB, using two transmit and two receive antennas. We then propose a near-capacity signaling method in which each transmit antenna uses a different carrier frequency. Using the near-capacity approach, we show that it is possible to achieve a BER of 2×10^{-5} at an average SNR per bit of just 2.5 dB, with one receive antenna for each transmit antenna. When the number of receive antennas for each transmit antenna is increased to 128, then a BER of 2×10^{-5} is attained at an average SNR per bit of 1.25 dB. In all cases, the number of transmit antennas is two and the spectral efficiency is 1 bit/transmission or 1 bit/sec/Hz. In other words, each transmit antenna sends 0.5 bit/transmission. It is possible to obtain higher spectral efficiency by increasing the number of transmit antennas, with no loss in BER performance, as long as each transmit antenna uses a different carrier frequency. The transmitted signal spectrum for the near-capacity approach can be restricted by pulse-shaping. In all the simulations, a four-state turbo code is used. The corresponding turbo decoder uses eight iterations. The algorithms can be implemented on programmable hardware and there is a large scope for parallel processing.**

Keywords–Channel capacity; coherent detection; frequency selective Rayleigh fading channel; massive multiple input multiple output (MIMO); orthogonal frequency division multiplexing (OFDM); spectral efficiency; turbo codes.

I. Introduction

We begin this article with an open question: what is the operating signal-to-noise (SNR) per bit or E_b/N_0 of the present day mobile phones [1]–[3]? The mobile phones indicate a typical received signal strength of -100 dBm (10^{-10} mW), however this is not the SNR per bit.

The above question assumes significance since future wireless communications, also called the 5th generation or 5G [4]–[7], is supposed to involve not only billions of people, but also smart machines and devices, e.g., driverless cars, remotely controlled washing machines, refrigerators, microwave ovens, robotic surgeries in health care and so on. Thus, we have to deal with an internet of things (IoT), which involves device-to-human, human-to-device and device-to-device communications. Due to the large number of devices involved, it becomes imperative that each device operates at the minimum possible average SNR per bit required for error-free communication.

Depending on the application, there are different requirements on the communication system. Critical applications like driverless cars and robotic surgeries require low to medium bit rates, e.g., 0.1 – 10 Mbps and low latency (the time taken to process the received information and send a response back to the transmitter) of the order of a fraction of a millisecond. Some applications like watching movies on a mobile phone require high bit rates, e.g., 10 – 1000 Mbps for high density and ultra high density (4k) video and can tolerate high latency, of the order of a fraction of a second. Whatever the application, the 5G wireless communication systems are expected to share some common features like having a large number of transmit and receive antennas also called massive multiple input multiple output (MIMO) [8]–[11] and the use of millimeter wave carrier frequencies (> 100 GHz) [12]–[16], to accommodate large bit-rates (> 1 Gbps) and large number of users. In this paper we deal with the physical layer of wireless systems that are also applicable to 5G. The main topics addressed in this work are timing and carrier synchronization, channel estimation, turbo codes and orthogonal frequency division multiplexing (OFDM). Recall that OFDM converts a frequency selective channel into a flat channel [17] [18].

Channel characteristics in the THz frequency range and at 17 GHz for 5G indoor wireless systems is studied in [19] [20]. Channel estimation for massive MIMO assuming spatial correlation between the receive antennas is considered in [21] [22]. In [23], a MIMO channel estimator and beamformer is described. Uplink channel estimation using compressive sensing for millimeter wave, multiuser MIMO systems is considered in [24] [25].

Waveform design for spectral containment of the transmitted signal, is an important aspect of wireless telecommunications, especially in the uplink, where many users access a base station. We require that the signal from one user does not interfere with the other user. This issue is addressed in [26]–[37]. Error control coding for 5G is discussed in [38] [39]. References to carrier and timing synchronization in OFDM can be found in [2] [3] [40].

The capacity of single-user MIMO systems under different

assumptions about the channel impulse response (also called the channel state information or CSI) and the statistics of the channel impulse response (also called channel distribution information or CDI) is discussed in [41]. The capacity of MIMO Rayleigh fading channels in the presence of interference and receive correlation is discussed in [42]. The low SNR capacity of MIMO fading channels with imperfect channel state information is presented in [43].

The main contribution of this paper is to develop discrete-time algorithms for coherently detecting multiple input, multiple output (MIMO), orthogonal frequency division multiplexed (OFDM) signals, transmitted over frequency selective Rayleigh fading channels. Carrier frequency offset and additive white Gaussian noise (AWGN) are the other impairments considered in this work. The minimum SNR per bit required for error-free transmission over frequency selective MIMO fading channels is derived. Finally we demonstrate how we can approach close to the channel capacity.

To the best of our knowledge, other than the work in [40], which deals with turbo coded single input single output (SISO) OFDM, and [2] [3], which deal with turbo coded single input multiple output (SIMO) OFDM, discrete-time algorithms for the coherent detection of turbo coded MIMO OFDM systems have not been discussed earlier in the literature. Coherent detectors for AWGN channels is discussed in [44] [45]. Simulations results for a 2×2 turbo coded MIMO OFDM system indicate that a BER of 10^{-5}, is obtained at an average SNR per bit of just 5.5 dB, which is a 2.5 dB improvement over the performance given in [2]. If each transmit antenna transmits at a different carrier frequency, then we show that it is possible to achieve a BER of 2×10^{-5} at an average SNR per bit of just 2.5 dB, with one receive antenna for each transmit antenna. When the number of receive antennas for each transmit antenna is increased to 128, then a BER of 2×10^{-5} is obtained at an average SNR per bit of 1.25 dB. In all cases, the number of transmit antennas is two and the spectral efficiency is 1 bit/transmission or 1 bit/sec/Hz. In other words, each transmit antenna sends 0.5 bit/transmission. It is possible to obtain higher spectral efficiency by increasing the number of transmit antennas, with no loss in BER performance, as long as each transmit antenna uses a different carrier frequency. It is possible to band limit the transmitted signal using pulse shaping. In all the simulations, a four-state turbo code is used. The corresponding turbo decoder uses eight iterations.

This paper is organized as follows. Section II presents the system model. The discrete-time algorithms and simulation results for the coherent receiver are given in Section III. Near-capacity signaling is presented in Section IV. Finally, Section V concludes the paper.

II. System Model

We assume a MIMO-OFDM system with N_t transmit and N_r receive antennas, with QPSK modulation. The data from each transmit antenna is organized into frames, as shown in Figure 1(a), similar to [2] [3] [40]. Note the presence of the cyclic suffix, whose purpose will be explained later. In Figure 1(b), we observe that only the data and postamble QPSK symbols are interleaved. The buffer QPSK symbols (B) are sent to the IFFT without interleaving. In Figure 1, the

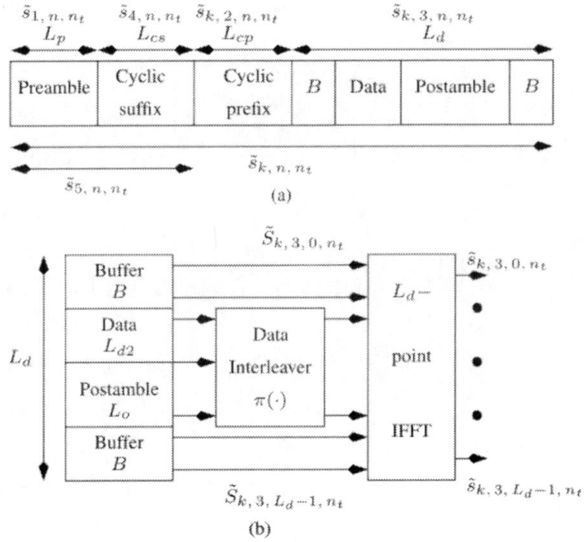

Figure 1. The frame structure in the time domain.

subscript k refers to the kth frame, n denotes the time index in a frame and $1 \le n_t \le N_t$ is the index to the transmit antenna. The total length of the frame is

$$L = L_p + L_{cs} + L_{cp} + L_d. \tag{1}$$

Let us assume a channel span equal to L_h. The channel span assumed by the receiver is [3] [40]

$$L_{hr} = 2L_h - 1 \tag{2}$$

Note that L_h depends on the delay spread of the channel, and is measured in terms of the number of symbols. Recall that, the delay spread is a measure of the time difference between the arrival of the first and the last multipath signal, as seen by the receiver. Typically

$$L_h = d_0/(cT_s) \tag{3}$$

where d_0 is the distance between the longest and shortest multipath, c is the velocity of light and T_s is the symbol duration which is equal to the sample spacing of $\tilde{s}_{k,n,n_t}$ in Figure 1(a). We have assumed a situation where the mobile is close to the base station and the longest path is reflected from the cell edge, which is approximately equal to the cell diameter d_0, as shown in Figure 2. The base stations, depicted by green dots, are interconnected by a high data-rate backhaul, shown by the blue lines. The cell edge is given by the red circles. Note that $d_1 < d_0$. In order to obtain symmetry, the backhaul forms an equilateral triangle of length d_1. The base station is at the center of each cell, whose diameter is d_0. For $L_h = 10$, $1/T_s = 10^7$ bauds and $c = 3 \times 10^8$ meters per sec, we get $d_0 = 300$ meters. Similarly with $L_h = 10$ and $1/T_s = 10^8$ bauds we obtain $d_0 = 30$ meters. In other words, as the baud rate increases, the cell size needs to decrease, and consequently the transmit power decreases, for the same channel span L_h. The length of the cyclic prefix and suffix is [17]:

$$L_{cp} = L_{cs} = L_{hr} - 1. \tag{4}$$

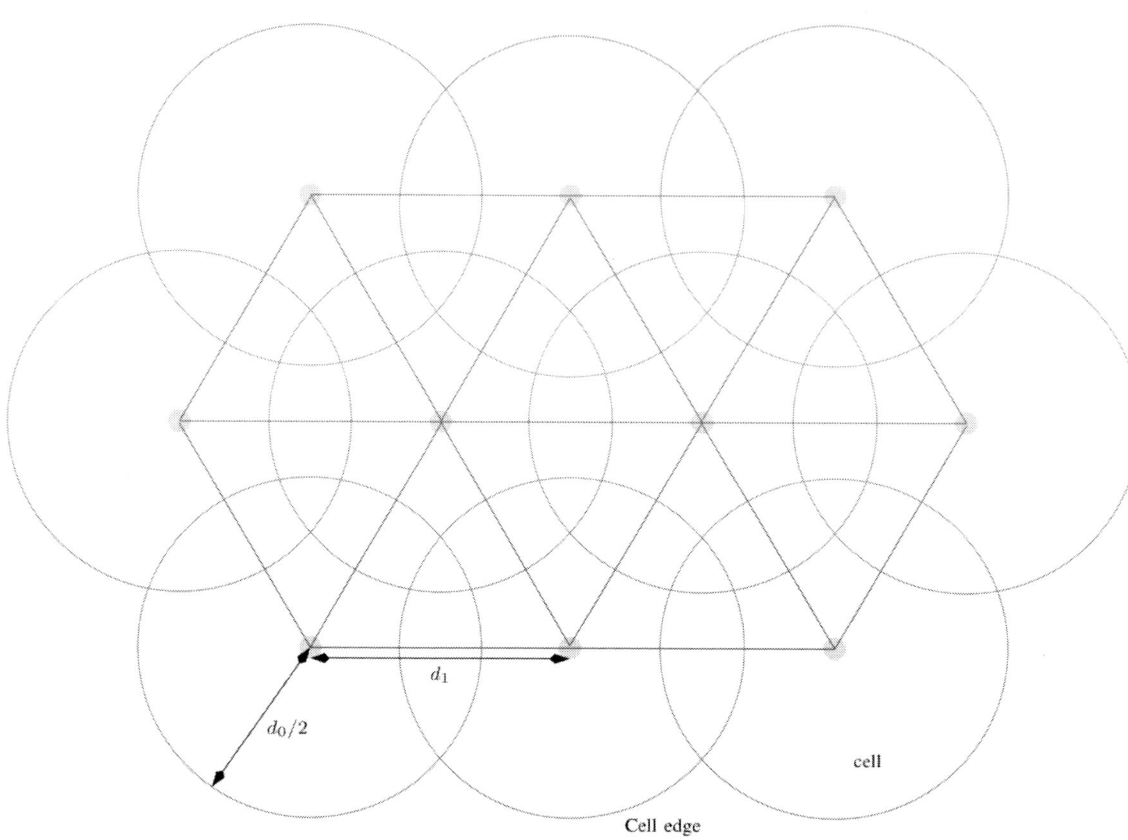

Figure 2. Arrangement of cells and base stations.

Throughout the manuscript, we use tilde to denote complex quantities. However, complex QPSK symbols will be denoted without a tilde, e.g., $S_{1,\,n,\,n_t}$. Boldface letters denote vectors or matrices. The channel coefficients $\tilde{h}_{k,\,n,\,n_r,\,n_t}$ associated with the receive antenna n_r ($1 \le n_r \le N_r$) and transmit antenna n_t ($1 \le n_t \le N_t$) for the kth frame are $\mathscr{C}\mathscr{N}(0,\,2\sigma_f^2)$ and independent over time n, that is:

$$\frac{1}{2}E\left[\tilde{h}_{k,\,n,\,n_r,\,n_t}\tilde{h}^*_{k,\,n-m,\,n_r,\,n_t}\right] = \sigma_f^2\delta_K(m) \tag{5}$$

where "*" denotes complex conjugate and $\delta_K(\cdot)$ is the Kronecker delta function. This implies a uniform power delay profile. Note that even though an exponential power delay profile is more realistic, we have used a uniform power delay profile, since it is expected to give the worst-case BER performance, as all the multipath components have the same power. The channel is assumed to be quasi-static, that is $\tilde{h}_{k,\,n,\,n_r,\,n_t}$ is time-invariant over one frame and varies independently from frame-to-frame, as given by:

$$\frac{1}{2}E\left[\tilde{h}_{k,\,n,\,n_r,\,n_t}\tilde{h}^*_{j,\,n,\,n_r,\,n_t}\right] = \sigma_f^2\delta_K(k-j) \tag{6}$$

where k and j denote the frame indices.

The AWGN noise samples $\tilde{w}_{k,n,n_r}$ for the kth frame at time n and receive antenna n_r are $\mathscr{C}\mathscr{N}(0,\,2\sigma_w^2)$. The frequency offset ω_k for the kth frame is uniformly distributed over $[-0.04,\,0.04]$ radian [46]. We assume that ω_k is fixed for a frame and varies randomly from frame-to-frame.

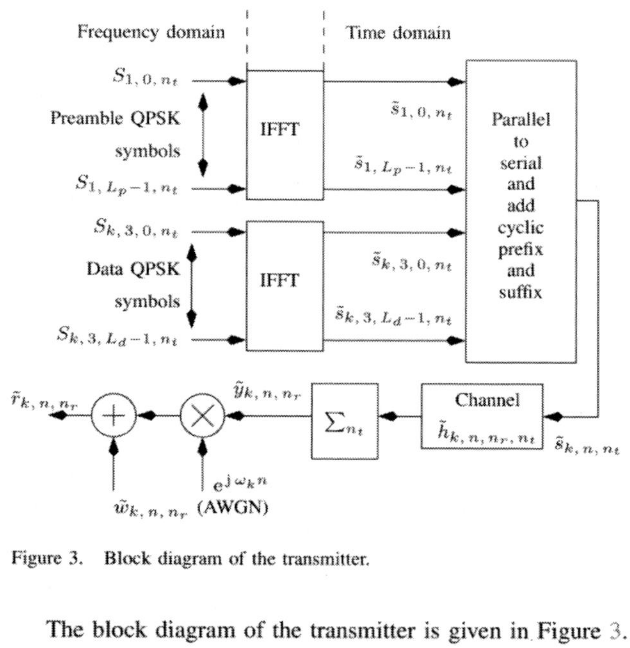

Figure 3. Block diagram of the transmitter.

The block diagram of the transmitter is given in Figure 3.

With reference to Figs. 1(a) and 3, note that:

$$\begin{aligned}
\tilde{s}_{1,\,n,\,n_t} &= \frac{1}{L_p}\sum_{i=0}^{L_p-1} S_{1,\,i,\,n_t}\mathrm{e}^{\mathrm{j}\,2\pi ni/L_p} \\
&\quad \text{for } 0 \le n \le L_p-1 \\
\tilde{s}_{k,\,3,\,n,\,n_t} &= \frac{1}{L_d}\sum_{i=0}^{L_d-1} S_{k,\,3,\,i,\,n_t}\mathrm{e}^{\mathrm{j}\,2\pi ni/L_d} \\
&\quad \text{for } 0 \le n \le L_d-1 \\
\tilde{s}_{k,\,2,\,n,\,n_t} &= \tilde{s}_{k,\,3,\,L_d-L_{cp}+n,\,n_t} \\
&\quad \text{for } 0 \le n \le L_{cp}-1 \\
\tilde{s}_{4,\,n,\,n_t} &= \tilde{s}_{1,\,n,\,n_t} \\
&\quad \text{for } 0 \le n \le L_{cs}-1 \\
\tilde{s}_{5,\,n,\,n_t} &= \tilde{s}_{1,\,n,\,n_t} + \tilde{s}_{4,\,n-L_p,\,n_t}.
\end{aligned} \tag{7}$$

From (7), it is clear that the preamble is independent of the frame k. However, each transmit antenna has its own preamble, for the purpose of synchronization and channel estimation at the receiver.

The preamble in the frequency domain, for each transmit antenna is generated as follows. Let $\pi_p(i)$, for $0 \le i \le L_p-1$, denote the interleaver map for the preamble. Let

$$\mathbf{S}_r = \left[\; S_{r,\,0} \quad \cdots \quad S_{r,\,L_p-1} \;\right]^T_{L_p\times 1} \tag{8}$$

denote a random vector of QPSK symbols. The preamble vector for the transmit antenna n_t is first initialized by

$$\begin{aligned}
\mathbf{S}_{1,\,n_t} &= \left[\; S_{1,\,0,\,n_t} \quad \cdots \quad S_{1,\,L_p-1,\,n_t} \;\right]^T_{L_p\times 1} \\
&= \mathbf{0}_{L_p\times 1}.
\end{aligned} \tag{9}$$

Next, we substitute

$$\mathbf{S}_{1,\,\pi_p(i_4:i_5),\,n_t} = \mathbf{S}_r(i_4:i_5). \tag{10}$$

where $i_4 : i_5$ denotes the range of indices from i_4 to i_5, both inclusive, and

$$\begin{aligned}
i_4 &= (n_t-1)L_p/N_t \\
i_5 &= i_4 + L_p/N_t - 1.
\end{aligned} \tag{11}$$

Note that the preamble in the frequency domain for each transmit antenna has only L_p/N_t non-zero elements, the rest of the elements are zero. Moreover, due to $\pi_p(\cdot)$, the L_p/N_t non-zero elements are randomly interspersed over the L_p subcarriers in the frequency domain, for each transmit antenna.

By virtue of the preamble construction in (9), (10) and (11), the preambles in the frequency and time domains corresponding to transmit antennas n_t and m_t satisfy the relation (using Parseval's energy theorem):

$$\begin{aligned}
S_{1,\,i,\,n_t}S^*_{1,\,i,\,m_t} &= (2N_tL_p/L_d)\delta_K(n_t-m_t) \\
&\quad \text{for } 0 \le i \le L_p-1 \\
\Rightarrow \tilde{s}_{1,\,n,\,n_t} \odot_{L_p} \tilde{s}^*_{1,\,-n,\,m_t} &= \begin{cases} 0 & \text{for } n_t \ne m_t, \\ & 0 \le n \le L_p-1 \\ (2L_p/L_d)\delta_K(n) & \\ & \text{for } n_t = m_t \end{cases}
\end{aligned} \tag{12}$$

where "$\odot_{L_p}$" denotes the L_p-point circular convolution. In other words, the preambles corresponding to distinct transmit antennas are orthogonal over L_p samples. Moreover, the autocorrelation of the preambles in frequency and time domain, can be approximated by a weighted Kronecker delta function (this condition is usually satisfied by random sequences having zero-mean; the approximation gets better as L_p increases).

We assume $S_{k,\,3,\,i,\,n_t} \in \{\pm 1 \pm \mathrm{j}\}$. Since we require:

$$E\left[\left|\tilde{s}_{1,\,n,\,n_t}\right|^2\right] = E\left[\left|\tilde{s}_{k,\,3,\,n,\,n_t}\right|^2\right] = 2/L_d \stackrel{\Delta}{=} \sigma_s^2 \tag{13}$$

we must have $S_{1,\,i,\,n_t} \in \sqrt{L_pN_t/L_d}\,(\pm 1 \pm \mathrm{j})$. In other words, the average power of the preamble part must be equal to the average power of the data part, in the time domain.

Due to the presence of the cyclic suffix in Figure 1 and (7), and due to (12), we have

$$\begin{aligned}
&\tilde{s}_{5,\,n,\,n_t} \star \tilde{s}^*_{1,\,L_p-1-n,\,m_t} \\
&= \begin{cases} 0 & \text{for } L_p-1 \le n \le L_p+L_{hr}-2, \\ & n_t \ne m_t \\ (2L_p/L_d)\delta_K(n-L_p+1) & \\ & \text{for } n_t = m_t \end{cases}
\end{aligned} \tag{14}$$

where "$\star$" denotes linear convolution.

The signal for the kth frame and receive antenna n_r can be written as (for $0 \le n \le L+L_h-2$):

$$\begin{aligned}
\tilde{r}_{k,\,n,\,n_r} &= \sum_{n_t=1}^{N_t}\left(\tilde{s}_{k,\,n,\,n_t} \star \tilde{h}_{k,\,n,\,n_r,\,n_t}\right)\mathrm{e}^{\mathrm{j}\,\omega_k n} + \tilde{w}_{k,\,n,\,n_r} \\
&= \tilde{y}_{k,\,n,\,n_r}\mathrm{e}^{\mathrm{j}\,\omega_k n} + \tilde{w}_{k,\,n,\,n_r}
\end{aligned} \tag{15}$$

where $\tilde{s}_{k,\,n,\,n_t}$ is depicted in Figure 1(a) and

$$\tilde{y}_{k,\,n,\,n_r} = \sum_{n_t=1}^{N_t} \tilde{s}_{k,\,n,\,n_t} \star \tilde{h}_{k,\,n,\,n_r,\,n_t}. \tag{16}$$

Note that any random carrier phase can be absorbed in the channel impulse response.

The uplink and downlink transmissions between the mobiles and base station could be carried out using time division duplex (TDD) or frequency division duplex (FDD). Time division (TDMA), frequency division (FDMA), code division (CDMA), orthogonal frequency division (OFDMA), for downlink transmissions and filterbank multicarrier (FBMC), for uplink transmissions [26], are the possible choices for multiple access (MA) techniques.

III. RECEIVER

In this section, we discuss the discrete-time receiver algorithms.

A. Start of Frame (SoF) and Coarse Frequency Offset Estimate

The start of frame (SoF) detection and coarse frequency offset estimation is performed for each receive antenna $1 \le n_r \le N_r$ and transmit antenna $1 \le n_t \le N_t$, as given by the following rule (similar to (22) in [40] and (24) in [3]): choose that value of m and ν_k which maximizes

$$\left|\left(\tilde{r}_{k,\,m,\,n_r}\,\mathrm{e}^{-\mathrm{j}\,\nu_k m}\right) \star \tilde{s}^*_{1,\,L_p-1-m,\,n_t}\right|. \tag{17}$$

Let $\hat{m}_k(\cdot)$ denote the time instant and $\hat{\nu}_k(\cdot)$ denote the coarse estimate of the frequency offset (both of which are functions of n_r and n_t), at which the maximum in (17) is obtained. Note that (17) is a two-dimensional search over m and ν_k, which can be efficiently implemented in hardware, and there is a large scope for parallel processing. In particular, the search over ν_k involves dividing the range of ω_k ($[-0.04, 0.04]$ radians) into B_1 frequency bins, and deciding in favour of that bin which maximizes (17). In our simulations, $B_1 = 64$ [3] [40].

Note that in the absence of noise and due to the properties given in (14)

$$\hat{m}_k(n_r, n_t) = L_p - 1 + \text{argmax}_m \left| \tilde{h}_{k,\, m,\, n_r,\, n_t} \right| \tag{18}$$

where argmax_m corresponds to the value of m for which $\left| \tilde{h}_{k,\, m,\, n_r,\, n_t} \right|$ is maximum. We also have

$$L_p - 1 \le \hat{m}_k(n_r, n_t) \le L_p + L_h - 2. \tag{19}$$

If $\hat{m}_k(\cdot)$ lies outside the range in (19), the frame is declared as erased (not detected). This implies that the peak in (17) is due to noise, and not due to the channel. The results for SoF detection at 0 dB SNR per bit for $L_p = 512, 1024, 4096$ are given in Figs. 4, 5, and 6, respectively, for $N_t = N_r = 2$. The parameter Z in the three figures denotes the correlation magnitude given by (17).

The average value of the coarse frequency offset estimate is given by

$$\hat{\omega}_k = \frac{\sum_{n_r=1}^{N_r} \sum_{n_t=1}^{N_t} \hat{\nu}_k(n_r, n_t)}{N_r N_t}. \tag{20}$$

B. Channel Estimation

We assume that the SoF has been estimated using (17) with outcome $m_{0,\, k}$ given by (assuming the condition in (19) is satisfied for all n_r and n_t):

$$m_{0,\, k} = \hat{m}_k(1, 1) - L_p + 1 \quad 0 \le m_{0,\, k} \le L_h - 1 \tag{21}$$

and the frequency offset has been perfectly canceled [3] [40]. Observe that any value of n_r and n_t can be used in the computation of (21). We have taken $n_r = n_t = 1$. Define

$$m_{1,\, k} = m_{0,\, k} + L_h - 1. \tag{22}$$

For the sake of notational simplicity, we drop the subscript k in $m_{1,\, k}$, and refer to it as m_1. The steady-state, preamble part of the received signal for the kth frame and receive antenna n_r can be written as:

$$\tilde{\mathbf{r}}_{k,\, m_1,\, n_r} = \sum_{n_t=1}^{N_t} \tilde{\mathbf{s}}_{5,\, n_t} \tilde{\mathbf{h}}_{k,\, n_r,\, n_t} + \tilde{\mathbf{w}}_{k,\, m_1,\, n_r} \tag{23}$$

where

$$\begin{aligned}
\tilde{\mathbf{r}}_{k,\, m_1,\, n_r} &= \begin{bmatrix} \tilde{r}_{k,\, m_1,\, n_r} & \ldots & \tilde{r}_{k,\, m_1+L_p-1,\, n_r} \end{bmatrix}^T \\
&\quad [L_p \times 1] \quad \text{vector} \\
\tilde{\mathbf{w}}_{k,\, m_1,\, n_r} &= \begin{bmatrix} \tilde{w}_{k,\, m_1,\, n_r} & \ldots & \tilde{w}_{k,\, m_1+L_p-1,\, n_r} \end{bmatrix}^T \\
&\quad [L_p \times 1] \quad \text{vector} \\
\tilde{\mathbf{h}}_{k,\, n_r,\, n_t} &= \begin{bmatrix} \tilde{h}_{k,\, 0,\, n_r,\, n_t} & \ldots & \tilde{h}_{k,\, L_{hr}-1,\, n_r,\, n_t} \end{bmatrix}^T \\
&\quad [L_{hr} \times 1] \quad \text{vector} \\
\tilde{\mathbf{s}}_{5,\, n_t} &= \begin{bmatrix} \tilde{s}_{5,\, L_{hr}-1,\, n_t} & \ldots & \tilde{s}_{5,\, 0,\, n_t} \\ \vdots & \ldots & \vdots \\ \tilde{s}_{5,\, L_p+L_{hr}-2,\, n_t} & \ldots & \tilde{s}_{5,\, L_p-1,\, n_t} \end{bmatrix} \\
&\quad [L_p \times L_{hr}] \quad \text{matrix}
\end{aligned} \tag{24}$$

where L_{hr} is the channel length assumed by the receiver (see (2)), $\tilde{\mathbf{s}}_{5,\, n_t}$ is the channel estimation matrix and $\tilde{\mathbf{r}}_{k,\, m_1,\, n_r}$ is the received signal vector *after* cancellation of the frequency offset. Observe that $\tilde{\mathbf{s}}_{5,\, n_t}$ is independent of m_1 and due to the relations in (12) and (14), we have

$$\tilde{\mathbf{s}}_{5,\, m_t}^H \tilde{\mathbf{s}}_{5,\, n_t} = \begin{cases} \mathbf{0}_{L_{hr} \times L_{hr}} & \text{for } n_t \ne m_t \\ (2L_p/L_d)\mathbf{I}_{L_{hr}} & \text{for } n_t = m_t \end{cases} \tag{25}$$

where $\mathbf{I}_{L_{hr}}$ is an $L_{hr} \times L_{hr}$ identity matrix and $\mathbf{0}_{L_{hr} \times L_{hr}}$ is an $L_{hr} \times L_{hr}$ null matrix. The statement of the ML channel estimation is as follows. Find $\hat{\mathbf{h}}_{k,\, n_r,\, m_t}$ (the estimate of $\tilde{\mathbf{h}}_{k,\, n_r,\, m_t}$) such that:

$$\left(\tilde{\mathbf{r}}_{k,\, m_1,\, n_r} - \sum_{m_t=1}^{N_t} \tilde{\mathbf{s}}_{5,\, m_t} \hat{\mathbf{h}}_{k,\, n_r,\, m_t} \right)^H \left(\tilde{\mathbf{r}}_{k,\, m_1,\, n_r} - \sum_{m_t=1}^{N_t} \tilde{\mathbf{s}}_{5,\, m_t} \hat{\mathbf{h}}_{k,\, n_r,\, m_t} \right) \tag{26}$$

is minimized. Differentiating with respect to $\hat{\mathbf{h}}_{k,\, n_r,\, m_t}^*$ and setting the result to zero yields [17] [47]:

$$\hat{\mathbf{h}}_{k,\, n_r,\, m_t} = \left(\tilde{\mathbf{s}}_{5,\, m_t}^H \tilde{\mathbf{s}}_{5,\, m_t} \right)^{-1} \tilde{\mathbf{s}}_{5,\, m_t}^H \tilde{\mathbf{r}}_{k,\, m_1,\, n_r}. \tag{27}$$

Observe that when $m_{0,\, k} = L_h - 1$ in (21), and noise is absent (see (29) in [40] and (35) in [3]), we obtain:

$$\begin{aligned}
&\hat{\mathbf{h}}_{k,\, n_r,\, m_t} \\
&= \begin{bmatrix} \tilde{h}_{k,\, 0,\, n_r,\, m_t} & \ldots & \tilde{h}_{k,\, L_h-1,\, n_r,\, m_t} & 0 & \ldots & 0 \end{bmatrix}^T.
\end{aligned} \tag{28}$$

Similarly, when $m_{0,\, k} = 0$ and in the absence of noise:

$$\begin{aligned}
&\hat{\mathbf{h}}_{k,\, n_r,\, m_t} \\
&= \begin{bmatrix} 0 & \ldots & 0 & \tilde{h}_{k,\, 0,\, n_r,\, m_t} & \ldots & \tilde{h}_{k,\, L_h-1,\, n_r,\, m_t} \end{bmatrix}^T.
\end{aligned} \tag{29}$$

To see the effect of noise on the channel estimate in (27), consider

$$\tilde{\mathbf{u}} = \left(\tilde{\mathbf{s}}_{5,\, m_t}^H \tilde{\mathbf{s}}_{5,\, m_t} \right)^{-1} \tilde{\mathbf{s}}_{5,\, m_t}^H \tilde{\mathbf{w}}_{k,\, m_1,\, n_r}. \tag{30}$$

It can be shown that

$$E\left[\tilde{\mathbf{u}} \tilde{\mathbf{u}}^H \right] = \frac{\sigma_w^2 L_d}{L_p} \mathbf{I}_{L_{hr}} \stackrel{\Delta}{=} 2\sigma_u^2 \mathbf{I}_{L_{hr}}. \tag{31}$$

Therefore, the variance of the ML channel estimate (σ_u^2) tends to zero as $L_p \to \infty$ and L_d is kept fixed. Conversely, when L_d is increased keeping L_p fixed, there is noise enhancement [2] [3]. The magnitude spectrum of the actual and estimated channel for various preamble lengths are shown in Figs. 7, 8 and 9 for $N_t = N_r = 2$ and 0 dB average SNR per bit. Note that $\tilde{H}_{k,\, i,\, n_r,\, n_t}$ denotes the L_d-point discrete Fourier transform (DFT) of $\tilde{h}_{k,\, n,\, n_r,\, n_t}$ in (5).

C. Fine Frequency Offset Estimation

The fine frequency offset estimate is obtained using the following rule: choose that value of time instant m and frequency offset $\nu_{k,\, f}$ which maximizes:

$$\left| \left(\tilde{r}_{k,\, m,\, n_r} \, \mathrm{e}^{-\mathrm{j}\,(\hat{\omega}_k + \nu_{k,\, f})m} \right) \star \tilde{y}_{1,\, k,\, L_2-1-m,\, n_r,\, n_t}^* \right| \tag{32}$$

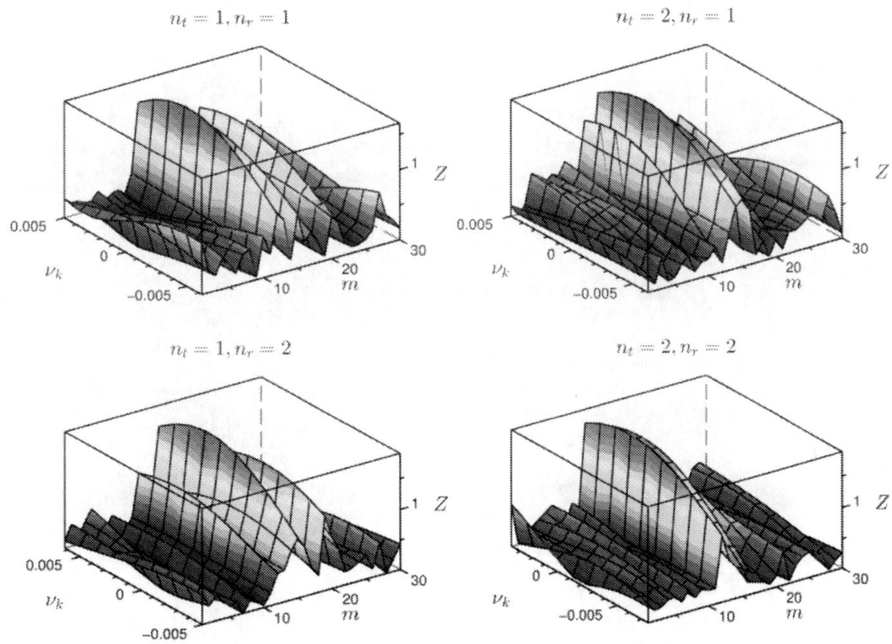

Figure 4. SoF detection at 0 dB SNR per bit, $L_p = 512$.

where

$$\begin{aligned} L_2 &= L_{hr} + L_p - 1 \\ \hat{y}_{1,\,k,\,m,\,n_r,\,n_t} &= \tilde{s}_{1,\,m,\,n_t} \star \hat{h}_{k,\,m,\,n_r,\,n_t} \end{aligned} \tag{33}$$

where $\hat{h}_{k,\,m,\,n_r,\,n_t}$ is obtained from (27). The fine frequency offset estimate ($\hat{\nu}_{k,\,f}(n_r,\,n_t)$) is obtained by dividing the interval $[\hat{\omega}_k - 0.005, \hat{\omega}_k + 0.005]$ radian ($\hat{\omega}_k$ is given in (20)) into $B_2 = 64$ frequency bins [44]. The reason for choosing 0.005 radian can be traced to Figure 5 of [3]. We find that the maximum error in the coarse estimate of the frequency offset is approximately 0.004 radian over 10^4 frames. Thus the probability that the maximum error exceeds 0.005 radian is less than 10^{-4}. However, from Table IV in this paper, we note that the maximum error in the frequency offset is 2.4×10^{-2} radians for $L_p = 512$, and 1.1×10^{-2} for $L_p = 1024$, both of which are larger than 0.005 radian. By observing this trend, we expect that for larger values of L_p, say $L_p = 4096$, the maximum error in the coarse frequency offset estimate would be less than 0.005 radians. Increasing L_p would also imply an increase in L_d, for the same throughput (see (54)). The average value of the fine frequency offset estimate is given by:

$$\hat{\omega}_{k,\,f} = \frac{\sum_{n_r=1}^{N_r} \sum_{n_t=1}^{N_t} \hat{\nu}_{k,\,f}(n_r,\,n_t)}{N_r N_t}. \tag{34}$$

D. Super Fine Frequency Offset Estimation

The fine frequency offset estimate in (34) is still inadequate for turbo decoding and data detection when $L_d \gg L_p$ [40]. Note that the residual frequency offset is equal to:

$$\omega_k - \hat{\omega}_k - \hat{\omega}_{k,\,f}. \tag{35}$$

This residual frequency offset is estimated by interpolating the FFT output and performing postamble matched filtering at the receiver [2] [3]. If the interpolation factor is I, then the FFT size is IL_d (interpolation in the frequency domain is achieved by zero-padding the FFT input in the time domain, and then taking the IL_d-point FFT). Let

$$m_{2,\,k} = m_{1,\,k} + L_p + L_{cs} \tag{36}$$

where $m_{1,\,k}$ is defined in (22). Once again, we drop the subscript k from $m_{2,\,k}$ and refer to it as m_2. Define the FFT input in the time domain as:

$$\tilde{\mathbf{r}}_{k,\,m_2,\,n_r} = [\ \tilde{r}_{k,\,m_2,\,n_r} \quad \cdots \quad \tilde{r}_{k,\,m_2+L_d-1,\,n_r}\ ]^T \tag{37}$$

which is the data part of the received signal in (15) for the kth frame and receive antenna n_r, assumed to have the residual frequency offset given by (35). The output of the IL_d-point FFT of $\tilde{\mathbf{r}}_{k,\,m_2,\,n_r}$ in (37) is denoted by

$$\tilde{R}_{k,\,i,\,n_r} = \sum_{n=0}^{L_d-1} \tilde{r}_{k,\,m_2+n,\,n_r} \mathrm{e}^{-\mathrm{j}\,2\pi i n/(IL_d)} \tag{38}$$

for $0 \le i \le IL_d - 1$.

The coefficients of the postamble matched filter is obtained as follows [2] [3]. Define

$$\tilde{G}''_{k,\,i,\,n_r} = \sum_{n_t=1}^{N_t} \hat{H}_{k,\,i_3,\,n_r,\,n_t} S_{k,\,3,\,i,\,n_t} \quad \text{for } i_0 \le i \le i_1 \tag{39}$$

where $\hat{H}_{k,\,i,\,n_r,\,n_t}$ is the L_d-point FFT of the channel estimate

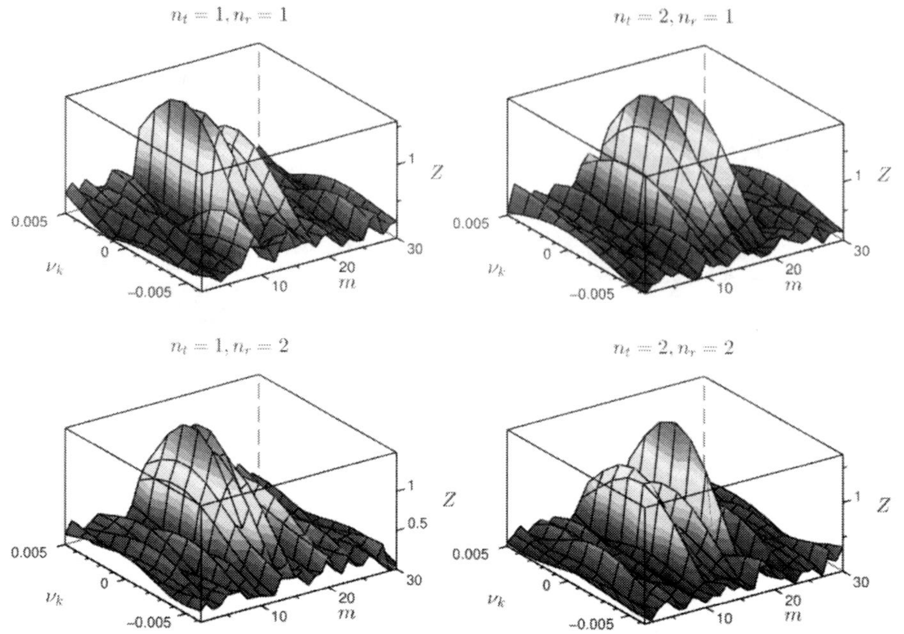

Figure 5. SoF detection at 0 dB SNR per bit, $L_p = 1024$.

in (27), and

$$
\begin{aligned}
i_0 &= B + L_{d2} \\
i_1 &= i_0 + L_o - 1 \\
i_3 &= B + \pi(i - B)
\end{aligned}
\tag{40}
$$

where $\pi(\cdot)$ is the data interleaver map, B, L_{d2} and L_o are the lengths of the buffer, data, and postamble, respectively, as shown in Figure 1(b). Let

$$
\tilde{G}'_{k,\,i_3,\,n_r} = \begin{cases} \tilde{G}''_{k,\,i,\,n_r} & \text{for } i_0 \le i \le i_1 \\ 0 & \text{otherwise} \end{cases} \tag{41}
$$

where $0 \le i_3 \le L_d - 1$, the relation between i_3 and i is given in (40). Next, we perform interpolation:

$$
\tilde{G}_{k,\,i_4,\,n_r} = \begin{cases} \tilde{G}'_{k,\,i,\,n_r} & \text{for } 0 \le i \le L_d - 1 \\ 0 & \text{otherwise} \end{cases} \tag{42}
$$

where $0 \le i_4 \le IL_d - 1$ and $i_4 = iI$. Finally, the postamble matched filter is $\tilde{G}^*_{k,\,IL_d-1-i,\,n_r}$, which is convolved with $\tilde{R}_{k,\,i,\,n_r}$ in (38). Note that due to the presence of the cyclic prefix, any residual frequency offset in the time domain, manifests as a circular shift in the frequency domain. The purpose of the postamble matched filter is to capture this shift. The role of the buffer symbols is explained in [2] [3]. Assume that the peak of the postamble matched filter output occurs at $m_{3,\,k}(n_r)$. Ideally, in the absence of noise and frequency offset

$$
m_{3,\,k}(n_r) = IL_d - 1. \tag{43}
$$

In the presence of the frequency offset, the peak occurs to the left or right of $IL_d - 1$. The average superfine estimate of the residual frequency offset is given by:

$$
\hat{\omega}_{k,\,sf} = 2\pi/(IL_d N_r) \sum_{n_r=1}^{N_r} \left[m_{3,\,k}(n_r) - IL_d + 1 \right]. \tag{44}
$$

E. Noise Variance Estimation

The noise variance is estimated as follows, for the purpose of turbo decoding:

$$
\hat{\sigma}_w^2 = \frac{1}{2L_pN_r} \sum_{n_r=1}^{N_r} \left(\tilde{\mathbf{r}}_{k,\,m_1,\,n_r} - \sum_{n_t=1}^{N_t} \tilde{\mathbf{s}}_{5,\,n_t} \hat{\mathbf{h}}_{k,\,n_r,\,n_t} \right)^H \left(\tilde{\mathbf{r}}_{k,\,m_1,\,n_r} - \sum_{n_t=1}^{N_t} \tilde{\mathbf{s}}_{5,\,n_t} \hat{\mathbf{h}}_{k,\,n_r,\,n_t} \right). \tag{45}
$$

F. Turbo Decoding

In this section, we assume that the frequency offset has been perfectly canceled, that is, $\tilde{\mathbf{r}}_{k,\,m_2,\,n_r}$ in (37) contains no frequency offset. The output of the L_d-point FFT of $\tilde{\mathbf{r}}_{k,\,m_2,\,n_r}$ for the kth frame is given by:

$$
\tilde{R}_{k,\,i,\,n_r} = \sum_{n_t=1}^{N_t} \tilde{H}_{k,\,i,\,n_r,\,n_t} S_{k,\,3,\,i,\,n_t} + \tilde{W}_{k,\,i,\,n_r} \tag{46}
$$

for $0 \le i \le L_d - 1$, where $\tilde{H}_{k,\,i,\,n_r,\,n_t}$ is the L_d-point FFT of $\tilde{h}_{k,\,n,\,n_r,\,n_t}$ and $\tilde{W}_{k,\,i,\,n_r}$ is the L_d-point FFT of $\tilde{w}_{k,\,n,\,n_r}$. It can be shown that [3] [40]

$$
\begin{aligned}
\frac{1}{2} E \left[\left| \tilde{W}_{k,\,i,\,n_r} \right|^2 \right] &= L_d \sigma_w^2 \\
\frac{1}{2} E \left[\left| \tilde{H}_{k,\,i,\,n_r,\,n_t} \right|^2 \right] &= L_h \sigma_f^2.
\end{aligned}
\tag{47}
$$

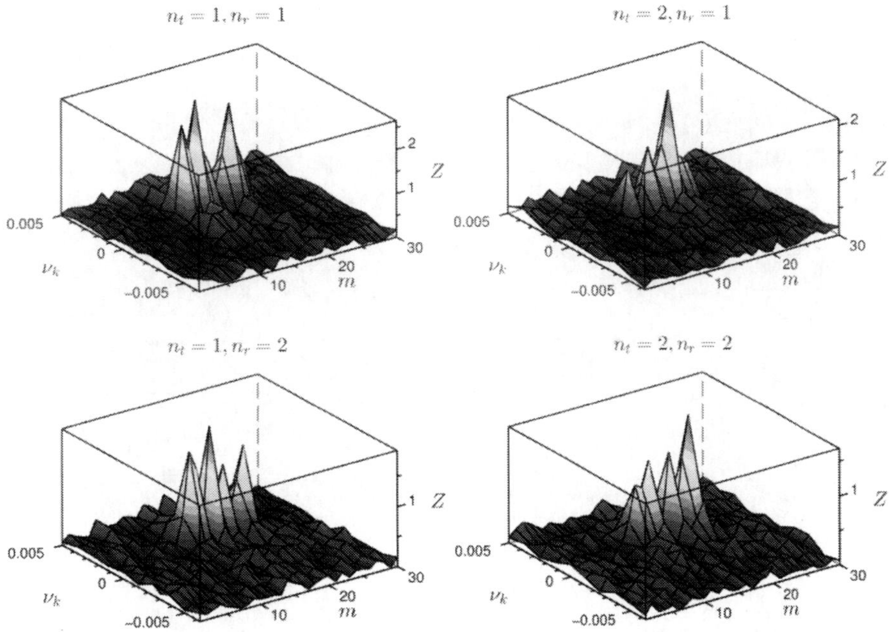

Figure 6. SoF detection at 0 dB SNR per bit, $L_p = 4096$.

The received signal in (46), for the kth frame and i^{th} subcarrier, can be written in matrix form as follows:

$$\tilde{\mathbf{R}}_{k,\,i} = \tilde{\mathbf{H}}_{k,\,i}\mathbf{S}_{k,\,3,\,i} + \tilde{\mathbf{W}}_{k,\,i} \tag{48}$$

where $\tilde{\mathbf{R}}_{k,\,i}$ is the $N_r \times 1$ received signal vector, $\tilde{\mathbf{H}}_{k,\,i}$ is the $N_r \times N_t$ channel matrix, $\mathbf{S}_{k,\,3,\,i}$ is the $N_t \times 1$ symbol vector and $\tilde{\mathbf{W}}_{k,\,i}$ is the $N_r \times 1$ noise vector.

The generating matrix of each of the constituent encoders is given by (41) in [ ], and is repeated here for convenience:

$$\mathbf{G}(D) = \left[\begin{array}{cc} 1 & \frac{1+D^2}{1+D+D^2} \end{array}\right]. \tag{49}$$

For the purpose of turbo decoding, we consider the case where $N_r = N_t = 2$. The details of turbo decoding can be found in [ ], and will not be discussed here. Suffices to say that corresponding to the transition from state m to state n, at decoder 1, for the kth frame, at time i, we define (for $0 \le i \le L_{d2} - 1$):

$$\gamma_{1,\,k,\,i,\,m,\,n} = \exp\left(-Z_{1,\,k,\,i,\,m,\,n} / \left(2L_d\hat{\sigma}_w^2\right)\right) \tag{50}$$

where $Z_{1,\,k,\,i,\,m,\,n}$ is given by

$$\min_{\text{all } S_{m,\,n,\,2}} \sum_{n_r=1}^{2} \left| \tilde{R}_{k,\,i,\,n_r} - \sum_{n_t=1}^{2} \hat{H}_{k,\,i,\,n_r,\,n_t} S_{m,\,n,\,n_t} \right|^2 \tag{51}$$

where $S_{m,\,n,\,n_t}$ denotes the QPSK symbol corresponding to the transition from state m to state n in the trellis, at transmit antenna n_t. Observe that $\hat{\sigma}_w^2$ is the estimate of σ_w^2 obtained from (45). Observe that the minimization in (51) is over all possible QPSK symbols, at $n_t = 2$ and index i. Similarly, for the transition from state m to state n, at decoder 2, for the kth frame, at time i, we define (for $0 \le i \le L_{d2} - 1$):

$$\gamma_{2,\,k,\,i,\,m,\,n} = \exp\left(-Z_{2,\,k,\,i,\,m,\,n} / \left(2L_d\hat{\sigma}_w^2\right)\right) \tag{52}$$

where $Z_{2,\,k,\,i,\,m,\,n}$ is given by

$$\min_{\text{all } S_{m,\,n,\,1}} \sum_{n_r=1}^{2} \left| \tilde{R}_{k,\,i,\,n_r} - \sum_{n_t=1}^{2} \hat{H}_{k,\,i,\,n_r,\,n_t} S_{m,\,n,\,n_t} \right|^2 . \tag{53}$$

Now, (50) and (52) are used in the forward and backward recursions of the BCJR algorithm [ ].

G. Summary of the Receiver Algorithms

The receiver algorithms are summarized as follows:

1) Estimate the start-of-frame and the frequency offset (coarse) using (17), for each receive antenna. Obtain the average value of the frequency offset ($\hat{\omega}_k$) using (20).
2) Cancel the frequency offset by multiplying $\tilde{r}_{k,\,n,\,n_r}$ in (15) by $\mathrm{e}^{-\mathrm{j}\,\hat{\omega}_k n}$, and estimate the channel using (27), for each n_r and n_t.
3) Obtain $\tilde{y}_{1,\,k,\,m,\,n_r,\,n_t}$ from (33) and the fine frequency offset using (34).
4) Cancel the frequency offset by multiplying $\tilde{r}_{k,\,n,\,n_r}$ in (15) by $\mathrm{e}^{-\mathrm{j}(\hat{\omega}_k + \hat{\omega}_{k,\,f})n}$, and estimate the channel again using (27), for each n_r and n_t.
5) Obtain the average superfine frequency offset estimate using (44). Cancel the offset by multiplying $\tilde{r}_{k,\,n,\,n_r}$ in (15) by $\mathrm{e}^{-\mathrm{j}(\hat{\omega}_k + \hat{\omega}_{k,\,f} + \hat{\omega}_{k,\,sf})n}$.
6) Obtain the noise variance estimate from (45).
7) Take the L_d-point FFT of $\tilde{\mathbf{r}}_{k,\,m2,\,n_r}$ and perform turbo decoding.

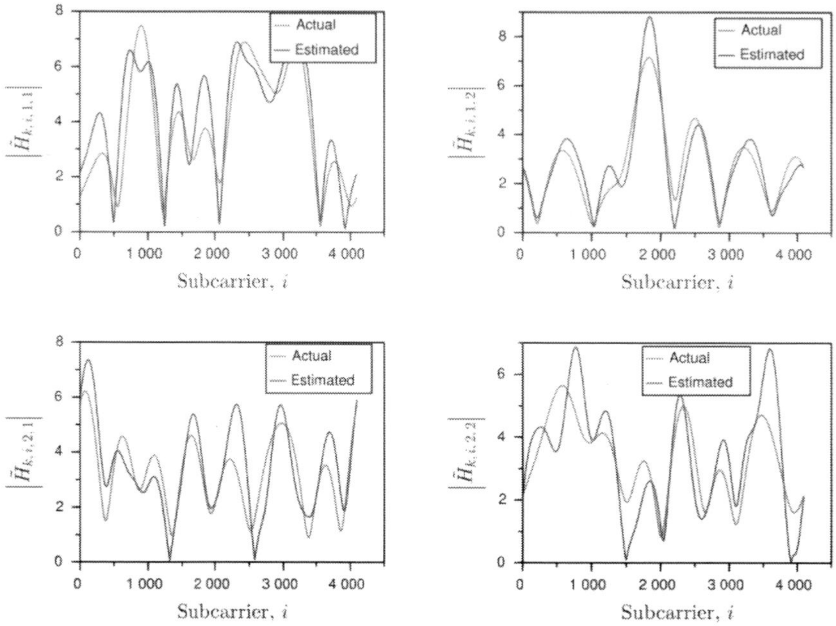

Figure 7. Magnitude spectrum of estimated and actual channel, $L_p = 512$.

H. Simulation Results

In this section, we present the simulation results for the proposed turbo coded MIMO OFDM system with $N_t = N_r = 2$. The SNR per bit is defined in (92). Note that one data bit (two coded QPSK symbols) is sent simultaneously from two transmit antennas. Hence, the number of data bits sent from each transmit antenna is $\kappa = 0.5$, as given in (92). We have also assumed that $\sigma_f^2 = 0.5$. The frame parameters are summarized in Table I. The maximum number of frames simulated is 2.2×10^4, at an average SNR per bit of 6.5 dB. Each simulation run is over 10^3 frames. Hence, the maximum number of independently seeded simulation runs is 22.

TABLE I. FRAME PARAMETERS.

Parameter	Value (QPSK symbols)
L_p	512, 1024
L_d	4096
B	4
L_o	256, 512
L_{d2}	3832, 3576
L_h	10
$L_{cp} = L_{cs}$	18

The throughput is defined as [2] [3]:

$$\mathscr{T} = \frac{L_{d2}}{L_d + L_p + L_{cp} + L_{cs}}. \tag{54}$$

The throughput of various frame configurations is given in Table II. The BER simulation results for the turbo coded MIMO OFDM system with $N_t = N_r = 2$ is shown in Figure 10. Here "Id" denotes the ideal receiver. For the practical receivers ("Pr"), the interpolation factor for superfine frequency offset estimation is $I = 16$. The practical receiver with $L_p = 1024$, $L_o = 512$ attains a BER of 10^{-5} at an SNR per bit of 5.5 dB, which is 1 dB better than the receiver with $L_p = 512$, $L_o = 256$. This is due to the fact that the variance of the channel estimation error with $L_p = 512$ is twice that of $L_p = 1024$ (see (31)). This difference in the variance of the channel estimation error affects the turbo decoding process. Moreover, the practical receiver in Figure 10 with $L_p = 1024$, $L_o = 512$ is 2.5 dB better than the practical receiver with one transmit and two receive antennas in Figure 10 of [2].

TABLE II. THROUGHPUT.

L_p	L_o	L_{d2}	$\mathscr{T}$
512	256	3832	82.515%
1024	512	3576	69.356%

TABLE III. PROBABILITY OF FRAME ERASURE.

Frame configuration	Probability of erasure
$L_p = 512$, $L_o = 256$	2.98×10^{-2}
$L_p = 1024$, $L_o = 512$	7×10^{-4}

The probability of frame erasure (this happens when (19)

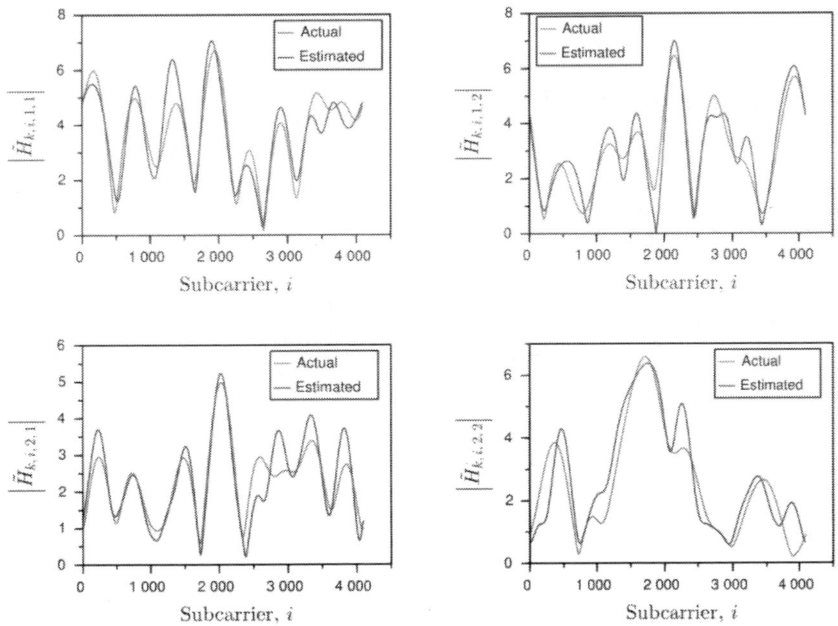

Figure 8. Magnitude spectrum of estimated and actual channel, $L_p = 1024$.

is not satisfied) at 0 dB SNR per bit is shown in Table III. Clearly, as L_p increases, the probability of erasure decreases. Finally, the root mean square (RMS) and maximum frequency offset estimation error in radians, at 0 dB SNR per bit, is given in Table IV.

IV. NEAR CAPACITY SIGNALING

In Sections II and III, we had presented the discrete-time algorithms for MIMO-OFDM. The inherent assumption in these two sections was that all transmit antennas use the same carrier frequency. The consequence of this assumption is that the signal at each receive antenna is a linear combination of the symbols from all the transmit antennas, as given in (46) and (48). This makes the estimation of symbols, $\mathbf{S}_{k,3,i}$ in (48), complicated for large values of N_t and N_r (massive MIMO). In this section, we assume that distinct transmit antennas use different carrier frequencies. Thus, the signals from distinct transmit antennas are orthogonal. To each transmit antenna, we associate N_r receive antennas, that are capable of receiving signals from one particular transmit antenna. The total number of receive antennas is now $N_r N_t$.

In order to restrict the transmitted signal spectrum, it is desirable to have a lowpass filter (LPF) at the output of the parallel-to-serial converter in Figure 3, for each transmit antenna. If we assume that the cut-off frequency of the LPF is $\pi/10$ radians and its transition bandwidth is $\pi/20$ radians, then the required length of the linear-phase, finite impulse response (FIR) LPF with Hamming window would be [48]

$$\begin{aligned} 8\pi/L_{\text{LPF}} &= \pi/20 \\ \Rightarrow L_{\text{LPF}} &= 160. \end{aligned} \tag{55}$$

Note that an infinite impulse response (IIR) filter could also be used. However, it may have stability problems when the cut-off frequency of the LPF is close to zero radians. If the physical channel has 10 taps as given by (3), then the length of the equivalent channel as seen by the receiver would be:

$$\begin{aligned} L_h &= L_{\text{LPF}} + 10 - 1 \\ &= 160 + 10 - 1 \\ &= 169. \end{aligned} \tag{56}$$

The values of L_p and L_d in Figure 1(a) have to be suitably increased to obtain a good estimate of the channel (see (31)) and maintain a high throughput (see 54). Let us denote the impulse response of the LPF by p_n. We assume that p_n is obtained by sampling the continuous-time impulse response $p(t)$ at a rate of $1/T_s$, where T_s is defined in (3). Note that p_n is real-valued [48]. The discrete-time Fourier transform (DTFT) of p_n is [17] [18]:

$$\begin{aligned} \tilde{P}_{\mathscr{P}}(F) &= \sum_{n=0}^{L_{\text{LPF}}-1} p_n \mathrm{e}^{-\mathrm{j}\,2\pi F n T_s} \\ &= \frac{1}{T_s} \sum_{m=-\infty}^{\infty} \tilde{P}(F - m/T_s) \end{aligned} \tag{57}$$

where the subscript $\mathscr{P}$ denotes a periodic function, F denotes the frequency in Hz and $\tilde{P}(F)$ is the continuous-time Fourier transform of $p(t)$. Observe that:

1) the digital frequency ω in radians is given by

$$\omega = 2\pi F T_s \tag{58}$$

2) $\tilde{P}_{\mathscr{P}}(F)$ is periodic with period $1/T_s$

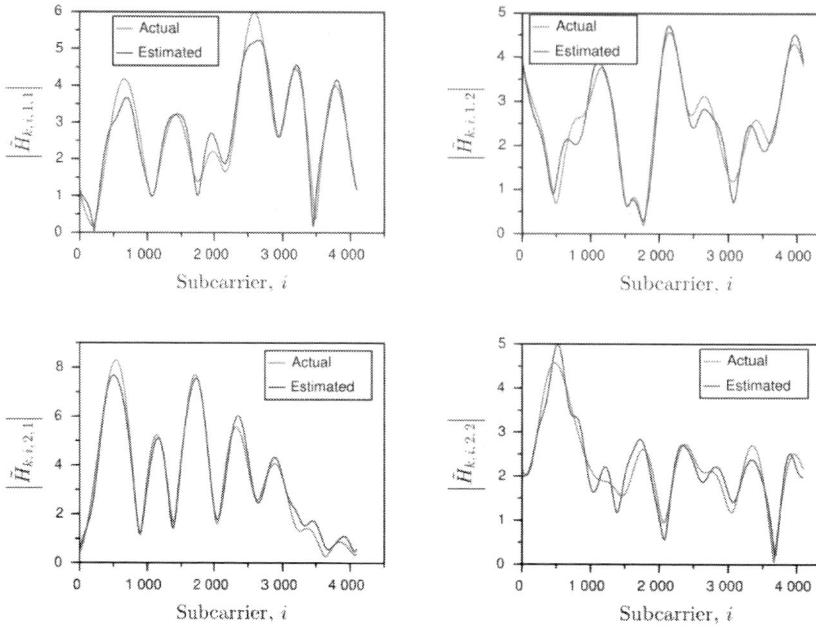

Figure 9. Magnitude spectrum of estimated and actual channel, $L_p = 4096$.

TABLE IV. FREQUENCY OFFSET ESTIMATION ERROR.

Frame configuration	Est. Error	Coarse	Fine	Superfine
$L_p = 512$ $L_o = 256$	RMS	1.71×10^{-3}	3.38×10^{-4}	5.85×10^{-5}
	Max.	2.4×10^{-2}	1.6×10^{-2}	2.6×10^{-4}
$L_p = 1024$ $L_o = 512$	RMS	3.3×10^{-4}	9.2×10^{-5}	4.3×10^{-5}
	Max.	1.2×10^{-2}	3.9×10^{-4}	1.82×10^{-4}

3) there is no aliasing in the second equation of (57), that is

$$\tilde{P}_{\mathscr{P}}(F) = \frac{\tilde{P}(F)}{T_s} \quad \text{for } -\tfrac{1}{2T_s} < F < \tfrac{1}{2T_s}. \tag{59}$$

Now, $\tilde{s}_{k,n,n_t}$ in Figure 1(a) is passed through the LPF. Let us denote the LPF output by $\tilde{v}_{k,n,n_t}$. After digital-to-analog (D/A) conversion, the continuous-time signal is denoted by $\tilde{v}_{k,n_t}(t)$. The power spectral density of $\tilde{v}_{k,n_t}(t)$ [17] [18]

$$S_{\tilde{v}}(F) = \frac{1}{T_s} \cdot \frac{\sigma_s^2}{2} \cdot \left|\tilde{P}(F)\right|^2 \tag{60}$$

where we have assumed that the samples of $\tilde{s}_{k,n,n_t}$ are uncorrelated with variance σ_s^2 given in (13). Thus the one-sided bandwidth of the complex baseband signal $\tilde{v}_{k,n_t}(t)$ is $1/(20T_s)$ Hz, for an LPF with cut-off frequency $\pi/10$ radians, since $1/T_s$ corresponds to 2π radians. Thus, the passband signal spectrum from a single transmit antenna would have a two-sided bandwidth of $1/(10T_s)$ Hz.

The frame structure is given by Figure 1. The average power of the preamble in the time domain must be equal to that of the data, as given by (13). Due to the use of different carrier frequencies for distinct transmit antennas, the same preamble pattern can be used for all the transmit antennas. Therefore, the subscript n_t can be dropped from the preamble signal, both in the time and frequency domain, in Figure 1(a) and (7). There are also no zero-valued preamble symbols in the frequency domain, that is [40]

$$S_{1,i} \in \sqrt{L_p/L_d}\,(\pm 1 \pm \mathrm{j}) \tag{61}$$

for $0 \le i \le L_p - 1$. The block diagram of the system for near capacity signaling is shown in Figure 11. The received signal vector at the output of the FFT for the N_r antennas associated with the transmit antenna n_t, for the kth frame and i^{th} $(0 \le i \le L_d - 1)$ subcarrier is:

$$\tilde{\mathbf{R}}_{k,i,n_t} = \tilde{\mathbf{H}}_{k,i,n_t} S_{k,3,i,n_t} + \tilde{\mathbf{W}}_{k,i,n_t} \tag{62}$$

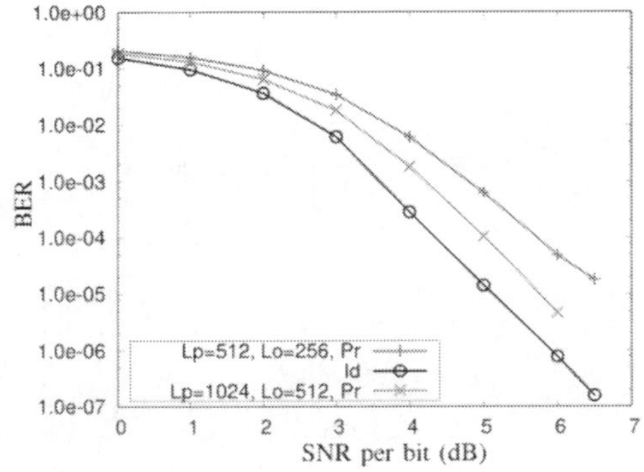

Figure 10. BER simulation results.

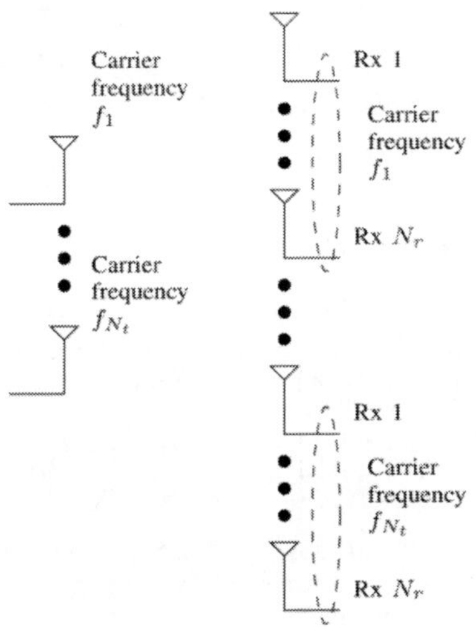

Figure 11. Near capacity signaling.

where $S_{k,\,3,\,i,\,n_t}$ is given in (7), $\tilde{\mathbf{R}}_{k,\,i,\,n_t}$, $\tilde{\mathbf{H}}_{k,\,i,\,n_t}$ and $\tilde{\mathbf{W}}_{k,\,i,\,n_t}$ are $N_r \times 1$ vectors given by:

$$\begin{aligned}\tilde{\mathbf{R}}_{k,\,i,\,n_t} &= \left[\begin{array}{ccc}\tilde{R}_{k,\,i,\,n_t,\,1} & \ldots & \tilde{R}_{k,\,i,\,n_t,\,N_r}\end{array}\right]^T \\ \tilde{\mathbf{H}}_{k,\,i,\,n_t} &= \left[\begin{array}{ccc}\tilde{H}_{k,\,i,\,n_t,\,1} & \ldots & \tilde{H}_{k,\,i,\,n_t,\,N_r}\end{array}\right]^T \\ \tilde{\mathbf{W}}_{k,\,i,\,n_t} &= \left[\begin{array}{ccc}\tilde{W}_{k,\,i,\,n_t,\,1} & \ldots & \tilde{W}_{k,\,i,\,n_t,\,N_r}\end{array}\right]^T.\end{aligned} \tag{63}$$

Similar to (47), it can be shown that for $1 \leq l \leq N_r$

$$\begin{aligned}\frac{1}{2}E\left[\left|\tilde{W}_{k,\,i,\,n_t,\,l}\right|^2\right] &= L_d\sigma_w^2 \\ \frac{1}{2}E\left[\left|\tilde{H}_{k,\,i,\,n_t,\,l}\right|^2\right] &= L_h\sigma_f^2.\end{aligned} \tag{64}$$

The synchronization and channel estimation algorithms are identical to that given in Section III with $N_t = 1$.

In the turbo decoding operation we assume that $N_t = 2$. The generating matrix of the constituent encoders is given by (49). For decoder 1 and $0 \leq i \leq L_{d2} - 1$, we define [2]:

$$\gamma_{1,\,k,\,i,\,m,\,n} = \prod_{l=1}^{N_r} \gamma_{1,\,k,\,i,\,m,\,n,\,l} \tag{65}$$

where

$$\gamma_{1,\,k,\,i,\,m,\,n,\,l} = \exp\left[-\frac{\left|\tilde{R}_{k,\,i,\,1,\,l} - \hat{H}_{k,\,i,\,1,\,l}S_{m,\,n}\right|^2}{2L_d\hat{\sigma}_w^2}\right] \tag{66}$$

where $\hat{\sigma}_w^2$ is the average estimate of the noise variance over all the N_r diversity arms, as given by (45) with $N_t = 1$, and $S_{m,\,n}$ is the QPSK symbol corresponding to the transition from state m to n in the encoder trellis. Similarly at decoder 2, for $0 \leq i \leq L_{d2} - 1$, we have:

$$\gamma_{2,\,k,\,i,\,m,\,n} = \prod_{l=1}^{N_r} \gamma_{2,\,k,\,i,\,m,\,n,\,l} \tag{67}$$

where

$$\gamma_{2,\,k,\,i,\,m,\,n,\,l} = \exp\left[-\frac{\left|\tilde{R}_{k,\,i,\,2,\,l} - \hat{H}_{k,\,i,\,2,\,l}S_{m,\,n}\right|^2}{2L_d\hat{\sigma}_w^2}\right]. \tag{68}$$

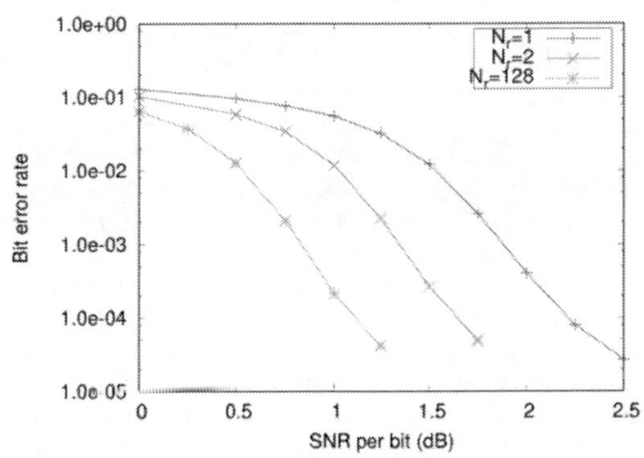

Figure 12. BER results for near capacity signaling with $N_t = 2$.

The simulation results assuming an ideal coherent receiver is given in Figure 12, for $L_d = 4096$, $L_p = L_o = B = L_{cp} = L_{cs} = 0$ (the preamble, postamble, buffer, cyclic prefix or suffix is not required, since this is an ideal coherent receiver), $N_t = 2$ and different values of N_r.

TABLE V. NUMBER OF SIMULATION RUNS FOR VARIOUS N_r.

N_r	SNR per bit (dB)	Max. no. of runs	Time for 1 run (minutes)
1	2.5	51	75
2	1.75	25	76
128	1.25	30	88

The maximum number of independently seeded simulation runs for various N_r and SNR per bit is given in Table V. For lower values of the SNR per bit, the number of runs is less than the maximum. Each run is over 10^3 frames. The time taken for one run using Scilab on an i5 processor is also given in Table V. The total time taken to obtain Figure 12 is approximately three months. The channel coefficients $\tilde{H}_{k,\,i,\,n_t,\,l}$ in (63) are assumed to be complex Gaussian and independent over i and l, that is

$$\begin{aligned}
\frac{1}{2}E\left[\tilde{H}_{k,\,i_1,\,n_t,\,l}\tilde{H}^*_{k,\,i_2,\,n_t,\,l}\right] &= L_h\sigma_f^2\delta_K(i_1-i_2)\\
\frac{1}{2}E\left[\tilde{H}_{k,\,i,\,n_t,\,l_1}\tilde{H}^*_{k,\,i,\,n_t,\,l_2}\right] &= L_h\sigma_f^2\delta_K(l_1-l_2).
\end{aligned} \tag{69}$$

The average SNR per bit is given by the second equation in (92) with

$$\begin{aligned}
P_{\text{av}} &= 2\\
L_h\sigma_f^2 &= 0.5\\
\kappa &= 0.5.
\end{aligned} \tag{70}$$

The turbo decoder uses eight iterations. Observe that in Figure 12, we obtain a BER of 2×10^{-5} at an average SNR per bit of just 2.5 dB, for $N_r=1$. It is also clear from Figure 12 that increasing N_r follows the law of diminishing returns. In fact there is only 1.25 dB difference in the average SNR per bit, between $N_r=1$ and $N_r=128$, at a BER of 2×10^{-5}. The slight change in slope at a BER of 2×10^{-5} is probably because the BER needs to averaged over more number of simulation runs. We do not expect an ideal coherent detector to exhibit an error floor.

It is interesting to compare the average SNR per bit definitions given by (70) and (92) for $N_r=1$ in this paper, with (38) in [40]. Observe that both definitions are identical. However, in Figure 12, we obtain a BER of 2×10^{-5} at an average SNR per bit of 2.5 dB, whereas in Figure 7 of [40] we obtain a similar BER at 8 dB average SNR per bit, for the ideal receiver. What could be the reason for this difference? Simply stated, in this section we have assumed a 4096-tap channel (see the first equation in (69) and equation (37) in [40] with $L_h=L_d$). However, in [40] we have considered a 10-tap channel. This is further explained below.

1) In this section, the SNR per bit for the kth frame and $N_r=1$ is proportional to (see also (22) in [2])

$$\text{SNR}_{k,\,\text{bit},\,1}\propto\frac{1}{L_d}\sum_{i=0}^{L_d-1}\left|\tilde{H}_{k,\,i,\,n_t,\,1}\right|^2 \tag{71}$$

where the subscript 1 in $\text{SNR}_{k,\,\text{bit},\,1}$ denotes case (1) and $\tilde{H}_{k,\,i,\,n_t,\,1}$ is defined in (63). Note that $\tilde{H}_{k,\,i,\,n_t,\,1}$ is a zero-mean Gaussian random variable which is independent over i and variance given by (64). Moreover, the right hand side of (71) gives the estimate of the variance of $\tilde{H}_{k,\,i,\,n_t,\,1}$. Let us now compute the variance of the estimate of the variance in (71), that is

$$\sigma_1^2=E\left[\left(\frac{1}{L_d}\sum_{i=0}^{L_d-1}\left|\tilde{H}_{k,\,i,\,n_t,\,1}\right|^2-2L_h\sigma_f^2\right)^2\right] \tag{72}$$

where we have used (64). It can be shown that

$$\sigma_1^2=\frac{\sigma_H^4}{L_d}=\frac{4L_h^2\sigma_f^4}{L_d} \tag{73}$$

where for $0\le i\le L_d-1$

$$\begin{aligned}
E\left[\left|\tilde{H}_{k,\,i,\,n_t,\,1}\right|^2\right] &= 2L_h\sigma_f^2\\
&\stackrel{\Delta}{=} \sigma_H^2\\
H_{k,\,i,\,n_t,\,1,\,I}+\mathrm{j}\,H_{k,\,i,\,n_t,\,1,\,Q} &= \tilde{H}_{k,\,i,\,n_t,\,1}\\
E\left[H^2_{k,\,i,\,n_t,\,1,\,I}\right] &= \sigma_H^2/2\\
&\stackrel{\Delta}{=} \sigma_{H,\,1}^2\\
E\left[H^2_{k,\,i,\,n_t,\,1,\,Q}\right] &= \sigma_H^2/2\\
&\stackrel{\Delta}{=} \sigma_{H,\,1}^2\\
E\left[H^4_{k,\,i,\,n_t,\,1,\,I}\right] &= 3\sigma_{H,\,1}^4\\
E\left[H^4_{k,\,i,\,n_t,\,1,\,Q}\right] &= 3\sigma_{H,\,1}^4\\
E\left[H^2_{k,\,i,\,n_t,\,1,\,I}H^2_{k,\,j,\,n_t,\,1,\,I}\right] &= \sigma_{H,\,1}^4 \quad i\ne j\\
E\left[H^2_{k,\,i,\,n_t,\,1,\,Q}H^2_{k,\,j,\,n_t,\,1,\,Q}\right] &= \sigma_{H,\,1}^4 \quad i\ne j\\
E\left[H^2_{k,\,i,\,n_t,\,1,\,I}H^2_{k,\,j,\,n_t,\,1,\,Q}\right] &= \sigma_{H,\,1}^4
\end{aligned} \tag{74}$$

where we have used the first equation in (69) and the assumption that $H_{k,\,i,\,n_t,\,1,\,I}$ and $H_{k,\,j,\,n_t,\,1,\,Q}$ are independent for all i, j.

2) Let us now compute the SNR per bit for each frame in [40]. Using the notation given in [40], we have

$$\text{SNR}_{k,\,\text{bit},\,2}\propto\frac{1}{L_d}\sum_{i=0}^{L_d-1}\left|\tilde{H}_{k,\,i}\right|^2 \tag{75}$$

where the subscript 2 in $\text{SNR}_{k,\,\text{bit},\,2}$ denotes case (2). Again, the variance of the estimate of the variance in the right hand side of (75) is

$$\sigma_2^2=E\left[\left(\frac{1}{L_d}\sum_{i=0}^{L_d-1}\left|\tilde{H}_{k,\,i}\right|^2-2L_h\sigma_f^2\right)^2\right]. \tag{76}$$

Observe that $\tilde{H}_{k,\,i}$ in (76) is obtained by taking the L_d-point FFT of an L_h-tap channel, and the autocorrelation of $\tilde{H}_{k,\,i}$ is given by (37) in [40]. Using Parseval's theorem we have

$$\frac{1}{L_d}\sum_{i=0}^{L_d-1}\left|\tilde{H}_{k,\,i}\right|^2=\sum_{n=0}^{L_h-1}\left|\tilde{h}_{k,\,n}\right|^2 \tag{77}$$

where $\tilde{h}_{k,\,n}$ denotes a sample of zero-mean Gaussian random variable with variance per dimension equal to σ_f^2. Note that $\tilde{h}_{k,\,n}$ is independent over n (see also (1) in [40]). Substituting (77) and the first equation of (74) in (76) we get

$$\sigma_2^2=E\left[\left(\sum_{n=0}^{L_h-1}\left|\tilde{h}_{k,\,n}\right|^2-\sigma_H^2\right)^2\right]. \tag{78}$$

It can be shown that

$$\sigma_2^2=4L_h\sigma_f^4 \tag{79}$$

where we have used the following relations:

$$\begin{aligned} E\left[\left|\tilde{h}_{k,n}\right|^2\right] &= 2\sigma_f^2 \\ h_{k,n,I} + \mathrm{j}\, h_{k,n,Q} &= \tilde{h}_{k,n} \\ E\left[h_{k,n,I}^2\right] &= \sigma_f^2 \\ E\left[h_{k,n,Q}^2\right] &= \sigma_f^2 \\ E\left[h_{k,n,I}^4\right] &= 3\sigma_f^4 \\ E\left[h_{k,n,Q}^4\right] &= 3\sigma_f^4 \\ E\left[h_{k,n,I}^2 h_{k,m,I}^2\right] &= \sigma_f^4 \quad n \neq m \\ E\left[h_{k,n,Q}^2 h_{k,m,Q}^2\right] &= \sigma_f^4 \quad n \neq m \\ E\left[h_{k,n,I}^2 h_{k,m,Q}^2\right] &= \sigma_f^4 \end{aligned} \tag{80}$$

where we have assumed that $h_{k,n,I}$ and $h_{k,m,Q}$ are independent for all n, m.

Substituting

$$\begin{aligned} L_h &= 10 \\ L_d &= 4096 \end{aligned} \tag{81}$$

in (74) and (80) we obtain

$$\begin{aligned} \sigma_1^2 &= 0.1\sigma_f^4 \\ \sigma_2^2 &= 40\sigma_f^4. \end{aligned} \tag{82}$$

Thus we find that the variation in the SNR per bit for each frame is 400 times larger in case (2) than in case (1). Therefore, in case (2) there are many frames whose SNR per bit is much smaller than the average value given by (92), resulting in a large number of bit errors. Conversely, the average SNR per bit in case (2) needs to be much higher than in case (1) for the same BER.

V. Conclusions

Discrete-time algorithms for the coherent detection of turbo coded MIMO OFDM system are presented. Simulations results for a 2×2 turbo coded MIMO OFDM system indicate that a BER of 10^{-5}, is obtained at an SNR per bit of just 5.5 dB, which is a 2.5 dB improvement over the performance given in the literature. The minimum average SNR per bit for error-free transmission over fading channels is derived and shown to be equal to -1.6 dB, which is the same as that for the AWGN channel.

Finally, an ideal near capacity signaling is proposed, where each transmit antenna uses a different carrier frequency. Simulation results for the ideal coherent receiver show that it is possible to achieve a BER of 2×10^{-5} at an average SNR per bit equal to 2.5 dB, with two transmit and two receive antennas. When the number of receive antennas for each transmit antenna is increased to 128, the average SNR per bit required to attain a BER of 2×10^{-5} is 1.25 dB. The spectral efficiency of the proposed near capacity system is 1 bit/sec/Hz. Higher spectral efficiency can be obtained by increasing the number of transmit antennas with no loss in BER performance. A pulse shaping technique is also proposed to reduce the bandwidth of the transmitted signal.

Future work could address the issues of peak-to-average power ratio (PAPR).

Appendix

A. The Minimum Average SNR per bit for Error-free Transmission over Fading Channels

In this appendix, we derive the minimum average SNR per bit for error-free transmission over MIMO fading channels. Consider the signal

$$\tilde{r}_n = \tilde{x}_n + \tilde{w}_n \qquad \text{for } 0 \le n < N \tag{83}$$

where $\tilde{x}_n$ is the transmitted signal (message) and $\tilde{w}_n$ denotes samples of zero-mean noise, not necessarily Gaussian. All the terms in (83) are complex-valued or two-dimensional and are transmitted over one complex dimension. Here the term dimension refers to a communication link between the transmitter and the receiver carrying only real-valued signals. We also assume that $\tilde{x}_n$ and $\tilde{w}_n$ are ergodic random processes, that is, the time average statistics is equal to the ensemble average. The time-averaged signal power over two-dimensions is given by, for large values of N:

$$\frac{1}{N}\sum_{n=0}^{N-1} |\tilde{x}_n|^2 = P'_{\text{av}}. \tag{84}$$

The time-averaged noise power per dimension is

$$\frac{1}{2N}\sum_{n=0}^{N-1} |\tilde{w}_n|^2 = \sigma'^2_w = \frac{1}{2N}\sum_{n=0}^{N-1} |\tilde{r}_n - \tilde{x}_n|^2. \tag{85}$$

The received signal power over two-dimensions is

$$\begin{aligned} \frac{1}{N}\sum_{n=0}^{N-1} |\tilde{r}_n|^2 &= \frac{1}{N}\sum_{n=0}^{N-1} |\tilde{x}_n + \tilde{w}_n|^2 \\ &= \frac{1}{N}\sum_{n=0}^{N-1} |\tilde{x}_n|^2 + |\tilde{w}_n|^2 \\ &= P'_{\text{av}} + 2\sigma'^2_w \\ &= E\left[|\tilde{x}_n + \tilde{w}_n|^2\right] \end{aligned} \tag{86}$$

where we have assumed independence between $\tilde{x}_n$ and $\tilde{w}_n$ and the fact that $\tilde{w}_n$ has zero-mean. Note that in (86) it is necessary that either $\tilde{x}_n$ or $\tilde{w}_n$ or both, have zero-mean.

Next, we observe that (85) is the expression for a $2N$-dimensional noise hypersphere with radius $\sigma'_w\sqrt{2N}$. Similarly, (86) is the expression for a $2N$-dimensional received signal hypersphere with radius $\sqrt{N(P'_{\text{av}} + 2\sigma'^2_w)}$.

Now, the problem statement is: how many noise hyperspheres (messages) can fit into the received signal hypersphere, such that the noise hyperspheres do not overlap (reliable decoding), for a given N, P'_{av} and σ'^2_w? The solution lies in the volume of the two hyperspheres. Note that a $2N$-dimensional hypersphere of radius R has a volume proportional to R^{2N}. Therefore, the number of possible messages is

$$M = \frac{\left(N\left(P'_{\text{av}} + 2\sigma'^2_w\right)\right)^N}{\left(2N\sigma'^2_w\right)^N} = \left(\frac{P'_{\text{av}} + 2\sigma'^2_w}{2\sigma'^2_w}\right)^N \tag{87}$$

over N samples (transmissions). The number of bits required to represent each message is $\log_2(M)$, over N transmissions.

Therefore, the number of bits per transmission, defined as the channel capacity, is given by [10]

$$\begin{aligned} C &= \frac{1}{N}\log_2(M) \\ &= \log_2\left(1+\frac{P'_{\text{av}}}{2\sigma'^2_w}\right) \quad \text{bits per transmission} \end{aligned} \tag{88}$$

over two dimensions or one complex dimension (here again the term "dimension" implies a communication link between the transmitter and receiver, carrying only real-valued signals. This is not to be confused with the $2N$-dimensional hypersphere mentioned earlier or the M-dimensional orthogonal constellations in [18]).

Proposition A.1: Clearly, the channel capacity is additive over the number of dimensions. In other words, channel capacity over D dimensions, is equal to the sum of the capacities over each dimension, provided the information is independent across dimensions [2]. Independence of information also implies that, the bits transmitted over one dimension is not the interleaved version of the bits transmitted over any other dimension.

Proposition A.2: Conversely, if C bits per transmission are sent over $2N_r$ dimensions, (N_r complex dimensions), it seems reasonable to assume that each complex dimension receives C/N_r bits per transmission [2].

The reasoning for *Proposition* A.2 is as follows. We assume that a "bit" denotes "information". Now, if each of the N_r antennas (complex dimensions) receive the "same" C bits of information, then we might as well have only one antenna, since the other antennas are not yielding any additional information. On the other hand, if each of the N_r antennas receive "different" C bits of information, then we end up receiving more information (CN_r bits) than what we transmit (C bits), which is not possible. Therefore, we assume that each complex dimension receives C/N_r bits of "different" information.

Note that, when

$$\begin{aligned} \tilde{x}_n &= \sum_{n_t=1}^{N_t} \tilde{H}_{k,\,n,\,n_r,\,n_t} S_{k,\,3,\,n,\,n_t} \\ \tilde{w}_n &= \tilde{W}_{k,\,n,\,n_r} \end{aligned} \tag{89}$$

as given in (46), the channel capacity remains the same as in (88). We now define the average SNR per bit for MIMO systems having N_t transmit and N_r receive antennas. We assume that κ information bits are transmitted simultaneously from each transmit antenna. The amount of information received by each receive antenna is $\kappa N_t/N_r$ bits per transmission, over two dimensions (due to Proposition A.2). Assuming independent channel frequency response and symbols across different transmit antennas, the average SNR of $\tilde{R}_{k,\,i,\,n_r}$ in (46) can be computed from (47) as:

$$\text{SNR}_{\text{av}} = \frac{2L_h\sigma_f^2 P_{\text{av}} N_t}{2L_d\sigma_w^2} = \frac{P'_{\text{av}}}{2\sigma'^2_w} \tag{90}$$

for $\kappa N_t/N_r$ bits, where

$$P_{\text{av}} = E\left[|S_{k,\,3,\,i,\,n_t}|^2\right]. \tag{91}$$

The average SNR per bit is

$$\begin{aligned} \text{SNR}_{\text{av},\,b} &= \frac{2L_h\sigma_f^2 P_{\text{av}} N_t}{2L_d\sigma_w^2}\cdot\frac{N_r}{\kappa N_t} \\ &= \frac{L_h\sigma_f^2 P_{\text{av}} N_r}{L_d\sigma_w^2\kappa} \\ &= \frac{P'_{\text{av}}}{2\sigma'^2_w}\cdot\frac{N_r}{\kappa N_t}. \end{aligned} \tag{92}$$

Moreover, for each receive antenna we have

$$C = \kappa N_t/N_r \quad \text{bits per transmission} \tag{93}$$

over two dimensions. Substituting (92) and (93) in (88) we get

$$\begin{aligned} C &= \log_2(1 + C\cdot\text{SNR}_{\text{av},\,b}) \\ \Rightarrow \text{SNR}_{\text{av},\,b} &= \frac{2^C-1}{C}. \end{aligned} \tag{94}$$

Clearly as $C \to 0$, $\text{SNR}_{\text{av},\,b} \to \ln(2)$, which is the minimum SNR required for error-free transmission over MIMO fading channels.

REFERENCES

[1] K. Vasudevan, "Coherent turbo coded mimo ofdm," in ICWMC 2016, The 12th International Conference on Wireless and Mobile Communications, Nov. 2016, pp. 91–99, [Online].

[2] ——, "Coherent detection of turbo-coded ofdm signals transmitted through frequency selective rayleigh fading channels with receiver diversity and increased throughput," Wireless Personal Communications, vol. 82, no. 3, 2015, pp. 1623–1642. [Online]. Available: http://dx.doi.org/10.1007/s11277-015-2303-8

[3] ——, "Coherent detection of turbo-coded OFDM signals transmitted through frequency selective rayleigh fading channels with receiver diversity and increased throughput," CoRR, vol. abs/1511.00776, 2015. [Online]. Available: http://arxiv.org/abs/1511.00776

[4] J. G. Andrews et al., "What will 5g be?" IEEE Journal on Selected Areas in Communications, vol. 32, no. 6, June 2014, pp. 1065–1082.

[5] O. Galinina, A. Pyattaev, S. Andreev, M. Dohler, and Y. Koucheryavy, "5g multi-rat lte-wifi ultra-dense small cells: Performance dynamics, architecture, and trends," IEEE Journal on Selected Areas in Communications, vol. 33, no. 6, June 2015, pp. 1224–1240.

[6] C. L. I et al., "New paradigm of 5g wireless internet," IEEE Journal on Selected Areas in Communications, vol. 34, no. 3, Mar. 2016, pp. 474–482.

[7] M. Agiwal, A. Roy, and N. Saxena, "Next generation 5g wireless networks: A comprehensive survey," IEEE Communications Surveys Tutorials, vol. 18, no. 3, thirdquarter 2016, pp. 1617–1655.

[8] F. Rusek et al., "Scaling up mimo: Opportunities and challenges with very large arrays," IEEE Signal Processing Magazine, vol. 30, no. 1, Jan. 2013, pp. 40–60.

[9] J. Hoydis, S. ten Brink, and M. Debbah, "Massive mimo in the ul/dl of cellular networks: How many antennas do we need?" IEEE Journal on Selected Areas in Communications, vol. 31, no. 2, Feb. 2013, pp. 160–171.

[10] E. Bjrnson, E. G. Larsson, and M. Debbah, "Massive mimo for maximal spectral efficiency: How many users and pilots should be allocated?" IEEE Transactions on Wireless Communications, vol. 15, no. 2, Feb. 2016, pp. 1293–1308.

[11] K. L. Wong, C. Y. Tsai, J. Y. Lu, D. M. Chian, and W. Y. Li, "Compact eight mimo antennas for 5g smartphones and their mimo capacity verification," in 2016 URSI Asia-Pacific Radio Science Conference (URSI AP-RASC), Aug. 2016, pp. 1054–1056.

[12] Z. Pi and F. Khan, "An introduction to millimeter-wave mobile broadband systems," IEEE Communications Magazine, vol. 49, no. 6, June 2011, pp. 101–107.

[13] T. S. Rappaport et al., "Broadband millimeter-wave propagation measurements and models using adaptive-beam antennas for outdoor urban cellular communications," IEEE Transactions on Antennas and Propagation, vol. 61, no. 4, Apr. 2013, pp. 1850–1859.

[14] ——, "Millimeter wave mobile communications for 5g cellular: It will work!" IEEE Access, vol. 1, 2013, pp. 335–349.

[15] T. S. Rappaport, W. Roh, and K. Cheun, "Mobile's millimeter-wave makeover," IEEE Spectrum, vol. 51, no. 9, Sept. 2014, pp. 34–58.

[16] S. Niknam, A. A. Nasir, H. Mehrpouyan, and B. Natarajan, "A multiband ofdma heterogeneous network for millimeter wave 5g wireless applications," IEEE Access, vol. 4, 2016, pp. 5640–5648.

[17] K. Vasudevan, Digital Communications and Signal Processing, Second edition (CDROM included). Universities Press (India), Hyderabad, www.universitiespress.com, 2010.

[18] ——, "Digital Communications and Signal Processing, Third edition," 2016, URL: http://home.iitk.ac.in/~vasu/book0.pdf [accessed: 2017-02-01].

[19] N. Khalid and O. B. Akan, "Wideband thz communication channel measurements for 5g indoor wireless networks," in 2016 IEEE International Conference on Communications (ICC), May 2016, pp. 1–6.

[20] N. R. Zulkefly et al., "Channel characterization for indoor environment at 17 ghz for 5g communications," in 2015 IEEE 12th Malaysia International Conference on Communications (MICC), Nov. 2015, pp. 241–245.

[21] Q. Guo, G. Gui, and F. Li, "Block-partition sparse channel estimation for spatially correlated massive mimo systems," in 2016 8th International Conference on Wireless Communications Signal Processing (WCSP), Oct. 2016, pp. 1–4.

[22] M. Kuerbis, N. M. Balasubramanya, L. Lampe, and A. Lampe, "On the use of channel models and channel estimation techniques for massive mimo systems," in 2016 24th European Signal Processing Conference (EUSIPCO), Aug. 2016, pp. 823–827.

[23] V. Sridhar, T. Gabillard, and A. Manikas, "Spatiotemporal-mimo channel estimator and beamformer for 5g," IEEE Transactions on Wireless Communications, vol. 15, no. 12, Dec. 2016, pp. 8025–8038.

[24] H. Xie, F. Gao, and S. Jin, "An overview of low-rank channel estimation for massive mimo systems," IEEE Access, vol. 4, 2016, pp. 7313–7321.

[25] Q. Wang, Z. Zhou, J. Fang, and Z. Chen, "Compressive channel estimation for millimeter wave multiuser mimo systems via pilot reuse," in 2016 8th International Conference on Wireless Communications Signal Processing (WCSP), Oct. 2016, pp. 1–6.

[26] B. Farhang-Boroujeny, "Ofdm versus filter bank multicarrier," IEEE Signal Processing Magazine, vol. 28, no. 3, May 2011, pp. 92–112.

[27] Y. Chen, F. Schaich, and T. Wild, "Multiple access and waveforms for 5g: Idma and universal filtered multi-carrier," in 2014 IEEE 79th Vehicular Technology Conference (VTC Spring), May 2014, pp. 1–5.

[28] B. Farhang-Boroujeny and H. Moradi, "Ofdm inspired waveforms for 5g," IEEE Communications Surveys Tutorials, vol. 18, no. 4, Fourthquarter 2016, pp. 2474–2492.

[29] E. Basar, "Index modulation techniques for 5g wireless networks," IEEE Communications Magazine, vol. 54, no. 7, July 2016, pp. 168–175.

[30] S. Venkatesan and R. A. Valenzuela, "Ofdm for 5g: Cyclic prefix versus zero postfix, and filtering versus windowing," in 2016 IEEE International Conference on Communications (ICC), May 2016, pp. 1–5.

[31] P. Weitkemper et al., "Hardware experiments on multi-carrier waveforms for 5g," in 2016 IEEE Wireless Communications and Networking Conference, April 2016, pp. 1–6.

[32] Z. Hraiech, F. Abdelkefi, and M. Siala, "Pops-ofdm with different tx/rx pulse shape durations for 5g systems," in 2015 5th International Conference on Communications and Networking (COMNET), Nov. 2015, pp. 1–6.

[33] X. Zhang, L. Chen, J. Qiu, and J. Abdoli, "On the waveform for 5g," IEEE Communications Magazine, vol. 54, no. 11, Nov. 2016, pp. 74–80.

[34] A. A. Zaidi et al., "Waveform and numerology to support 5g services and requirements," IEEE Communications Magazine, vol. 54, no. 11, Nov. 2016, pp. 90–98.

[35] G. Berardinelli, K. I. Pedersen, T. B. Sorensen, and P. Mogensen, "Generalized dft-spread-ofdm as 5g waveform," IEEE Communications Magazine, vol. 54, no. 11, Nov. 2016, pp. 99–105.

[36] C. An, B. Kim, and H. G. Ryu, "Design of w-ofdm and nonlinear performance comparison for 5g waveform," in 2016 International Conference on Information and Communication Technology Convergence (ICTC), Oct. 2016, pp. 1006–1009.

[37] Y. Qi and M. Al-Imari, "An enabling waveform for 5g – qam-fbmc: Initial analysis," in 2016 IEEE Conference on Standards for Communications and Networking (CSCN), Oct. 2016, pp. 1–6.

[38] R. Garzn-Bohrquez, C. A. Nour, and C. Douillard, "Improving turbo codes for 5g with parity puncture-constrained interleavers," in 2016 9th International Symposium on Turbo Codes and Iterative Information Processing (ISTC), Sept. 2016, pp. 151–155.

[39] L. Guo, Z. Ning, Q. Song, Y. Cui, and Z. Chen, "Toward efficient 5g transmission: Ser performance analysis for asynchronous physical-layer network coding," IEEE Access, vol. 4, 2016, pp. 5083–5097.

[40] K. Vasudevan, "Coherent detection of turbo coded ofdm signals transmitted through frequency selective rayleigh fading channels," in Signal Processing, Computing and Control (ISPCC), 2013 IEEE International Conference on, Sept. 2013, pp. 1–6.

[41] A. Goldsmith, S. A. Jafar, N. Jindal, and S. Vishwanath, "Capacity limits of mimo channels," IEEE Journal on Selected Areas in Communications, vol. 21, no. 5, June 2003, pp. 684–702.

[42] Y. Wang and D. W. Yue, "Capacity of mimo rayleigh fading channels in the presence of interference and receive correlation," IEEE Transactions on Vehicular Technology, vol. 58, no. 8, Oct. 2009, pp. 4398–4405.

[43] F. Benkhelifa, A. Tall, Z. Rezki, and M. S. Alouini, "On the low snr capacity of mimo fading channels with imperfect channel state information," IEEE Transactions on Communications, vol. 62, no. 6, June 2014, pp. 1921–1930.

[44] K. Vasudevan, "Iterative Detection of Turbo Coded Offset QPSK in the Presence of Frequency and Clock Offsets and AWGN," Signal, Image and Video Processing, Springer, vol. 6, no. 4, Nov. 2012, pp. 557–567.

[45] ——, "Design and development of a burst acquisition system for geosynchronous satcom channels," CoRR, vol. abs/1510.07106, 2015. [Online]. Available: http://arxiv.org/abs/1510.07106

[46] H. Minn, V. K. Bhargava, and K. B. Letaief, "A Robust Timing and Frequency Synchronization for OFDM Systems," IEEE Trans. on Wireless Commun., vol. 2, no. 4, July 2003, pp. 822–839.

[47] S. Haykin, Adaptive Filter Theory, 3rd ed. Prentice Hall, 1996.

[48] J. G. Proakis and D. G. Manolakis, Digital Signal Processing: Principles, Algorithms and Applications, 2nd ed. Maxwell MacMillan, 1992.

[49] J. G. Proakis and M. Salehi, Fundamentals of Communication Systems. Pearson Education Inc., 2005.

Modelling and Characterization of Customer Behavior in Cellular Networks

Thomas Couronné
Orange Labs
France Telecom R&D,
Paris, France
Email:Thomas.Couronne@orange-ftgroup.com

Valery Kirzner
Institute of Evolution
University of Haifa
Haifa, Israel
Email:valery@research.haifa.ac.il

Katerina Korenblat
Software Engineering Department
Ort Braude College
Karmiel, Israel
Email:katerina@braude.ac.il

Elena V. Ravve
Software Engineering Department
Ort Braude College
Karmiel, Israel
Email:cselena@braude.ac.il

Zeev Volkovich
Software Engineering Department
Ort Braude College
Karmiel, Israel
Email:vlvolkov@braude.ac.il

***Abstract*—In this paper, we extend a model of the fundamental user profiles, developed in our previous works. We explore customer behavior in cellular networks. The study is based on investigation of activities of millions of customers of Orange, France. We propose a way of decomposition of the observed distributions according to certain external criteria. We analyze distribution of customers, having the same number of calls during a fixed period. A segmentation of the population is provided by an approximation of the considered distribution by means of a mixture of several more "basic" distributions presenting the "granularity" of the user's activity. In order to examine the meaning of the found approximation, a clustering of the customers is provided using their daily activity, and a new clustering procedure is constructed. The optimal number of clusters turned out to be three. The approximation is reduced in the optimal partition to a single-exponential one in one of the clusters and to two double-exponential in others. This fact confirms that the proposed partition corresponds to reliable consequential social groups.**

Keywords*–Customer behavior pattern; Market segmentation; Probability distribution; Mixture distribution model; Machine learning; Unsupervised classification; Clustering.

I. Introduction

This paper presents an extended and improved version of [1], where we introduced the general framework of modelling behavior patterns in cellular networks.

Customer behavior is a way people, groups and companies purchase, operate with and organize goods, services, ideas and knowledge in order to suit to their needs and wants [2], [3]. Multidisciplinary studies of the customer behavior strive to comprehend the decision-making processes of customers and serve as a basis for market segmentation. Through market segmentation, large mixed markets are partitioned into smaller sufficiently homogeneous sectors having similar needs, wants, or demand characteristics.

In the cellular networks context, the mentioned products and services can be expressed in spending of the networks resources such as the number of calls, SMS messages and bandwidth. Market segmentation in this area is able to characterize behavior usage or preferences for each sector of customers. In other words, typifying of the customers' profiles is aimed at using this pattern in order to suitably adapt specific products and services to the clients in each market segment.

A segmentation of the population is provided by an approximation of the considered distribution by means of a mixture of several more "basic" distributions, which represent the "granularity" of the user's activity. Such mixture distribution models are conventional in machine learning due to their fruitful applications in unsupervised classification (clustering). In this framework, the underling probability distribution is decomposed into a mixture of several simple ones, which correspond to subgroups (clusters) with high inner homogeneity. In our application, hypothetically, each one of these clusters corresponds to a social group of users, having its own dynamics of calls depending upon the individual group social parameters.

The common applications of the known Expectation Maximization algorithm [4], which estimates parameters of the mixture models (for instance, in the clustering), suggest the Gaussian Mixture Model of the data. This well-understood technique is much admired because it satisfies a monotonic convergence property and can be easily implemented. Nevertheless, there are several known drawbacks. If there are multiple maxima, the algorithm may discover a local maximum, which is not a global one. In addition, the obtained solution strongly depends on the initial values [5]. Moreover, many studies are recently devoted to analysis of non-Gaussian processes, which are often related to the power law distributions.

While in clustering as a rule the Gaussian Mixture Model of the data is assumed, we treat the user activity in a cellular network as a mechanism generating *non-Gaussian* distributions.

In physics, hyperbolic dependencies are often observed (e.g., theories during phase transitions that clarify the corresponding mechanism). On the other hand, there are a number of general formal models (for example, the law of Yule [6]), where such a distribution appears. In these models, hyperbolic behavior is often observed as asymptotic or applicable to certain parts of the distribution.

Our research develops *a novel model of the fundamental user behavior patterns* (user profiles) in cellular networks. We adopt the standard simple regression methodology of [7] to our purposes. We show that empirical densities of the studied underlying distributions are monotone decreasing and do not exhibit multi-modality. These properties characterize mixtures of *the exponential distribution* [8], [9]. In this sense, we extend the study of [10], where it was shown that a parallel user activity in recording in an email address book leads to an appropriate exponential distribution of the clients.

In order to explore the meaning of the found approximation, a clustering of the customers is provided, based on their daily activity, and a *new clustering procedure* is constructed in the spirit of the bi-clustering methodology of [11], [12].

We base our study on analysis of the underlying distribution of customers, who have the same number of calls during a fixed period, say a day. In this research, an exponential distribution mixture model is applied. It is shown that a three-exponential distribution fits well the needed target.

The estimated optimal number of clusters turned out to be three. A straightforward clustering of the original data is hardly expected to deliver a robust and meaningful partition. Such a situation is a common place in the current practice. Moreover, in many applications the aim is to reveal not merely potential clusters, but also a quite small number of variables, which adequately settle that partition. For instance, the sparse K-means (SK-means) proposed in [13], at once discovers the clusters and the key clustering variables.

A *new procedure* in the spirit of such a bi-clustering methodology, where features and items are simultaneously clustered, is applied in this paper. Firstly, 24 hours inside a day (the features) are clustered consistent with the corresponding users' activity. In the next step, the users are divided in groups according to their occurrences in the previous partition of hours. As a result, a sufficiently robust clustering of users is obtained together with a description of the clusters in terms of call activity.

The observed dissimilarity between hours (from the point of view of the users' behavior) can be naturally characterized by a distance between the corresponding distributions. In this paper, we employ Kolmogorov-Smirnov two sample test statistic [14], [15], which is actually the maximal distance between two empirical normalized cumulative distribution functions.

Then we use the Partitioning Around Medoids clustering algorithm [16], in order to cluster the data. This algorithm operates with a distance matrix, but not with the items themselves. This is feasible for small data sets (such as the considered one, composed of 24 hours) and a small number of clusters three in our case. One of the input parameters of the algorithm is the number of clusters. We estimate the optimal number of their hours clusters, using the Silhouette coefficient of [17]. Here ideas of both cohesion and separation are combined: for individual points as well as for partitions. The number of clusters was checked in the interval of $[2-10]$, and the optimal one was found to be 3 for all the considered data sets.

When we obtain classification of users' activity across the hour clusters, we built a vector, composed of the fractions of calls falling within each hour cluster. At this stage, we produce user clustering employing this new data representation. Note that, due to the large amount of data, we deal here with a high complexity clustering task. It means that the traditional clustering algorithms cannot be directly applied to this situation. In order to resolve this problem we apply a resampling clustering procedure, according to which the whole data set is partitioned based on clustering of its samples.

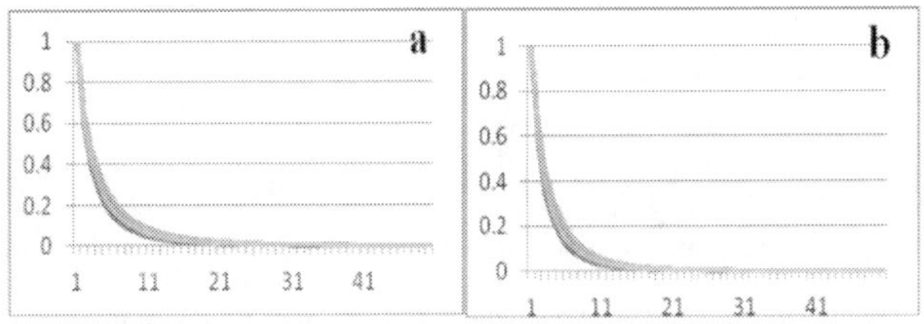

Figure 1. DSN curves for $InCalls$ (a) and $OutCalls$ (b), obtained on each day of the whole period of observation (13 days).

Finally, we obtain the optimal partition with a single-exponential call distribution in one of the clusters and two double-exponential call distributions in others. This fact confirms that the proposed partition corresponds to reliable consequential social groups. We emphasize the fact that the similarity measure, applied in the clustering process, is formed without any reference to the previously discussed mixture model.

The results, presented in the paper, are obtained by means of a study of the daily activity of a real group of users during the period from March 31, 2009 through April 11, 2009. For each considered day, several million users in this group are active (making one or more calls). The time of each input or output call is known. Note that the sets of active users on different days vary.

The paper is structured as follows. Section II is devoted to a distribution model of user activity and its decomposition. Section III describes the customer clustering procedure and its evaluations. The section presents model-based evaluation of the proposed customer classification. Section IV summarizes the paper and provides outlook.

II. Distribution Model of User Activity

In this section, we consider a mixture model approximation of the underlying distribution of users having the same number of calls during a day. We denote by DSN the *Day Same Number* distribution. We distinguish two types of user activity: input calls, denoted by $InCalls$, and output calls, denoted by $OutCalls$.

All users (about five millions) are divided into groups according to their number of calls per day, so that the i-th group contains all customers having exactly i calls per a particular day. The size of the i-th group is denoted by N_i. Obviously, the contents and sizes of the groups are not the same for different days. In addition, the number of groups with $i > 100$ is very small in the dataset, and these groups most likely contain "non-standard" users such that sales agents, call centers and so on. We omit such groups together with users, who do not call at all in a given day, since this lack of activity could be explained by factors that are not directly related to the user activity on the network.

The DSN curves, normalized to 1, of $InCalls$ (a) and $OutCalls$ (b) as well as the corresponding numbers of calls ranging from 1 to 50, are shown in Fig. 1. We note that the curves are of almost the same monotonically decreasing form for all 13 days of the observation.

TABLE I. p-values for different numbers of components

Number of components	1	2	**3**	4
p-value	0	$8.6e-06$	**0.025**	0.282

As it was mentioned in Section I, a mixture distribution model with exponential components seems to be an appropriate approximation of DSN. In our context, it is natural to assume that the underlying population is actually a mix of several different sub-populations. Mixture distribution models appear in many applications as an inherent and straightforward tool to pattern population heterogeneity. The assumption about *exponentially distributed* components of the mixture is commonly invoked in the study of lifetime or more universal duration data. Here you have a simple k-finite exponential mixture model, having a density function of the following form

$$f(x) = \sum_{j=1}^{k} A_j exp(-t_j \cdot x), \qquad (1)$$

where A_j and t_j, $j = 1, ...k$ are nonnegative numbers, and $\sum_{j=1}^{k} A_j = 1$. For a given number of components k, the Expectation–Maximization (EM) algorithm [4] is a traditional method for maximum likelihood estimation of finite mixtures.

However, we apply another approach in the spirit of the linear regression methodology without any prior assumption about k - the number of components. For this purpose, we initially form explanatory variable $X = (1, 2, ..., 100)$ and response Y. For each value $x \in X$, $Y = ln\left(f(x)\right)$, where $f(x)$ is the normalized frequencies of DSN in a day.

Using the standard simple regression methodology of [7], a linear regression model is identified as $Y = a + b \cdot X$ and the first estimation of the density $f(x)$ in (1) is constructed: $f^{(1)}(x) = A_1 \exp(-t_1 \cdot x)$, for $A_1 = \exp(a)$ and $t_1 = -b$. In the next step, the new response is built: $Y = ln\left(f(x) - f^{(1)}(x) + C\right)$, where C is a sufficiently big positive number insuring that $f(x) - f^{(1)}(x) + C > 0$ for all x and j. In each step, p-value coefficient of significance:

$$F = \frac{R^2(X,Y)}{1 - R^2(X,Y)}(100 - 1) \qquad (2)$$

is calculated. Here $R(X, Y)$ is the Pearson correlation coefficient between X and Y [18]. The described procedure is repeated until the actual p-value is less than the traditional level of significance 0.05. In our particular application, for all cases of daily activity, the procedure has been stopped after three components were extracted.

The parameters of (1), calculated for each of the 13 days of the observation, are presented in Tables II and III. They demonstrate high stability of the exponent indexes t_1, t_2, t_3, which are practically independent of time but are somewhat different on the weekends, i.e., Saturdays 4 and 11 of April 2009 and Sunday 5 of April 2009. Amplitudes A_1, A_2, A_3 differ to a greater degree (in percentage terms). Thus, the absolute number of active users varies from day to day to a greater extent than the distribution pattern, which actually corresponds to a set of exponent indexes. The p-values, calculated for the first of the considered days, are presented in Table I.

TABLE II. Values of the approximation function parameters on different days for $InCalls$. (The designations of the amplitudes (A) and indexes (t) correspond to (1))

Dates	A_1	t_1	A_2	t_2	A_3	t_3
03_30	80001	0.12	399893	0.32	420568	1.02
03_31	110555	0.12	441268	0.33	380258	1.15
04_01	94021	0.11	421456	0.31	401002	1.01
04_02	99683	0.11	419564	0.3	411258	1.05
04_03	96660	0.11	409176	0.29	405050	0.98
04_04	90424	0.12	406385	0.34	420161	1.07
04_05	59971	0.12	399873	0.36	530064	1.08
04_06	91189	0.11	425022	0.31	450957	1.04
04_07	83467	0.11	415012	0.3	431301	0.96
04_08	93358	0.11	430842	0.31	422297	1
04_09	102169	0.11	426124	0.31	416794	1.07
04_10	97814	0.11	402832	0.3	408717	1
04_11	65206	0.11	353998	0.33	439797	1.01

TABLE III. Values of the approximation function parameters on different days for $OutCalls$. (The designations of the amplitudes (A) and indexes (t) correspond to (1))

Dates	A_1	t_1	A_2	t_2	A_3	t_3
03_30	100684	0.16	561222	0.37	527907	1.25
03_31	119660	0.16	560344	0.36	514682	1.32
04_01	116329	0.16	564578	0.35	498085	1.32
04_02	118910	0.16	546314	0.35	494688	1.27
04_03	130193	0.16	538984	0.34	497177	1.3
04_04	95354	0.16	524779	0.39	548041	1.34
04_05	87109	0.17	522660	0.46	617407	1.41
04_06	110086	0.16	562064	0.36	548389	1.34
04_07	102030	0.15	560233	0.35	497784	1.22
04_08	90481	0.15	568191	0.34	510487	1.21
04_09	115820	0.16	543334	0.34	505349	1.26
04_10	121782	0.16	518418	0.34	500068	1.24
04_11	80915	0.15	445910	0.39	538691	1.22

In the case of $InCalls$ (Table II), the ratio of the exponent indexes is: $3{\cdot}t_1 \approx t_2, 3{\cdot}t_2 \approx t_3$. In the case of $OutCalls$ (Table III), this ratio is somewhat different: $2 \cdot t_1 \approx t_2, 3.5 \cdot t_2 \approx t_3$. The decay value x_0 of each component in (1) is chosen in order to normalize the component value at this point to 1.

The components are not equivalent in the sense of their decay value (see Table IV). In fact, the exponent with index $t_3 = 1.0$ and amplitude $A_3 = 500,000$ (these values are typical for one of the three exponents, which describe the daily activity) already decays at $x_0 = 13$. For the second typical pair of the values: $t_2 = 0.33$ and $A_2 = 400,000$, the decay occurs at $x_0 = 39$. Moreover, the exponent with $t_1 = 0.12$ and $A_1 = 90,000$ has the longest effect on DSN: $x_0 = 95$. Accordingly, two of the three components, which describe the user activity, disappear in the middle of the considered interval of calls. Only the third exponent continues, and its values may be considered as the "asymptotic behavior" of the distribution.

The relatively complex nature of the obtained empirical distribution model of user activity may indicate the heterogeneity of the entire set of the users. This set is conceivably composed of a few groups such that the total user activity in a group is described by a certain simpler distribution.

TABLE IV. Decay value for each component of DSN on different days. Columns 1, 2, 3 show decay values, x_0, of the corresponding components.

Date	$InCalls$			$OutCalls$		
	1	2	3	1	2	3
03_30	94	40	12	71	35	10
03_31	96	39	11	73	36	9
04_01	104	41	12	72	37	9
04_02	104	43	12	73	37	10
04_03	104	44	13	73	38	10
04_04	95	37	12	71	33	9
04_05	91	35	12	66	28	9
04_06	103	41	12	72	36	9
04_07	103	43	13	76	37	10
04_08	104	41	12	76	38	10
04_09	104	41	12	72	38	10
04_10	104	43	12	73	38	10
04_11	100	38	12	75	33	10

Obviously, the social status, gender and age of the users affect their activity on telephone networks. However, such types of personal data are not available for us. Therefore, in the following section, we divide the users into groups, based merely on the features of their individual activity during a given day. It is assumed that these features are related to some of the social characteristics of the users. A justification for this assumption may be found, for example in [19].

III. User classification

We assume that the obtained three-component exponential mixture model reflects the inner customers' behavior patterns, exposed by the observed data. In order to identify these patterns, all the users are divided into groups according to a comparable daily performance. In this way, analysis of the overall cluster behavior can characterize the corresponding pattern.

We apply a procedure in the spirit of the bi-clustering methodology of [13]. First of all, we cluster 24 hours inside a day (the features) according to the corresponding users' activity. Then, the users are divided in groups according to their occurrences in the hour's partition. As a result, a sufficiently robust clustering of users is obtained together with a description of the clusters in terms of call activity.

A. Clustering of hours

First of all, we try to outline a similarity between hours in a day. For this purpose, we consider each hour as a distribution of users across the actual numbers of calls within this hour. It means that we examine how many people did not call at all in this hour, how many people called just one time, two times and so on.

The observed dissimilarity between hours can be naturally characterized by a distance between the corresponding distributions. Generally speaking, any asymptotically distribution-free statistic is suitable for this purpose. In fact, the distribution of an asymptotically distribution-free statistic does not depend on the underlying distribution of the populations for samples of sufficiently large size. Here, we employ the well-known Kolmogorov-Smirnov (KS) two sample test statistic [14], [15].

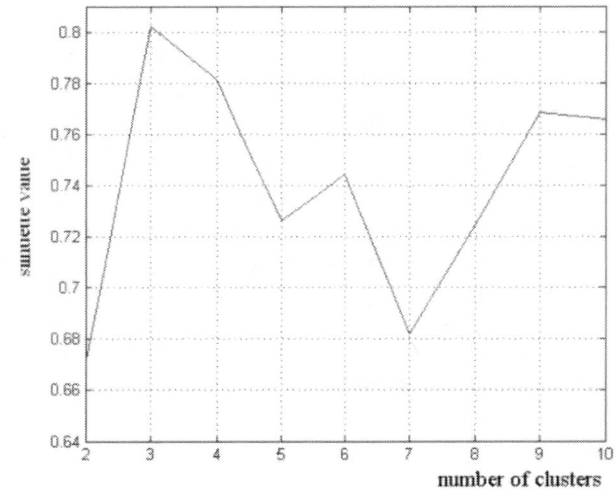

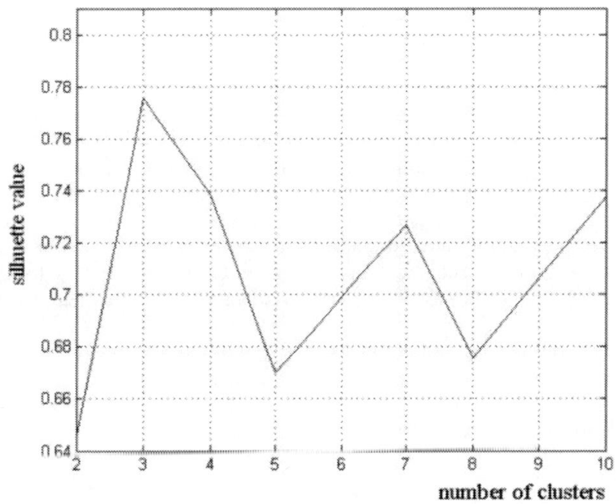

Figure 2. Silhouette plots for April 5 and April 10

Calculating the KS-distance for each pair of hours, we get a 24×24 distance matrix. The Partitioning Around Medoids (PAM) clustering algorithm [16] is applied now to cluster the data. In order to divide a data set into k clusters using PAM, firstly, k objects from the data are chosen as initial cluster centers (medoids) with the intention to attain the minimal total scattering around them (to reduce the loss function value). Then, the procedure iteratively replaces each one of these center points by non-center ones with the same purpose. If no one of further changes can improve the value of the loss function then the procedure ends.

In addition to the clustered data, PAM requires as an input parameter the number of clusters k. Hence, the first step of our procedure is devoted to estimation of the optimal number of the hour's clusters. For this purpose, we use the

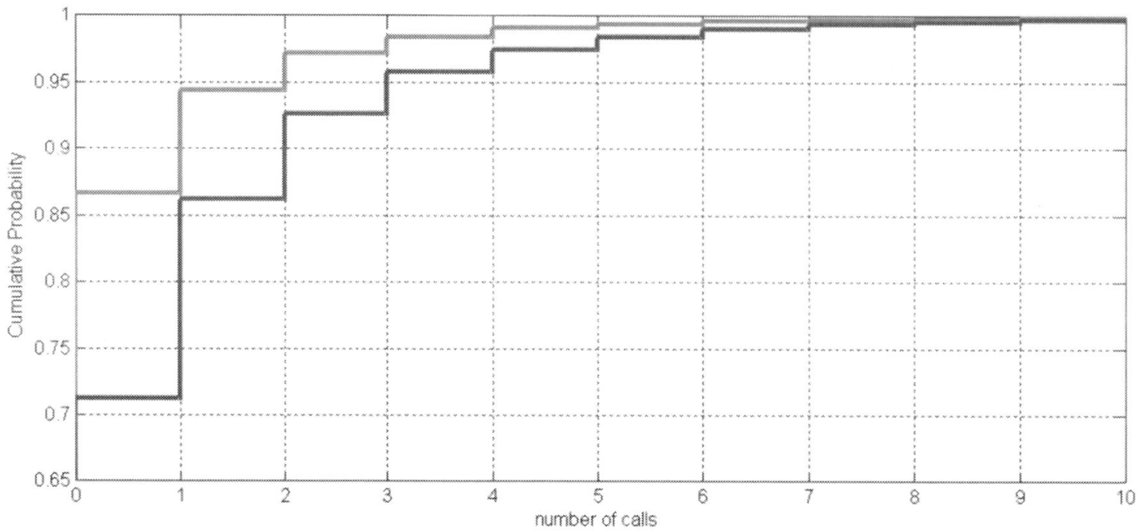

Figure 3. Empirical cumulative distribution functions for hours 9 (upper) and 19 (lower).

Silhouette coefficient of [17]. For each point, the Silhouette index takes values in $[-1, 1]$ interval, if that the Silhouette mean value, calculated across the whole data, is close to 1 specifies "well clustered" data, and value -1 characterizes a very "poor" clustering solution. Therefore, the Silhouette mean value, found for several different numbers of clusters, can indicate the most appropriate number of clusters by its maximal value. The number of clusters was checked in the interval of $[2-10]$, and the optimal one was found to be 3 for all the considered data sets (i.e., for all considered days). An example of Silhouette plots (for 5 of April and 10 of April) is shown in Fig. 2. Fig. 3 presents examples of two different normalized cumulative distribution curves, calculated for hours 9 and 19.

The partition of 24 hours into 3 hour clusters is presented in Fig. 4 for three different dates. It can be concluded that although the partitions slightly depend on the particular data set (date), the overall structure of the clusters is preserved. Namely, there is a silent 'night' cluster (red), an active 'day' cluster (blue), and a 'morning/evening' cluster (green). Table V shows the same distribution of 24 hours with another color convention: 'night' cluster (dark gray), 'morning/evening' cluster (light gray) and 'day' cluster (white) for all the considered dates. The procedure was successfully applied to our data sets, which contains information on the activity of about 5 million users during the period of observation: 13 days. We recall that only active users, those having at least one, are considered in our procedure. Based on the results of this clustering of hours, we can obtain information from the original data regarding the user activity during those hours, which correspond to the clusters.

B. Clustering of users

We obtained classification of users' activity across the hour clusters. Apparently, a user can move from cluster to cluster, for example, in case when the corresponding SIM card is transferred to another person like a family member. However, as it was mentioned, the clustering structure is very similar for different working days, e.g., the most of the users do not change their behavior in a cellular network.

Now, for each user we built a vector, composed of the fractions of calls falling within each hour cluster. We produce user clustering employing this new data representation. Due to the large amount of data, we are dealing here with a high complexity clustering task. We apply a resampling clustering procedure. User behavior patterns are obtained from analysis of the users falling within a certain cluster. In this section, we describe the proposed classification procedure and its results.

1) Clusterization procedure: The main aim of the users clustering procedure is to divide the clients into groups, using information about their activity in each one of the hour clusters, obtained in the previous stage. We present each user as three dimensional vector (r_1, r_2, r_3), where r_i is the ratio of a user's activity during a cluster of hours number i. More precisely, r_i is a fraction of a user's calls during the cluster i in the total number of calls during a day.

The proposed resampling clustering procedure is based on the well-known K-means algorithm [20], and implementing de-facto the idea, proposed in [21]. The K-means algorithm has two input parameters: the number of clusters k and the data set to be clustered X. It strives to find a partition $\pi(X) = \{\pi_1(X), \dots, \pi_k(X)\}$ minimizing the following loss function

$$\rho_{\{c_1,\dots c_k\}}(\pi(X)) = \frac{1}{N}\sum_{j=1}^{k}\sum_{x\in\pi_j(X)}\|x-c_j\|^2, \quad (3)$$

where c_j, $j = 1,...,k$ is the mean position (the cluster centroid) of the objects belonging to cluster $\pi_j(X)$, and N is the size of X.

TABLE V. 24 hours partition into dark gray (night), light gray (morning/evening) and white (day) clusters for different dates.

	1	2	3	4	5	6	7	8	9	10	11	12	13	14	15	16	17	18	19	20	21	22	23	24
30.03	2	2	2	2	2	2	2	2	1	1	1	3	3	3	3	3	3	3	3	3	3	1	1	2
31.03	2	2	2	2	2	2	2	2	1	1	1	3	3	3	1	3	3	3	3	3	3	1	1	2
01.04	2	2	2	2	2	2	2	2	1	1	3	3	3	3	3	3	3	3	3	3	3	1	1	1
02.04	2	2	2	2	2	2	2	2	1	1	1	1	3	3	1	1	3	3	3	3	3	1	1	2
03.04	2	2	2	2	2	2	2	2	1	1	1	3	3	3	3	3	3	3	3	3	3	1	1	2
04.04	2	2	2	2	2	2	2	2	2	1	3	3	3	3	3	3	3	3	3	3	3	1	1	1
05.04	1	2	2	2	2	2	2	2	1	1	3	3	3	3	3	3	3	3	3	3	3	3	1	1
06.04	2	2	2	2	2	2	2	2	1	1	1	3	3	3	3	3	3	3	3	3	3	1	1	2
07.04	2	2	2	2	2	2	2	2	1	1	1	3	3	3	1	3	3	3	3	3	3	1	1	2
08.04	2	2	2	2	2	2	2	2	1	1	3	3	3	3	3	3	3	3	3	3	3	1	1	1
09.04	2	2	2	2	2	2	2	2	1	1	1	3	3	3	3	3	3	3	3	3	3	1	1	2
10.04	2	2	2	2	2	2	2	2	1	1	3	3	3	3	3	3	3	3	3	3	3	1	1	1
11.04	2	2	2	2	2	2	2	2	1	1	1	3	3	3	3	3	3	3	3	3	3	1	1	2

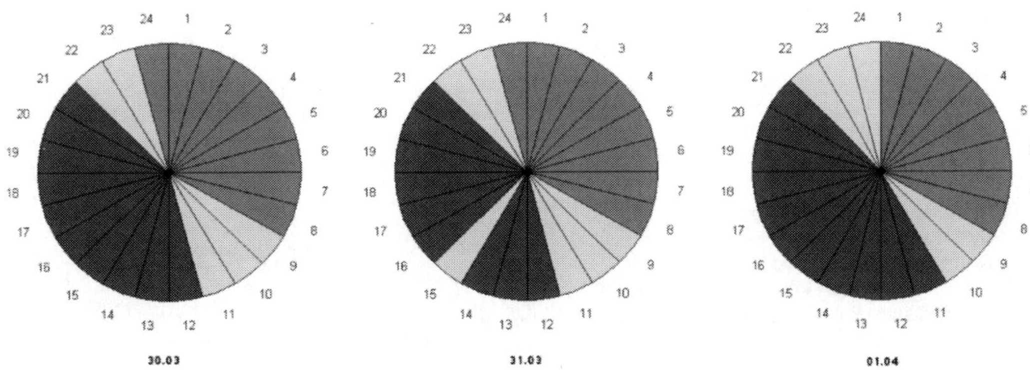

Figure 4. 24-hour partition for Mars 30, Mars 31, April 01: 'night' cluster (red), 'day' cluster (blue), and 'morning/evening' cluster (green).

Initially, the centroid set can be predefined or chosen randomly. Using the current centroid set, the K-means algorithm assigns each point to the nearest centroid aiming to form the current clusters and then recalculates centroids as the clusters means. The process is reiterated until the centroids are stabilized. In the general case, as a result of this procedure, the objective function (3) reaches its local minimum. Note that in the K-means algorithm, a partition is unambiguously defined by the centroid set and vise versa. Moreover, in the general case, the loss function (3) can be used for assessing the quality of arbitrary partition $\widehat{\pi}(X)$ with respect to given centroid set $\{c_1, \dots c_k\}$. The resampling procedure allows partitioning a large data set based on partitioning its parts as presented in Algorithm 1.

2) Choosing the number of users clusters: In order to evaluate the optimal number of clusters, usually, one compares stability of the obtained partition for different numbers of clusters. To this aim, we repeat the users' clustering procedure ten times on the same data set and evaluate the Rand index value between all obtained partitions. The Rand index [22] represents the measure of similarity between two partitions. It is calculated by counting the pairs of samples, which are assigned to the same or to different clusters in these partitions. The closeness of the Rand index value to 1 indicates similarity of the considered partitions.

For the same purpose, the Adjusted Rand index of [23], which is the corrected-for-chance version of the Rand index, can be used as well. However, in our consideration, it is more suitable to use the regular one because it still reflects well the closeness of the partitions. The mean values of the obtained Rand indexes naturally characterize stability of the partition by the maximal value. So, the "true" number of clusters corresponds to the most stable partition.

C. Experimental study

In this section, we are mostly concentrated on the data set for April 1, which is taken as a typical example of the original data sets. The results (obtained for other data sets) are very similar including all the parameters, considered below.

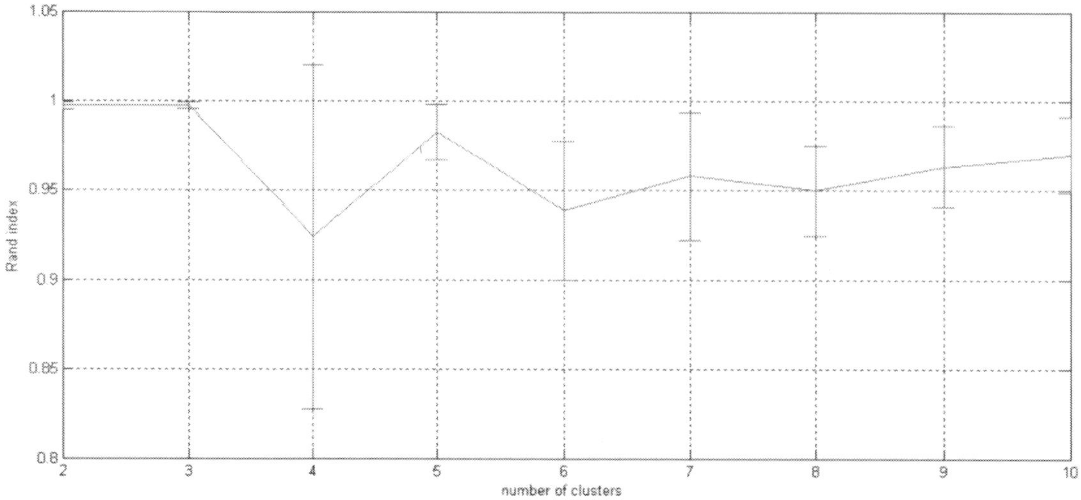

Figure 5. Rand index plot for the data set of April 1.

Algorithm 1: Partitioning
Input:
X dataset to be clustered;
k the number of clusters;
N the number of samples;
m the sample size;
ε the threshold value.
Resampling procedure: *Randomly draw* N *samples* S_i *of size* m *from* X *without replacement.*
1: **for all** S_i **do**
2: In the first iteration, set of centroids C is chosen randomly.
3: Cluster S_i by K-means algorithm, starting from the given centroid set C.
4: Cluster X by assignment to the nearest centroid, using the centroids, obtained in the previous step.
5: Calculate the object function value of the partition $\pi(X)$ from the previous step according to (3).
6: **end for**
7: Choose from the set $\{S_1, \dots, S_N\}$ a sample S_0 with the minimal object function value.
8: **if** the first iteration is being processed or if the absolute difference between two minimal object function values, which are calculated for two sequential iterations, is greater than ε **then**
9: replace C with the set of centroids of $\pi(S_0)$, and return to step 1
10: **else**
11: stop
12: **end if**
end

1) Estimation of the "true" number of clusters: In order to estimate the optimal number of clusters in the users' clusterization procedure described in Section III-B1, we repeat the clustering stability evaluation procedure described in Section III-B2 for each of the possible number of clusters in interval $[2, 10]$. The results for all dates are very similar. Fig. 5 demonstrates an example of Rand-index curve for April 1. It is easy to see that the maximal stability attitudes appear for $N = 2$ and $N = 3$.

Recall that the main purpose of the user clustering is to recognize behavior patterns, which represent the general structure of the users' population. Let us consider two possible estimators for the "true" number of clusters from this point of view. We describe a behavior pattern via an average level of the users' activity within each of the three hour clusters, defined in Section III-A. So, we take a three-dimensional representation of users, introduced in Section III-B1, and calculate the mean and standard deviation of each coordinate in each user cluster.

The user activity patterns for April 1 are shown in Fig. 6 by means of the error bar plot of values in each hour cluster. Recall that for the given date we obtained a 'night' cluster (red) with hours 1-8; a 'day' cluster (blue) with hours 11-21; and a 'morning/evening' cluster (green) containing hours 9-10 and 22-24 (see Fig. 4). For example, pattern A (the left panel in the picture) is characterized by the prevalence of the day activity since the average activity value is 0.84 for the 'day' hour cluster, in comparison with the values of 0.09 and 0.06 for the other hour clusters. Similarly, the behavior pattern B (the middle panel) describes users with significant activity in all hour clusters, while pattern C (the right panel) is characterized by high activity in the morning-evening hours.

The obtained result shows that we have a "clear" partition into 2 clusters and that one of them is well divided into 2 more sub-clusters. In fact, the two-clusters partitions contain the cluster corresponding to Pattern B and the united cluster for Patterns A and C. For our purposes, therefore,

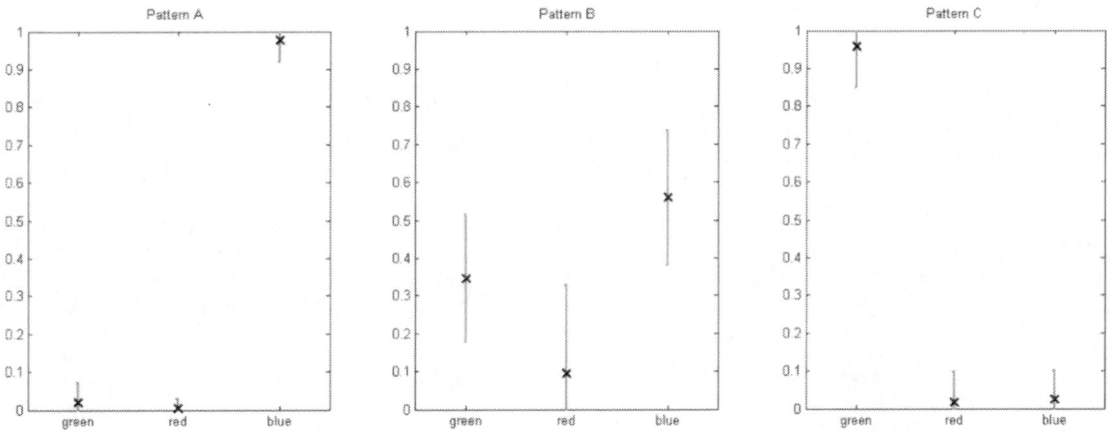

Figure 6. Profiles of 3 customer clusters (green, red, blue) for work day (April 1; $InCalls$).

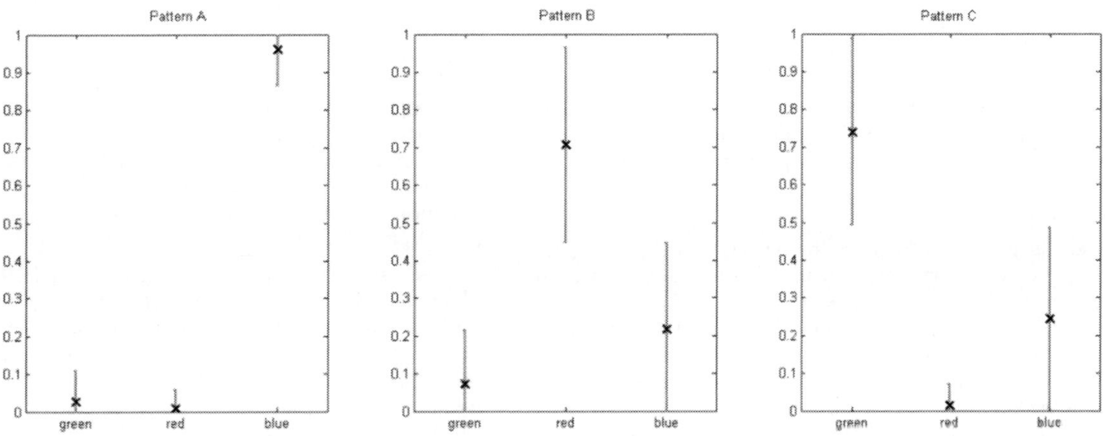

Figure 7. Profiles of 3 customer clusters (green, red, blue) for off day (April 5; $InCalls$).

it is natural to choose 3 as the "true" number of clusters. Note, that it is common situation in cluster analysis: the "ill-pose" number of clusters determination task can have several solutions depending on the model resolution. In the most cases, the population is partitioned into three clusters, with about 70, 20, and 10 user percentages in these clusters. This fact demonstrates the distribution within the population, connected to the call activity. This fact may be related to the nature of the people working time.

2) Procedure convergence: Now, we demonstrate that the resampling clustering procedure (Algorithm 1) converges very fast. In fact, Table VI shows the minimal objective function values for the first five iterations of the resampling procedure, executed on 100 samples for $k = 3$ (for others k, the situation is similar). The results show that, even in the second iteration, the minimal average of the distances does not change significantly as compared to the first iteration. In the subsequent iterations, this value remains constant to within 0.0001.

3) Profile stability: Further, we use behavior patterns for comparison of the results of our procedure on different datasets. The profiles for each considered date are shown in Tables VII and VIII. It is easy to see that they are stable both for work days and off days. However, the difference between work and off days is significant (see Fig. 6 and Fig. 7 for comparison). Although qualitative descriptions of profiles are very similar in both cases (pattern A with prevalent "day" activity; pattern B with significant activity throughout 24 hours and pattern C with prevalent "morning-evening" activity), in off days higher "night" activity is detected.

D. Call activity, associated within patterns

Now, we consider the call activity of the users, who correspond to each one of the three found clusters. The total activity of all the users within a day has a density with two

TABLE VI. Minimum of average distances to the nearest centroid for the first 5 iterations of the resampling procedure of Algorithm 1.

Iteration	1	2	3	4	5
Minimum	0.014487	0.013302	0.013295	0.013309	0.0132901

TABLE VII. Mean values for different Patterns in 3 clusters partition. (For Pattern X mean values for each hour cluster (red - 'night', green - 'morning/evening' and blue - 'day')).

	Pattern A			Pattern B			Pattern C		
	green	red	blue	green	red	blue	green	red	blue
30.03	0.9704	0.0086	0.021	0.0187	0.0047	0.9766	0.33	0.1397	0.53
31.03	0.9104	0.0269	0.0627	0.0199	0.0056	0.9745	0.2966	0.1589	0.545
1.04	0.9575	0.0166	0.026	0.0194	0.0037	0.977	0.3469	0.0942	0.559
2.04	0.9071	0.0279	0.065	0.0206	0.006	0.9734	0.2975	0.1594	0.543
3.04	0.9464	0.0276	0.026	0.0236	0.0066	0.9698	0.3395	0.13	0.53
4.04	0.6909	0.0257	0.2834	0.0387	0.0135	0.9478	0.0563	0.7429	0.201
5.04	0.7394	0.0149	0.2457	0.0289	0.0105	0.9606	0.0747	0.7062	0.219
6.04	0.9113	0.027	0.0617	0.0182	0.0054	0.9764	0.296	0.1571	0.547
7.04	0.9684	0.0098	0.0217	0.0205	0.0065	0.973	0.3179	0.1579	0.524
8.04	0.9688	0.0097	0.0215	0.0194	0.0062	0.9743	0.3164	0.1551	0.529
9.04	0.9633	0.0098	0.0269	0.0239	0.0062	0.9698	0.346	0.1278	0.526
10.04	0.9527	0.0192	0.0281	0.0204	0.0048	0.9748	0.339	0.1088	0.552
11.04	0.7045	0.0327	0.2628	0.0392	0.0151	0.9457	0.0284	0.7945	0.177

peaks. One of them is placed in the workday middle, and the second one, the higher peak, is located in the period after 7 p.m such that a local activity minimum is observed immediately after.

The shape of the corresponding density in the first cluster (A) is actually the same. However, the user's activity almost does not vary in the second cluster (B), i.e., the density curve has several insignificant peaks, and the activity decreases at 10 p.m. The total activity of the users belonging to cluster three (C) has two peaks, which are located in the morning and in the evening of a day.

The corresponding curves are shown in Fig. 8 and Fig. 9, where columns A, C present $InCalls$, and columns B, D present $OutCalls$. Here, the blue curves corresponds to the total activity densities of all the users; the red, green and brown ones give the total activity densities for clusters 1, 2 and 3, respectively. Note that both activity types have the same distribution shapes. Furthermore, the distribution of calls during a day for all three clusters is almost independent on the activity type (see Fig. 10a).

1) Features of the cluster model parameters: The model that we use reveals major differences between the DSN of the entire set of users and the DSNs for the individual clusters. In fact, for $InCalls$, the DSN for Cluster 1 is almost always best fitted by a single exponent. On the other hand, in more than half of the observed cases, the DSN for Cluster 2 is fitted by two exponents. Moreover, during the weekend period, the curve is fitted by three exponents. The DSN for Cluster 3 is usually fitted by two exponents, while the three-exponent fit sometimes arises without regard for the day of the week (Table IX). For $OutCalls$ (Table X), the above irregularities are more pronounced for Clusters 1 and 2, since all the best fits for Cluster 3 are two-exponential.

TABLE VIII. Standard deviation for different Patterns in 3 clusters partition. (For Pattern X std values for each hour cluster (red - 'night', green - 'morning/evening' and blue - 'day')).

	Pattern A			Pattern B			Pattern C		
	green	red	blue	green	red	blue	green	red	blue
30.03	0.0515	0.0285	0.0593	0.1796	0.2713	0.2002	0.083	0.0488	0.0666
31.03	0.0528	0.0309	0.0612	0.1701	0.2818	0.1962	0.1523	0.1025	0.1224
1.04	0.0516	0.0253	0.0578	0.1684	0.2325	0.1777	0.1087	0.0816	0.0733
2.04	0.0536	0.0319	0.0623	0.1699	0.2807	0.1957	0.1537	0.1038	0.1236
3.04	0.058	0.034	0.0675	0.178	0.2599	0.1875	0.1241	0.104	0.0732
4.04	0.0889	0.0543	0.1066	0.1276	0.2452	0.2232	0.255	0.0762	0.2371
5.04	0.079	0.0479	0.0961	0.1411	0.2574	0.2254	0.2472	0.0565	0.2396
6.04	0.0502	0.0303	0.0588	0.169	0.283	0.1982	0.1521	0.1027	0.1216
7.04	0.0537	0.0332	0.0636	0.1831	0.2797	0.2033	0.0859	0.0525	0.0677
8.04	0.0522	0.0327	0.062	0.1823	0.2773	0.2024	0.0854	0.052	0.0675
9.04	0.0584	0.033	0.0674	0.1762	0.2566	0.1927	0.0908	0.0517	0.0745
10.04	0.0529	0.0287	0.0604	0.1726	0.2467	0.1835	0.1142	0.0867	0.0758
11.04	0.09	0.0579	0.1108	0.0775	0.2361	0.2175	0.2502	0.0977	0.2359

Tables IX and X demonstrate comparison of the DSNs performance in Clusters 1-3 with the DSN, which is found within the total set of users. Each one of the curves exhibits its own cluster behavior characterizing the group. Nevertheless, joining any two of these clusters results in a three-component DSN. At the same time, we split the data randomly. This random partition into three clusters (with the same number of users as in the calculation of Clusters 1, 2, 3 as mentioned above) yields the same three exponent indexes, $t1 = 0.11$, $t2 = 0.31$ and $t3 = 1.01$ for all three clusters, which coincide with those calculated for the total set of users on the same day (see Table XI).

Thus, simplification of the cluster model shows that the partition into Clusters 1-3 actually reflects different activity characteristics for different groups of users. There are some differences on the weekends. However, in general, the parameters of a particular DSN are the same for each day. Note also that the DSNs of Clusters 2 and 3 are not in the least close to the second or third component (exponent) of the total set DSN. Indeed, in our model, the DSN of Cluster 2 consists mainly of two exponents, with one exponent disappearing at the decay value of 30, while the other (as a rule) is not decaying up to the value of 70. The DSN of Cluster 3 also has long-lasting components (up to 100 and more - see Table XII).

IV. CONCLUSION AND FURTHER STUDIES

Most of the recent studies, which consider the analysis of non-Gaussian processes, are related to hyperbolic distribution. The mere existence of such a distribution does not depend on the particular model, but rather is the result of the process being non-Gaussian in nature. Indeed, the Gnedenko-Doeblin limit theorem imposes restrictions on the form of a non-Gaussian distribution. Namely, its asymptotic behavior coincides with the Zipf distribution to within a slowly varying function.

For example, the hyperbolic distribution was first observed in some fields of human endeavor, e.g., Pareto distribution of people according to their income and Zipf's law for the frequency of words in a text, [24]. It later turned out that the

TABLE IX. Parameters of the approximating curves for Clusters 1-3 during the days of observation ($InCalls$).

	Cluster 1						Cluster 2						Cluster 3					
	A1	t1	A2	t2	A3	t3	A1	t1	A2	t2	A3	t3	A1	t1	A2	t2	A3	t3
03_30	75595	0.14					192142	0.2	613143	1			47803	0.31	507346	1.96		
03_31	99881	0.12					183988	0.21	617336	1.08			760	0.05	68228	0.3	693935	2
04_01	67779	0.13					34652	0.3	346267	1.63			237500	0.19	603396	0.96		
04_02	75929	0.13					42852	0.3	500546	1.97			223697	0.19	623453	0.99		
04_03	102570	0.14					22086	0.08	293554	0.26	757514	1.63	35196	0.29	16495	0.31	546056	1.95
04_04	9222	0.11	96032	0.43			67172	0.12	379913	0.34	6.27E+08	8.94	2267	0.08	55826	0.52		
04_05	117294	0.49					59033	0.13	426361	0.4	2.55E+08	7.97	1541	0.08	26157	0.47		
04_06	81775	0.14					28985	0.09	311895	0.29	931890	1.92	53561	0.3	604540	1.97		
04_07	101825	0.12					66891	0.28	683759	1.93			5214	0.06	192583	0.23	633898	1.11
04_08	82563	0.13					234989	0.19	627543	0.96			37836	0.31	485223	1.95		
04_09	93323	0.13					54257	0.3	596335	1.98			7664	0.06	214184	0.21	635576	1.09
04_10	81522	0.12					106849	0.36	817000000	9.84			205885	0.19	609365	1.04		
04_11	6587	0.1	92657	0.43			59427	0.12	346767	0.36	4.58E+08	8.71	3391	0.11	69657	0.63		

TABLE X. Parameters of the approximating curves for Clusters 1-3 during the days of observation ($OutCalls$)

	Cluster 1						Cluster 2						Cluster 3					
	A1	t1	A2	t2	A3	t3	A1	t1	A2	t2	A3	t3	A1	t1	A2	t2	A3	t3
03_30	84800	0.16					29389	0.4	710400	2.27			282378	0.25	864407	1.09		
03_31	85229	0.15					78809	0.46	25900000	6.3			294449	0.24	856164	1.13		
04_01	82321	0.14					317001	0.25	814726	1.11			26982	0.35	494050	1.84		
04_02	88472	0.14					292626	0.24	832276	1.12			80758	0.45	818000000	9.77		
04_03	109623	0.14					258084	0.24	863402	1.16			43339	0.36	537802	1.71		
04_04	5974	0.1	100551	0.4			32822	0.11	485256	0.35	7.59E+08	8.79	15437	0.47	30837	0.47		
04_05	90602	0.47					46062	0.14	506705	0.44	3.85E+08	8.13	837	0.07	32721	0.43		
04_06	84352	0.15					75673	0.47	725000000	9.63			301425	0.25	868863	1.15		
04_07	94715	0.15					31373	0.4	740493	2.29			285742	0.24	851642	1.1		
04_08	91272	0.15					309021	0.24	858547	1.11			28508	0.4	690454	2.27		
04_09	114017	0.14					48479	0.38	907529	2.21			243980	0.24	880043	1.16		
04_10	85846	0.14					28740	0.33	485367	1.78			304700	0.24	797224	1.12		
04_11	2699	0.07	95655	0.42			36654	0.12	424785	0.37	5.87E+08	8.6	2246	0.11	59476	0.63		

same laws could be detected in other areas of human endeavor (e.g., the distribution of cities according to population) as well as in natural phenomena (e.g., time distribution of disasters). Internet activity and, in particular, user activity on social networks, appears to be an appropriate area for such analysis. Numerous studies suggest different models of social networks and try to link particular network characteristics with some measure of user activity. These characteristics often obey the hyperbolic law in one form or another.

From a practical point of view, the difference between non-Gaussian distributions (sometimes referred to as heavy-tailed) and the Gaussian distribution is quite important. The frequencies of extreme deviations in the two distributions are very different. The moments of non-Gaussian distributions increase with sample size, but do not tend to be limited as in the Gaussian case.

Although the social activity distribution of a population takes a specific and constant form, it can be assumed that the observed distribution is in some sense an averaged one. Obviously, it is composed of various types of distributions, generated by different social layers. We have in mind not only the groups, arising from the simplest types of differences, such as age and gender, but also the more complex features of the population under consideration. The purpose of this paper is to analyze the phenom as well as to decompose the observed distributions, according to certain external criteria.

It can be assumed that the hyperbolic law or the combination of distribution laws for various social groups, depend on the nature of the user joint activity. In some cases, each user's actions are in some sense sequential, so that their average behavior can be considered in the framework of a single law.

In the cases where users' actions occur in parallel, each user group, which is uniform with respect to some criterion, can generate its own law of activity distribution. Typically,

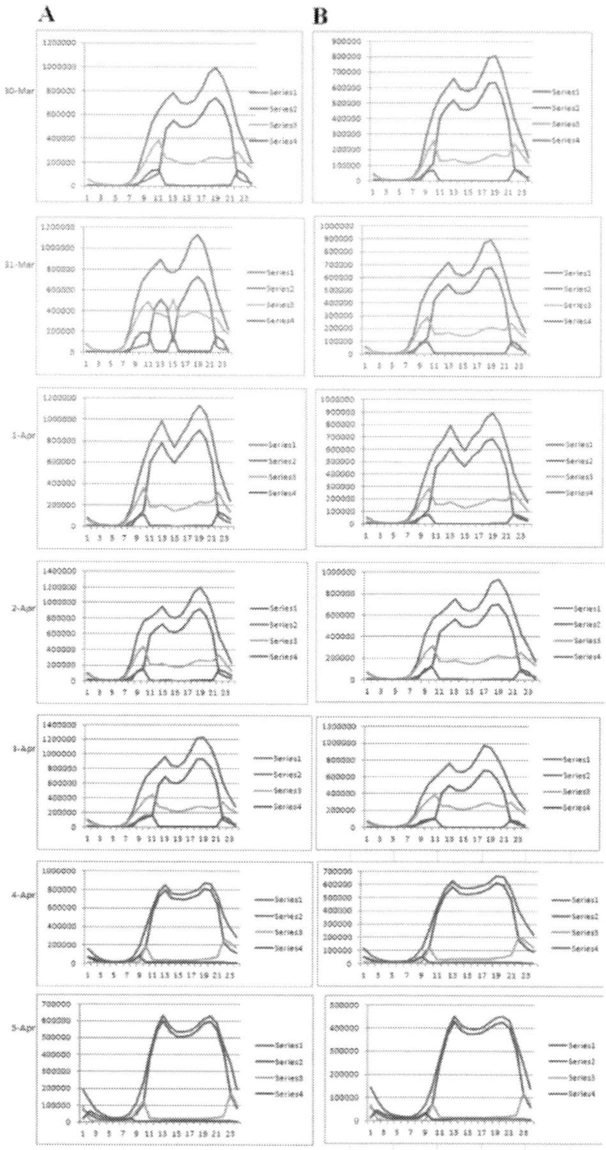

Figure 8. Distribution of $InCalls$ and $OutCalls$ during the day in the three clusters of users (A) and (B).

users actions in such a group are aggregated in order to pattern the group behavior. Researchers, who study the parameters of such networks, often find fractal properties and hyperbolic distributions. An example of parallel user activity is the number of records in an email address book. In a population of 16,881 users of a large university computer system, the cumulative distribution is not a powerful one, [10].

Since telephone calls are also more likely to be a parallel user's activity in the sense described above, we expected to find that the observed distribution of calls is the sum of several distribution functions, corresponding to different social groups

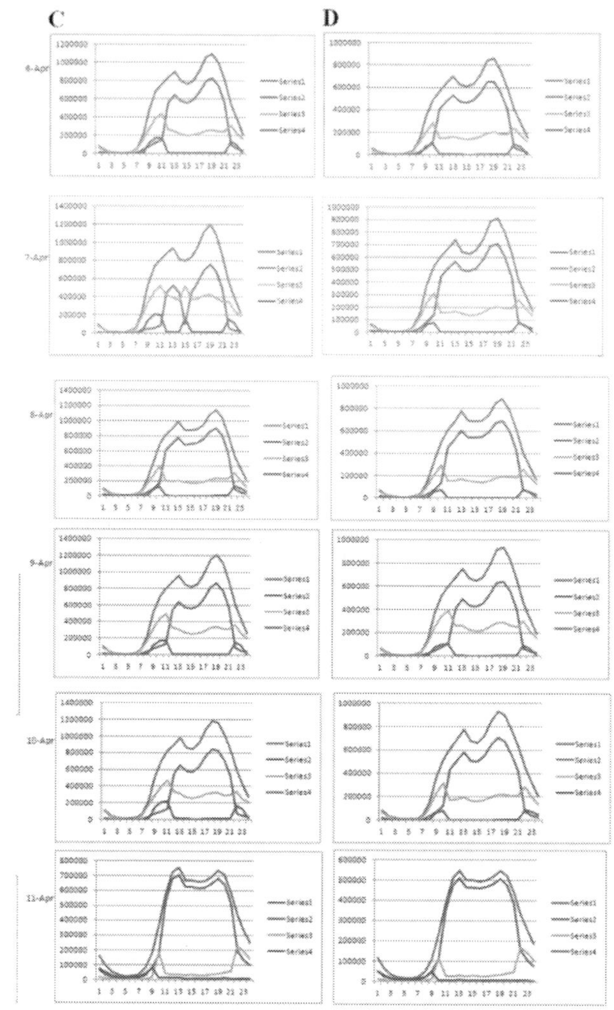

Figure 9. Distribution of $InCalls$ and $OutCalls$ during the day in the three clusters of users (C) and (D).

TABLE XI. Decay value of each DSN component in the activity/cluster model for all the three clusters considered ($InCalls$)

	cluster 1			cluster 2			cluster 3		
	1	2	3	1	2	3	1	2	3
03_30	80	0	0	60	13	0	34	6	0
03_31	95	0	0	57	12	0	132	37	6
04_01	85	0	0	34	7	0	65	13	0
04_02	86	0	0	35	6	0	64	13	0
04_03	82	0	0	125	48	8	36	31	6
04_04	82	26	0	92	37	2	96	21	0
04_05	23	0	0	84	32	2	91	21	0
04_06	80	0	0	114	43	7	36	6	0
04_07	96	0	0	39	6	0	142	52	12
04_08	87	0	0	65	13	0	34	6	0
04_09	88	0	0	36	6	0	149	58	12
04_10	94	0	0	32	2	0	64	12	0
04_11	87	26	0	91	35	2	73	17	0

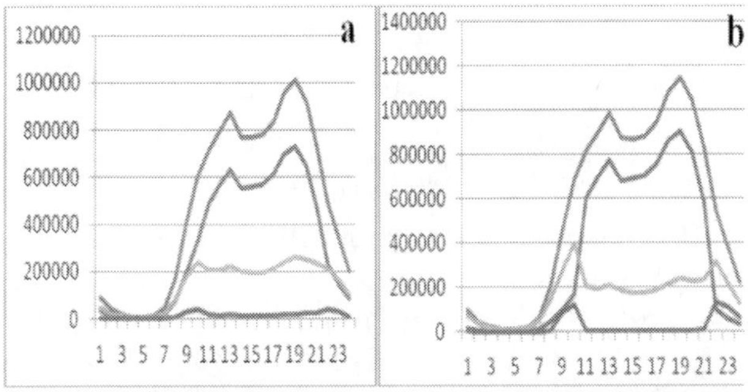

Figure 10. (a) Distribution of $InCalls$ for the clusters obtained for $OutCalls$. (b) Distribution of $InCalls$ for the clusters obtained for $InCalls$. Date: April 8. Notations of the curves are the same as in Fig. 8.

TABLE XII. Decay value of each DSN component in the activity/cluster model for all the three clusters considered ($OutCalls$)

	cluster 1			cluster 2			cluster 3		
	1	2	3	1	2	3	1	2	3
03_30	70	0	0	25	5	0	50	12	0
03_31	75	0	0	24	2	0	52	12	0
04_01	80	0	0	50	12	0	29	7	0
04_02	81	0	0	52	12	0	25	2	0
04_03	82	0	0	51	11	0	29	7	0
04_04	86	28	0	94	37	2	20	21	0
04_05	24	0	0	76	29	2	96	24	0
04_06	75	0	0	23	2	0	50	11	0
04_07	76	0	0	25	5	0	52	12	0
04_08	76	0	0	52	12	0	25	5	0
04_09	83	0	0	28	6	0	51	11	0
04_10	81	0	0	31	7	0	52	12	0
04_11	112	27	0	87	35	2	70	17	0

of users. The limited number of these groups is an important prerequisite for such differentiation because averaging over the groups is absent in this case. In [25], we introduced the notion of user strategy and showed that the number of different strategies is small. Therefore, we expected to obtain a small number of groups with equivalent user activity. Having no real-life socio-relevant parameters, we assumed that the peculiarities of a user's activity during a day may correlate with the user's social status.

We split the population into three clusters and showed that these clusters have simpler distribution functions than those for the total population. Yet, it is quite possible that a more detailed partition exists with even simpler distributions for each group.

References

[1] T. Couronne, V. Kirzner, K. Korenblat, E. Ravve, and Z. Volkovich, "Modelling behavior patterns in cellular networks," in Proceedings of ICCGI-2016, The Eleventh International Multi-Conference on Computing in the Global Information Technology, November 13-17, 2016, 2017, pp. 64–71.

[2] I. Simonson, Z. Carmon, R. Dhar, A. Drolet, and S. Nowlis, "Consumer research: in search of identity," Annual Review of Psychology, vol. 52, 2001, pp. 249–275.

[3] P. Kotler and K. Keller, Marketing Management, ser. MARKETING MANAGEMENT. Pearson Prentice Hall, 2006.

[4] A. Dempster, N. Laird, and D. Rubin, "Maximum likelihood from incomplete data via the EM algorithm," Journal of the Royal Statistical Society, vol. 39, no. 1, 1977, pp. 1–38.

[5] G. McLachlan and D. Peel, Finite mixture models, ser. Wiley series in probability and statistics. New York: J. Wiley & Sons, 2000.

[6] J. Willis and G. Yule, "Some statistics of evolution and geographical distribution in plants and animals, and their significance," Nature, vol. 109, 1922, pp. 177–179.

[7] J. Kenney and E. Keeping, "Linear regression and correlation," in Mathematics of Statistics: Part 1, 3rd ed. NJ: Princeton, Van Nostrand, 1962, ch. 15, pp. 252–285.

[8] N. Jewell, "Mixtures of exponential distributions," The Annals of Statistics, vol. 10, no. 2, 1982, pp. 479–848.

[9] J. Heckman, R. Robb, and J. Walker, "Testing the mixture of exponentials hypothesis and estimating the mixing distribution by the method of moments," Journal of the American Statistical Association, vol. 85, no. 410, 1990, pp. 582–589.

[10] M. Newman, S. Forrest, and J. Balthrop, "Email networks and the spread of computer viruses," Physical Review E, vol. 66, Sep 2002, p. 035101.

[11] J. Hartigan, "Direct clustering of a data matrix," J. Amer. Statist. Assoc, vol. 67, 1972, pp. 123–132.

[12] Y. Cheng and G. Church, "Biclustering of expression data," in Proceedings of the Eighth International Conference on Intelligent Systems for Molecular Biology. AAAI Press, 2000, pp. 93–103.

[13] D. Witten and R. Tibshirani, "A framework for feature selection in clustering," Journal of the American Statistical Association, vol. 105, no. 490, 2010, pp. 713–726.

[14] R. Lopes, P. Hobson, and I. Reid, "The two-dimensional Kolmogorov-Smirnov test," in Proceeding of the XI International Workshop on Advanced Computing and Analysis Techniques in Physics Research, Nikhef, Amsterdam, the Netherlands, April 23-27, 2007. Proceedings of Science, 2007.

[15] ——, "Computationally efficient algorithms for the two-dimensional Kolmogorov-Smirnov test," Journal of Physics: Conference Series, vol. 119, no. 4, 2008, p. 042019.

[16] L. Kaufman and P. Rousseeuw, Finding groups in data: an introduction to cluster analysis, ser. Wiley series in probability and mathematical statistics. New York: Wiley, 1990, a Wiley-Interscience publication.

[17] P. Rousseeuw, "Silhouettes: A graphical aid to the interpretation and validation of cluster analysis," Journal of Computational and Applied Mathematics, vol. 20, 1987, pp. 53 – 65.

[18] F. Galton, "Typical laws of heredity," Nature, vol. 12, 1877, pp. 492–495, 512–533.

[19] S. Phithakkitnukoon, T. Horanont, G. D. Lorenzo, R. Shibasaki, and C. Ratti, "Activity-aware map: Identifying human daily activity pattern using mobile phone data," in Human Behavior Understanding: First International Workshop, HBU 2010, Istanbul, Turkey, August 22, 2010. Proceedings, A. Salah, T. Gevers, N. Sebe, and A. Vinciarelli, Eds. Berlin, Heidelberg: Springer Berlin Heidelberg, 2010, pp. 14–25.

[20] D. MacKay, Information Theory, Inference & Learning Algorithms. New York, NY, USA: Cambridge University Press, 2002.

[21] J. Kogan, C. Nicholas, and M. Teboulle, Grouping Multidimensional Data: Recent Advances in Clustering, 1st ed. Springer Publishing Company, Incorporated, 2010.

[22] N. Vinh, J. Epps, and J. Bailey, "Information theoretic measures for clusterings comparison: Is a correction for chance necessary?" in Proceedings of the 26th Annual International Conference on Machine Learning, ser. ICML '09. New York, NY, USA: ACM, 2009, pp. 1073–1080.

[23] S. Wagner and D. Wagner, "Comparing Clusterings – An Overview," Universität Karlsruhe (TH), Tech. Rep. 2006-04, 2007.

[24] R. Baayen, Word Frequency Distributions, ser. Text, Speech and Language Technology. Springer Netherlands, 2001, no. 1.

[25] T. Couronné, V. Kirzhner, K. Korenblat, and Z. Volkovich, "Some features of the users activities in the mobile telephone network," Journal of Pattern Recognition Research, vol. 1, 2013, pp. 59–65.

A Constraint Programming Approach to Optimize Network Calls by Minimizing Variance in Data Availability Times

Luis Neto[1], Henrique Lopes Cardoso[2], Carlos Soares[3], Gil Gonçalves[4]
{lcneto, hlc, csoares, gil}@fe.up.pt
Faculdade de Engenharia, Universidade do Porto, Porto, Portugal

[14]ISR-P, Instituto de Sistemas e Robótica - Porto, Portugal

[2]LIACC, Laboratório de Inteligência Artificial e Ciência de Computadores, Porto, Portugal

[3]INESC TEC, Instituto de Engenharia de Sistemas e Computadores, Tecnologia e Ciência, Porto, Portugal

***Abstract*—Smart Nodes are intelligent components of sensor networks that perform data acquisition and treatment, by performing virtualization of sensor instances. Smart Factories are an application domain in which dozens of these cyber-physical components are used, flooding the network with messages. In this work, we present a methodology to reduce the number of calls a Smart Node makes to the network. We propose grouping individual communications within a Smart Node to reduce the number of calls, which is important to improve the efficiency of the factory network. The paper exposes and explains the Smart Node internal structure, formally describing the problem of minimizing the number of calls Smart Nodes make to Cloud Services, by means of a combinatorial *Constraint Optimization Problem*. Using two *Constraint Satisfaction Solvers*, we have addressed the problem using distinct approaches. In this extended version of the work, an additional constraint is added to cut the search space, by eliminating infeasible solutions. Optimal and sub-optimal solutions for an actual problem instance have been found with both approaches. Furthermore, we present a comparison between both solvers in terms of computational efficiency, constraints created in the extended vs original version and show the solution is feasible to apply in a real case scenario.**

Keywords–Sensor Simulation; Combinatorial Optimization; Time Synchronization; Smart Nodes; Industrial Wireless Sensor Networks.

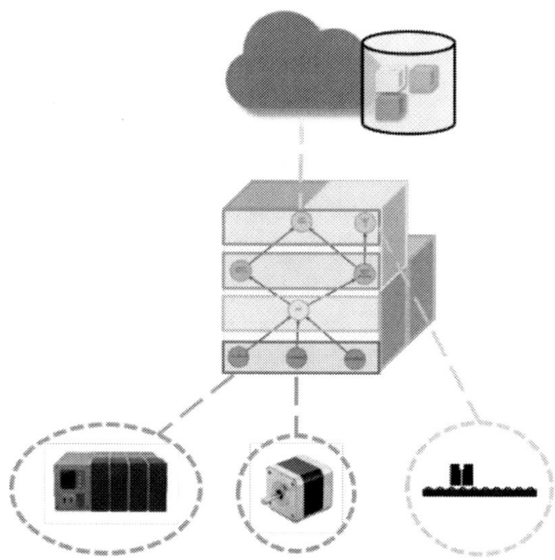

Figure 1. A Smart Node gateway.

I. INTRODUCTION

Wireless Sensor Networks (WSN) consist of sensors sparsely distributed over a given area to sense physical properties, such as luminosity, temperature, current, etc. They are composed of sensor nodes, which pass data until a destination gateway is reached. Common applications are industrial and environment sensing, where they can be used to perceive the state of a machine and prevent natural disasters, respectively. Gateways in WSN play a preponderant role, since they acquire data from sensors, do pre-processing and are responsible to send sensors data to cloud systems for other forms advanced processing.

In this work we present an extension to a previous formulation [1] that solves the problem presented in the following sections. In this extended version, the problem was revised with the intent to increase the time efficiency of the previous proposed solution and also to explore in more detail the previous results. For this analysis, it was planned to run the same tests again, but for a longer period of time. After getting a second set of results, the problem was once again analysed. The analysis objective was try to find some constraint, formulation improvement or domain reduction that decreases the complexity for finding a solution.

The presented technology, a sensor gateway, inherits its main characteristics from the Smart Component philosophy. This philosophy is based in a consistent study of the Smart Manufacturing initiative and it is being systematically refined and matured by past and present European projects

(*XPress [2], IRamp3 [3], ReBORN [4] and SelSus [5]*). There are five essential characteristics to a Smart Component:

- **Reconfigurable and modular**: the solution must be capable to extend its capabilities by adding new software modules and it must be capable to reconfigure its internal operation in runtime.
- **Data processing capabilities**: system state assessment, event detection and fault alarm requires data processing capabilities.
- **Omnidirectional communication and interface capabilities**: omnidirectional means that the system must be capable to talk with devices at a lower level (sensors and machines), same level (other Smart Component's) and higher level (cloud servers, manufacturing systems).
- **Process events and take actions**: this capability provides the system with a certain degree of smartness and autonomy. In case any event of interest, the system must be capable of detecting it and take the proper actions.
- **Real-time acquisition, processing and delivering**: typically, field devices operate at variable real-time scales, performing multiple tasks in a coordinated way. Providing actions in real time is a vital factor for industrial scenarios.

What introduces the complexity that we are trying to address in the Smart Component is the fact that it was designed to be modular, according with Component-Based Software Engineering methodologies. It was developed as "a composite of sub-parts rather than a monolithic entity" [6]. The advantages of such tackle many objectives of the software industry, some of them are: reduction of production cost, code reuse, code portability, fast time to market, systematic approach to system construction and guided system design by formalization and use of domain specific modelling languages.

The component model is the foundation of a component based design. It defines, briefly, the composition standard, that is: how components are composed into larger pieces; how and if they can be composed at design and/or runtime phases of a component life-cycle; how they interact; how the component repository (if any) is managed and the runtime environment that contains the assembled application. Because all of this, component models are hard to build. Some known problems are: achieving deterministic and real-time characteristics; managing parallel flows of component and system development; maintaining components for reuse; different levels of granularity [7] and portability problems [8].

According to [6], components can be divided into 2 main classes: 1) objects, as in OO languages; 2) architectural units, that together compose a software architecture. According to the authors, there are no standard criteria for what constitutes a component model. Components syntax is the language used to component definition and which may be different from implementation language. Typically, the containers and runtime environments are designed and maintained in a server. In this case, we are dealing with an embedded system; being itself the runtime environment and container. The Smart Node uses architectural units as encapsulation for drivers that gather sensor and machine data, objects are used to implement algorithms for data treatment.

Figure 1 shows a Smart Node from an external operation of perspective. These components are nodes in Industrial Cyber Physical Systems that operate and control *Industrial Wireless Sensor Networks*. To introduce the problem this paper addresses, let us consider a scenario in which a reasonable number of these components operate simultaneously. In this operation the following conditions applies:

- Gateways are in constant synchronization with Intra/Inter Enterprise Cloud systems.
- Gateways perform collaborative tasks by talking over the network.
- Human Machine Interface devices proceed to on demand requests to the Smart Nodes.

A large quantity of messages is expected, generated by a large number of devices and services.

Gateways collect data from different sensor types (e.g., humidity, current, pressure). These cyber-physical components are coupled to industrial machines, along with several sensors, which collect data about the operation of machines; finally, the data collected is treated and synchronized with Cloud systems for multiple purposes. The majority of sensors coupled to industrial machines sample data at very different rates and synchronize the collected data with the Smart Node, in the respective sampling frequency. A Smart Node can embed a set of different data treatment modules. These modules can be instantiated to provide different ways of treating sensor data in a way that can be represented as a graph (Figure 2). A gateway internal logic arrangement is represented using a *directed acyclic graph (DAG)*. The graph structure in Figure 2 can be divided into three levels, each with a different label and colour assignment: the Sensor Level (bottom level), includes sensor instances providing data to the gateway; the Data Treatment Level (middle level), includes nodes representing instances of algorithms embedded at the gateway that can treat information in several ways (e.g., aggregate data using moving average, perform trend analysis or other functions); the Network Level (top level), includes nodes where the flow resulting from the lower level nodes can be redirected to subscribing hosts in the network. This internal structure can be dynamically rearranged: new sensors and data modules can be loaded into the Smart Node; the connections between nodes can be reformulated to synchronize and treat data in new ways.

A problem of efficiency emerges due to the different rates at which the data is gathered from all kinds of connected sensors. When data reaches the Network Level nodes, it is immediately sent to the subscriber, a node in the network, in this case, some cloud service. Slight time differences in the availability of data lead the different Network Level nodes to perform new and individual calls. If those time differences were eliminated, Network Level nodes would be synchronized and data from the different nodes could be packed together, reducing the total number of calls made and the network traffic heavily. To accomplish synchronization among Network Level nodes, data buffers for all the edges connecting nodes previous to a particular Network node must be resized to compensate: (1) different time to process data by Data Treatment level nodes, since each module takes different time to process data; (2) different sampling rates of sensors, a same number of samples is accumulated at different times.

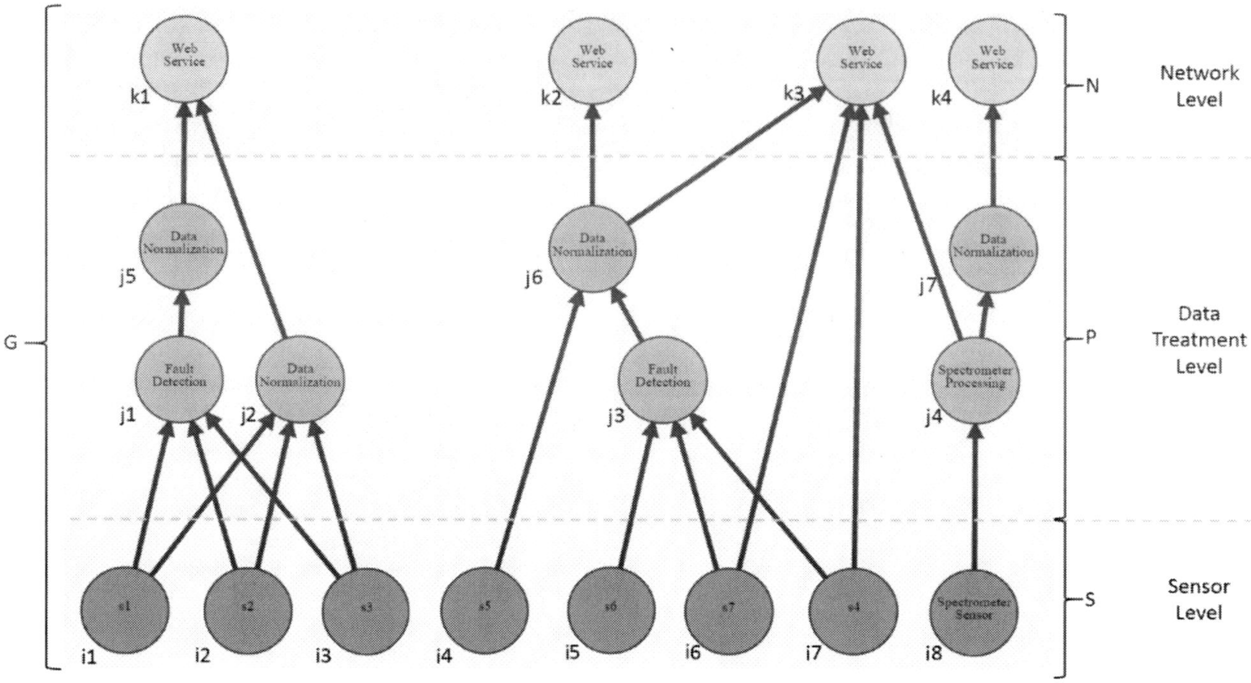

Figure 2. Internal Gateway configuration.

Taking advantage of the DAG representation of the gateway, we formulate and propose a solution to the problem as a combinatorial *Constraint Optimization Problem.*

The remaining chapters in this work describe the following: In Section II, a formal definition of the problem is presented. Section III shows literature review, the problem formulation basis. In Section IV, the solving process is detailed along with assumptions, constraints and technology that has been used. In Section V, the initial set of results is presented. Section VI explains the revision made to the initial problem solution, a new constraint is formally defined and the application of that constraint is reported in comparison with extended result sets. In section VII, conclusions and future work are described.

II. Problem Definition

Each arc in the graph (see Figure 2) has an associated buffer $b_{n,m}$. Given the fact that sensors are sampling at different frequencies $freq$, these buffers are filled at different rates. We define G as the set of nodes in a particular Gateway instance; three subsets of nodes are contained in $G: N \subset G$ is the subset of Network Nodes (index k nodes); $P \subset G$ is the subset of data Processing Nodes (index j nodes); $S \subset G$ is the subset of Sensor Nodes (index i nodes). The subsets obey to the following conditions:

$$G = N \cup P \cup S; N \cap P = \emptyset; P \cap S = \emptyset; N \cap S = \emptyset \quad (1)$$

Nodes in N can be classified as consumers; nodes in S are exclusively producers; nodes in P are both producers and consumers. Edges between nodes can be defined as:

$$e_{n,m} = \begin{cases} 1 \text{ if } n \text{ is consumer of } m : n \neq m; \\ \quad m \in P \cup S \text{ and } n \in N \cup P \\ \quad 0 \text{ otherwise} \end{cases} \quad (2)$$

As an example, we can observe in Figure 2 that node j_6 consumes from i_4 (Sensor Level) and j_3, which is in same level (Processing Level) and all the k nodes (Network Level) only consume from inferior levels. To help in the definition of this problem, two additional subsets of nodes, containing the connections of a given node, are defined as follows:

$$W_n = \{j : j \in P \wedge e_{n,j} = 1\}, n \in N \cup P \quad (3)$$

Equation (3) defines a subset of nodes in P, which are producers for the given node $n \in N \cup P$. As an example (Figure 2), for $n = j_6 : W_{j_6} = \{j_3\}$; for $n = k_3 : W_{k_3} = \{j_6, j_4\}$; and for $n = j_3 : W_{j_3} = \emptyset$ since it does not consume from any Data Processing nodes.

$$X_n = \{i : i \in S \wedge x_{n,i} = 1\}, n \in N \cup P \quad (4)$$

Equation (4) defines a subset of nodes in S, which, are producers for the given node $n \in N \cup P$. In Figure 2, these are the nodes i in the Sensor Level, from which, Processing Level nodes and Network Level nodes consume. As an example (Figure 2), for $n = k_3 : X_{k_3} = \{i_6, i_7\}$; for $n = k_1 : W_{k_1} = \emptyset$ since it does not consume from any Sensor Level node and for $n = j_6 : W_{j_6} = \{i_4\}$.

A processing node in P applies an algorithm to transform the data coming from its associated producers. The data generated at the sensor level is delivered to the processing nodes as a batch, which contains the number of samples equal to the size of the buffer for the corresponding edge.

In order to the processing to be possible, the number of elements in each collection must be the same. This constraint must be applied to the subsets W_n and X_n of a given node n in $N \cup P$, respectively; for that constraint to be respected, the size of every buffer associated to each element in $W_n \cup X_n$ must be the same. Formally this constraint can be represented as:

$$\forall n \in N \cup P, \forall m \in W_n \cup X_n : |b_{n,m}| = f(n) \quad (5)$$

Where $|b_{n,m}|$ represents the size of the given buffer for the given edge $e_{n,m}$ and $f(n)$ is the size of any buffer from which node n consumes.

The size of a buffer is adjustable and can vary from 1 to 1000. The objective of this problem is to arrange a combination of values to parametrize the size of every buffer $|b|$, for every arc in the graph, which minimizes the differences between times at the Network Nodes in which data is available to be sent to the network. To calculate the time that takes data to be available at every node $k \in N$, the times for all its providers in the graph must be calculated. As data comes in collections (sets of single values), let us define *burst* as the exact time at which data is sent from one provider node to a consumer node and represent the *burst* of a node n as B_n.

The *burst* of a Sensor Node i is defined by the product of its sampling frequency and the size of the buffer associated to the edge $e_{n,i}$ we are assuming. That way, every time a sample from a sensor is collected, that sample is sent to all consumers of that sensor. A *burst* of a Sensor Node to an adjacent consumer node, m, occurs when the buffer for the edge $e_{i,m}$ is completely filled, and is formally represented by the expression:

$$B_{i,m} = freq(i) \times |b_{i,m}| \times e_{i,m} = 1; \forall i \in S \wedge m \in P \cup N \quad (6)$$

For a Data Processing Node, the burst time must contemplate all the burst times from its providers, the time that takes for the associated function $T(f(n))$ to treat one data sample and the size of the buffer associated to the edge $e_{n,m}$ we are assuming. The expression which determines the burst time for a Data Processing Node j to a consumer node m is defined as:

$$B_{j,m} = (\max_{i \in W_j \cup X_j}(B_{i,j}) + T(f_j) \times (|W_j| + |X_j|)) \times |b_{j,m}|; e_{j,m} = 1 \quad (7)$$

We assume that the growth in time complexity of the function $T(f_n) : n \in P$ is linear with the number of samples to process. Since the size of each producer buffer is equal, we multiply the total number of producers of j by the cost of treating a single sample. To calculate the *burst* for j_1 (see Figure 2), we take the max *burst* of X_{j_1} and sum the product of $T(f_{j_1})$ (time to process one sensor sample) with the number of elements in X_{j_1} (which corresponds to the producers i_1, i_2 and i_3).

Finally, to calculate the *burst* of a Network Node $k \in N$:

$$B_k = \max_{i \in X_k \cup W_k}(B_{i,k}) \quad (8)$$

Using the expression to calculate the *burst* for each Network Node, the objective is to minimize the variance of *burst* for all the Network Nodes and also minimize the sum of all buffer sizes in the DAG. By varying the size of the buffers in the graph, the variance of all burst times for Network Nodes and the sum of all buffer sizes are minimized. With a variance of zero or closer, data from different Network Nodes can be packed in the same payload and sent to the subscribers in the network. Even if the quantity of data exceeds the maximum payload size for the protocol in use, or the physical link being used, the number of connections needed is far less than it is when using the original strategy of independent calls. The number of buffers $|P \cup N|$, times an upper bound buffer size of 1000 is multiplied by the variance. This way, the variance has more impact in the search of an optimal solution than the sum of all buffer sizes.

$$\hat{V}(B_k) \times 1000 \times |P \cup N| + \sum_{n \in |P \cup N|} \sum_{m \in W_n \cup X_n} |bn, m| \quad (9)$$

As follows from Equation (9), minimizing variance of burst times for network nodes is the major concern. To reflect this, the variance is multiplied by the maximum possible size for a buffer (1000, which is a reasonable number of samples for a sensor), times the number of Processing and Network nodes. This will drive the solver to focus on a solution with less variance, and break ties by considering the minimal buffer sizes (as these incur a cost). With a variance of 0 at the Network Level nodes, all data produced can be sent to the cloud using the same call. If variance is higher than 0, a threshold must be used to decide the maximum reasonable time to wait between bursts. In comparison with individual calls strategy – a call made every time a burst at the Network Level occurs – the number of calls to the cloud is minimized as a consequence. The theoretical search space of the problem is E^n, where E represents the total number of edges in the graph and $n = 1000$ is the *Buffer Size* domain upper bound. The real search space, imposed by the constraint of Equation (5), can be determined by F^n, where $F = |P| + |N|$ is the total number of Processing and Network nodes in the graph.

III. Related Work

To the best of our knowledge, there is no scientific literature or works that cover this exact problem. The problem presented in this work emerged due to the very specific nature of Smart Nodes applied to industrial monitoring situations. Since an exact formulation or solution to this problem could not be found, the related works presented are analogous in the sense that some knowledge could be used to refine the modelling and solutions presented.

The theoretical background behind this problem has a large spectrum of application. The problem of modelling buffer sizes is mostly applied to network routing, to which the works [9],[10] and [11] are examples. As we are not interested in dealing with networks intrinsic characteristics, those buffer optimization problems can hardly be extrapolated to this work. The domain of Wireless Sensor Networks (WSN) is another scope of application of buffer modelling optimization, with relevant literature in this domain; the section of *Routing* problems in [12] covers a great number of important works regarding Flow Based Optimization Models, for data aggregation and routing problems. WSN optimization models care with constraints that this problem modulation does not cover, such as: residual energy of nodes, link properties, network lifetime, network organization and routing strategies.

A relevant work in WSN revealed to be of the major interest for this work. The authors presented and solved the problem of removing inconsistent time offsets, in time synchronization protocols for WSN [13]. The problem presented has a high degree of similarity with the case we are dealing. The problem is represented by a *Time Difference Graph (TDG)*, where each node is a sensor, every sensor has local time and every arc has an associated cost time given by a function. The solution to the problem is given by a Constraint Satisfaction Problem (CSP) approach. For every arc in the graph there exists an *adjustment variable* (analogous to the buffer size in this case), assignments are made to the variables to find the largest consistent sub-graph, i.e., a sub-graph in which inconsistent time offsets are eliminated.

Focusing the search in the literature domain of CSP problems, several works were revealed in the sub-domain of balancing, planning and scheduling activities that can be related to this application [14][15][16][17][18]. Namely, models of combinatorial optimization for minimizing the maximum/total lateness/tardiness of directed graphs of tasks with precedence and time constraints [14][18]. These problems are analogous to this work, and due to a simplified formulation with the same constraints (precedences and time between nodes), can be easily extrapolated to our case.

IV. Implementing and Testing

A. Problem Assumptions

The Smart Node application has several interfaces for real sensors, the physical connections range from radio frequency to cabled protocols. By testing this model with simulated scenarios, we assume no interference or noise of any type can cause disturbance in the sampling frequency. In a real case scenario, a sensor could enter in an idle state for a variety of reasons. In that case, data would not be transmitted at all, causing the transmission of data to the Cloud to be postponed for undefined time, waiting for the Network Level node burst depending on the idle sensor. For simplification, we assume a sensor never enters an idle state. Also, it is assumed that the time that takes to treat one sample of data will increase linearly for more than one sample, as mentioned for $T(f_j)$ when introducing Equation (7).

B. Constraint Satisfaction Problem Solvers

For comparison of performance purposes we implemented the problem using both *OptaPlanner* and *SICStus Prolog*. As the Smart Node is implemented in Java we can take advantage of a direct integration with *OptaPlanner* in future. On the other hand, we expected that *SICStus Prolog* would produce the same results with better computation times because of the lightweight implementation and optimized constraint library. Using these premises and the results presented in the next section a grounded decision about what solver to use in future implementations of the Smart Node can be made.

C. Tests

To validate the problem solutions, several DAG configurations were tested using the two implemented versions, based on *OptaPlanner* and *SICStus Prolog*, as described in Section IV. To test the implementations an algorithm to generate instances of the problem was built. The script generates instances of the Smart Node internal structure, DAG's, with a given number of Processing and Network nodes. Algorithm 1 briefly illustrates the approach:

```
Data: G ← S ∪ P ∪ N
Result: Smart Node internal configuration G
notVisitedNodes ← G;
Pnodes ← randomInteger(|P∪N|/2, |P ∪ N| − 2);
Nnodes ← nNodes − Pnodes;
Snodes ←
  randomInteger(nNodes/2, nNodes + nNodes/2);
G ← S, P, N ←
  generateNodes(Snodes, Pnodes, Nnodes);
remainingEdges ← Pnodes × 2 + Nnodes + Snodes;
while remainingEdges > 0 do
    if node ← notVisitedNodes.nextNode() then
        notVisitedNodes.remove(node);
    else
        node ← G.randomNode();
    end
    if node is S then
        connect to a random P or S node, disconnected
          nodes first;
        remainingEdges − −;
    else if node is P then
        get connection from a random P or S node,
          disconnected nodes first;
        connect to a random P or S node, disconnected
          nodes first;
        remainingEdges − −;
        remainingEdges − −;
    else
        get connection from random a P or S node,
          disconnected nodes first;
        remainingEdges − −;
    end
end
```

Algorithm 1: Smart Node instance generation.

Real scenarios generally have a higher number of Sensor Nodes, followed by a small number of Processing Nodes and an even smaller number of Network Nodes. Typically, the total number of nodes does not exceed 30 per operation. The instance generator picks aleatory numbers for the nodes bounded by a real case scenario application. Sampling frequencies for the sensors are assumed to vary from 400 to 2000 milliseconds. Functions to treat data in Processing Nodes are not typically complex. We measured the real case scenario functions to treat the minimum amount of data (1 sample) and we got values ranging from 0.19 to 0.38 milliseconds. To cover the buffer size domain, we need to take the worst case, 1000 samples. Given best and worst cases, the values attributed to cost of

Processing Nodes ($T(f_j)$ in Equation (7)) are between 1 and 40 milliseconds.

1) OptaPlanner: This solver [19] is a pure *Java* constraint satisfaction *API* and solver that is maintained by the *RedHat* community. It can be embedded within the Smart Node application to execute and provide on-demand solutions to this optimization problem. Because of the reconfigurable property of the Smart Node internal structure, each time the structure is rearranged, the solution obtained to the problem instance prior to the reconfiguration becomes infeasible. The integration (see Figure 3) between the two technologies is accomplished by defining the problem in the OptaPlanner notation: (1) *Buffer Size* class corresponds to the *Planning Variable*, during the solving process it will be assigned by the different solver configurations; (2) *Edge* class is the *Planning Entity*, the object of the problem that holds the *Planning Variable*; (3) *SmartNodeGraph* class is the *Planning Solution*, the object that holds the problem instance along with a class that allows to calculate the score of a certain problem instance. The score is given by implementing Equation (9); the best hard score is 0, which corresponds to null variance between the Network Levels nodes. The soft score corresponds to the minimization of the sum of all buffer sizes and does not weight as much as a hard score in search phase.

Since the search space is exponential, heuristics can be implemented to help the *OptaPlanner* solver to determine the easiest buffers to change. The implemented heuristic sorts the buffers from the easiest to the hardest. The sorting values are given by the number of ancestors of a given edge, an edge with a greater number of ancestors is more difficult to plan. Also, if an edge leads to a Network Node, it is considered more difficult to plan. *OptaPlanner* offers a great variety of algorithms to avoid the huge search space of most *CSPs*. These algorithms can be consulted in the documentation [20] and configured to achieve best search performances. For a correct comparison we used the *Branch and Bound* algorithm, which is the same algorithm that *SICStus Prolog* uses by default, without heuristics.

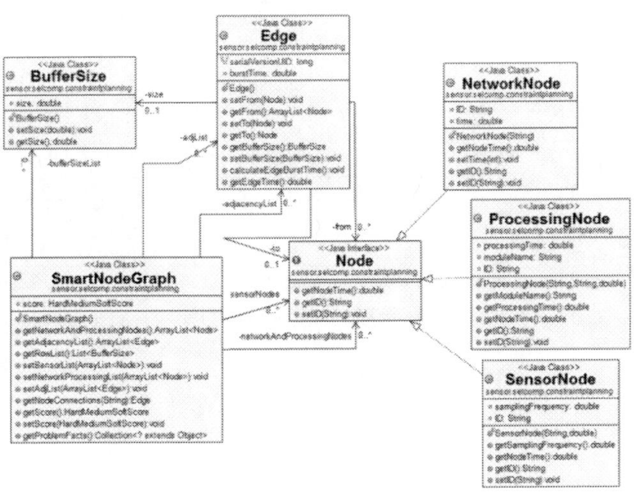

Figure 3. UML for Smart Node and OptaPlanner integration.

The UML diagram in Figure 3 shows the modelling of the problem using the *OptaPlanner* methodology.

2) SICStus Prolog: SICStus Prolog [21] provides several libraries of constraints that allow to model constraint satisfaction problems much more naturally than the *OptaPlanner* approach, which follows from the fact that modelling a problem in *SICStus Prolog* takes advantage of the declarative nature of logic programming. The problem modelling involved four types of facts (to represent N, P and S nodes, and to represent edges) and six predicates (to gather variables, express domain and constraints). The *clpfd* (Constraint Logic Programming over Finite Domains) [22] library was used to model and solve the problem. This library contains several options of modelling that can be used to optimize the labelling process. In our case, the labelling process takes as objective the minimization of the difference between the Network Node with the maximum burst time and the one with the lowest burst time (Equation (9)). The variables of the problem are given by a list of all the facts *edge(from,to,buffer_size).*, where *buffer_size* are the variables to solve in a finite domain from 1 to 1000. In future implementations of the problem, global constraints and labelling options must be analysed to ensure the modulation is the most optimized.

V. RESULTS

For both implementations the first set of results is shown in Tables I and II. The results shown are an average of 5 different problem instances for each problem size, which is determined by $|P \cup N|$, see Section II. To gather results, the generator was used to generate 5 instances of the problem for each row. Then, both solvers were used in the same machine (Intel(R) Core(TM) i7-4710HQ CPU @ 2.50GHz (8 CPUs), 2.5GHz, 16384MB RAM), with the same conditions (Windows 10 Home 64-bit), to run the tests. We established a limit of 60s to run the tests, which was considered acceptable for the solvers to find a feasible solution in a real case. Another limit was the number of nodes used in the experiences. With a number of nodes in the order of 100, and a time window of 8 hours, both solvers were unable to give a response to most cases. Given the complexity stated, and the fact that in real cases the number of nodes normally does not exceed 30, 50 nodes was the limit used for the tests.

The quality of the solutions found is mostly given by the second column, which represents the constraint of minimizing the burst times at the Network Level. As we can be seen in Table II, the *SICStus Prolog* implementation shows the best results for the most relevant quality factor. In the third column, the sum of all the buffer sizes is lower in the *OptaPlanner* implementation (Table I). During the tests, it was observed in the logs that the *OptaPlanner* was much slower traversing the search tree. Regarding all the columns, a clear tendency to worst results is obvious along the table, but in the last line of both tables, a sudden improvement in the variance occurs. This behaviour enforces the NP-Completeness nature of this kind of problems. In every row of both tables, in which a *Solution time* of 60 seconds is found, that row matches a sub-optimal solution. Since both solvers were programmed to stop at 60 seconds, most solutions are not optimal. Sub-optimal solutions are feasible in a real case, even if the variance between call times is not zero, because the gap is heavily reduced. The

TABLE I. OptaPlanner results

OptaPlanner			
$\|P \cup S\|$	$\Delta V(B_k)$(ms)	$\sum \|b_{n,m}\|$	*Solution time(s)*
5	15.600	264.400	48.133
10	82.200	30.600	60.000
15	205.800	241.400	48.037
20	637.600	189.800	60.000
25	1494.000	56.600	60.000
30	1218.600	128.800	60.000
35	979.000	74.400	60.000
40	1434.400	74.600	60.000
45	1138.200	89.000	60.000
50	646.600	118.600	60.000

TABLE II. SICStus results

SICStus			
$\|P \cup S\|$	$\Delta V(B_k)$(ms)	$\sum \|b_{n,m}\|$	*Solution time(s)*
5	0.400	731.800	38.022
10	1.800	738.000	48.894
15	73.000	1738.600	60.000
20	102.400	4912.600	60.000
25	600.000	8210.800	60.000
30	457.800	6214.800	60.000
35	351.800	7986.200	60.000
40	564.000	5792.200	60.000
45	630.000	10457.000	60.000
50	321.200	14706.400	60.000

Smart Component can define a time window with the size of the variance, and this way, include all results in the same call.

VI. PROBLEM REVISION

In this section, the second set of results is presented and discussed. A deeper problem analysis was conducted and the conclusions of this analysis are applied in a third set of tests.

Firstly, the time limit imposed to the search conducted in the previous results (Table I and Table II), was extended to 9 hours. To add more detail to the study, two new columns were added to the new results (Table III, Table IV and Table V). The initial variance $\Delta V_i(B_k)$, introduced in the first column, is the variance calculated with all buffer sizes set to the minimum size of 1. This column was introduced to give an idea of by how much is the time difference between the optimized version is produced and the first approach - set all buffers to same value, 1. The second column introduced was *"Total Search time (s)"*, it indicates the total amount of time that the search process took. For 32400 seconds (or 9 hours), it indicates a non optimal solution, because the search phase surpassed the time limit established. When the time indicated is the same as in *"Total Search time (s)"*, it means that an optimal solution was found timely. *"Total Search time (s)"* indicates the time that took to find the solution presented in the table, which is the last optimization found before the time limit was exceeded. With this separation it is possible to see that most of the results ($\Delta V_f(B_k)$) are found in a average time of 2.46 hours for the *SICStus* implementation. These results motivated a problem revision to decrease the search time and that is addressed in the following sections.

TABLE III. OptaPlanner Extended Results

OptaPlanner					
$\|P \cup U\|$	$\Delta V_i(B_k)$ *(ms)*	$\Delta V_f(B_k)$ *(ms)*	$\sum \|b_{n,m}\|$	*Solution time (s)*	*Total Search time (s)*
5	35	0	805	611.654	611.654
	1325	3	42	32400.000	32400.000
10	571	17	46	32400.000	32400.000
	1565	337	25	32400.000	32400.000
15	657	657	1122	32400.000	32400.000
	1313	520	29	32400.000	32400.000
20	320	51	1258	32400.000	32400.000
	1071	1071	43	32400.000	32400.000
25	1833	1833	44	32400.000	32400.000
	332	332	53	32400.000	32400.000
30	1553	1553	55	32400.000	32400.000
	1192	1192	52	32400.000	32400.000
35	2096	2096	56	32400.000	32400.000
	464	464	89	32400.000	32400.000
40	251	251	106	32400.000	32400.000
	464	464	89	32400.000	32400.000
45	6	0	98	12896.000	32400.000
	365	365	64	32400.000	32400.000
50	1364	1364	112	32400.000	32400.000
	496	496	101	32400.000	32400.000

TABLE IV. SICStus Extended Results

SICStus					
$\|P \cup U\|$	$\Delta V_i(B_k)$ *(ms)*	$\Delta V_f(B_k)$ *(ms)*	$\sum \|b_{n,m}\|$	*Solution time (s)*	*Total Search time (s)*
5	35	0	805	40.594	40.594
	1325	0	83	192.076	192.076
10	571	24	4059	6609.570	6609.570
	1565	42	1420	32400.000	32400.000
15	657	87	1122	19933.302	32400.000
	1303	102	3834	1867.245	32400.000
20	320	0	1258	1183981.000	11839.810
	1071	2	3666	32400.000	32400.000
25	1833	0	1258	32400.000	32400.000
	332	2	3666	655.428	32400.000
30	1553	44	49	32400.000	32400.000
	1192	397	741	3564.869	32400.000
35	2096	661	380	2.409	32400.000
	464	464	89	631.403	32400.000
40	251	44	7398	2341415.000	32400.000
	464	191	15790	29237.796	32400.000
45	6	0	12387	9862.394	32400.000
	365	102	1459	11052.058	32400.000
50	1364	922	8630	7666.592	32400.000
	496	15	19318	150.605	32400.000

A. *Proposed Enhancement*

To analyse the problem more deeply, let us consider the buffers in the graph were adjusting its size is really critical. The buffers in inferior levels, all that connect P and S nodes, although their size may impact the final solution, are less critical. The unique constraint that must hold on these is the one of Equation (5). This constraint implies that buffers connecting P nodes must have the same size. In these cases, the impact on the superior level is dictated by the burst time of the latest provider to send data. There is nothing that can be done beyond this constraint. On the other hand, let us consider buffers that connect directly to network nodes N. These buffers dictate the optimization function defined in Equation (9). By increasing the buffer size, we are multiplying it by the burst time of the latest consumer to provide data. That is to say, if the values of these buffers are different, we cannot multiply the same value on two or more different buffers. If the same value is multiplied, we are maintaining the difference between them. Taking this in consideration, there is an obvious constraint to apply in this case, constrain buffers with different burst times of having the same size. Although this seems a little improvement, the impact of this constraint grows in function of the number of different buffers being considered.

To formalize this constraint, let us first define a set that contains the buffers of all edges that connect directly Network Nodes. Let us denote this set by NBs, which stands for "Network Buffer's". We can define this set recurring to the previous set definitions in Equation (3) and Equation (4), as follows:

$$NBs = \{b_{k,m} : \forall k \in N, m \in X_k \cup W_k\} \tag{10}$$

Relying on the DAG of Figure 2 to give a clearer example, this set would contain the following buffers $NBs = \{b_{k_1,j_5}, b_{k_1,j_2}, b_{k_2,j_6}, b_{k_3,j_6}, b_{k_3,i_6}, b_{k_3,i_7}, b_{k_3,j_4}, b_{k_4,j_7}\}$.

Having at this point a clear view of types of buffers that will be the target of this optimization, we can introduce the constraint that will be only applied when the buffers belong to edges were the following conditions apply. The first condition for applicability of this constraint is that it can only be applied to buffers with different burst times ($B_{i,n_1} \neq B_{j,n_2}$). The second condition is that the source of data cannot be the same, because implicitly the burst time will be the same. Considering Figure 2, the buffers b_{k_2,j_6} and b_{k_3,j_6} fall in these two conditions. They have the same source, implicitly they have the same burst time. The logic of this constraint is: if we multiply the same factor (buffer size) by the same value (burst time), we are maintaining the variance between the two buffers being considered.

$$\forall i \in BNs, \forall j \in BNs, i \neq j, B_{i,n_1} \neq B_{j,n_2}, n_1 \neq n_2 : |b_{i,n_1}| \neq |b_{i,n_2}| \tag{11}$$

The impact of this constraint can be theoretically calculated for the worst search case, i.e., explore all the possible combinations of buffers sizes in NBs. Let us define the number of possible combinations for buffer sizes as 1000^B. In which 1000 is the domain size for a buffer and B is the number of buffers in NBs. Now we need to obtain the number of buffers that correspond to edges with different burst times. If we apply the conditions of Equation (11) to NBs, specifically the part that guarantees different burst times ($B_{i,n_1} \neq B_{j,n_2}$), we obtain the number of buffers D to which this constraint can be applied. Considering the previous definitions for B and D, by relying on combinatorics, we can apply simple arrangements to calculate the number of times that two ore more buffers in a search assignment will be equal. By subtracting the number of combinations cut from the search space (due to the application of Equation (11)) to the total number of assignments, we get the optimized number of possible combinations.

$$1000^B - \frac{1000!}{(1000-D)!} \tag{12}$$

Considering the most basic case, five buffers ($B = 5$), and only two different among them ($D = 2$), this would give us a reduction in the search space of 999000 possibilities. In the most optimistic case, in which all buffers are different ($B = 5$ and $D = 5$), the reduction in search space is exponentially best, resulting in a cut of $9.90034950024 \times 10^{14}$ possibilities.

B. Enhancement Tests

This subsection reports the results of implementing the optimization constraint developed in the previous section. The same conditions (hardware and time limit) and problem instances (same graphs) as in the previous tests were used. Because of the results obtained by the *OptaPlanner* implementation (Table III), the optimization constraint was only implemented in the *SICStus* solution. Table V shows the results for optimized version of the problem.

TABLE V. SICStus Enhancement Results

SICStus Optimized					
$\|P \cup U\|$	$\Delta V_i(B_k)ms$	$\Delta V_f(B_k)ms$	$\sum \|b_{n,m}\|$	*Solution time (s)*	*Total Search time (s)*
5	35	0	805	1.284	1.284
	1325	0	83	57.004	57.004
10	571	2	424	3526.065	32400.000
	1565	42	1420	2.817	32400.000
15	657	182	75	491.078	32400.000
	1313	163	490	1438.775	32400.000
20	320	1	261	2282.241	32400.000
	1071	278	3492	71.76	32400.000
25	1833	797	3677	7358.274	32400.000
	332	8	204	322.932	32400.000
30	1553	388	285	1653.479	32400.000
	1192	351	7002	1396.515	32400.000
35	2096	5129	301	213.453	32400.000
	464	330	9827	382.596	32400.000
40	251	216	948	2379.582	32400.000
	464	944	2001	12295.929	32400.000
45	6	0	121	556.953	556.953
	365	508	827	7684.82	32400.000
50	1364	20771	495	79.019	32400.000
	496	78	1365	110.605	32400.000

In Table VI, a comparison between the number of prunings for the same iterations and versions (in each table, for the same number of nodes $|P \cup U|$, there are two rows for the two different problem graphs tested) of the test is presented. The number of prunings was obtained by SICStus, using the *fdstats* predicate. As can be verified, the number of prunings was increased, which means that the improvement introduced is reducing the search space by cutting the search tree more times in the optimized version of the implementation.

TABLE VI. SICStus Enhancement Statistics

	$\|P \cup U\|$	5	10	15	20	25	30	35	40	45	50
Prunings	1st. Optimized	43192808	4.122E+10	1.23E+10	6.24E+10	6.76E+10	4.78E+10	1.69E+11	4.14E+10	3.8E+10	2.78E+10
	1st. Non Opt.	74079794	151387289	5.67E+08	3.04E+10	2.03E+10	1.14E+10	3.97E+10	1.67E+10	6.64E+10	2.78E+10
	2nd. Optimized	51587328	4.423E+10	2.58E+10	2.13E+10	2.78E+10	2.84E+10	6.3E+10	6.58E+10	7.11E+10	3.19E+10
	2nd. Non Opt	45262552	539864744	2.29E+10	2.99E+10	3.01E+10	2.05E+10	2.39E+10	4.44E+10	3.06E+10	4.21E+10

Despite the optimized version having reached faster solutions in practically all cases, as shown in the graph of Figure 4, the solution quality was affected negatively as can be seen in the graph of Figure 5. Although this might seem a worse strategy at first sight, it will always guarantee that the ideal solution of $\Delta V_f(B_k) = 0$ is found faster than in the previous implementation.

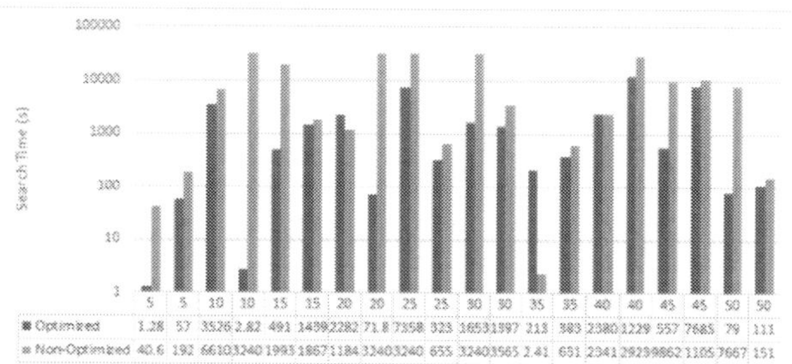

Figure 4. Search Time Comparison, Optimized vs Non-Optimized

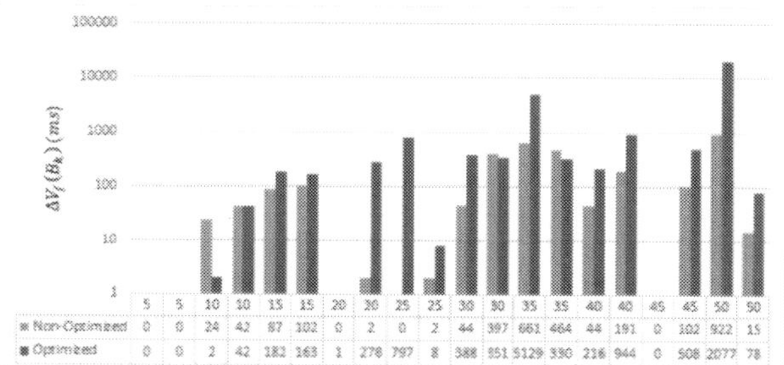

Figure 5. Solution Quality Comparison, Optimized vs Non-Optimized

VII. Conclusion and Future Work

Despite the search space of the problem, both solvers reached optimal solutions in cases that are feasible to real application. In the future tuning options of the solvers must be explored. Another additional constraint to this problem could be the introduction of a case in which a single or several sensors are producing data with a higher priority. The problem can be easily reformulated to embrace that kind of situation by modifying the objective function Equation (9). *SICStus Prolog* shows a clear advantage in computation time. That difference can be the reflex of the number of code lines needed to model the problem. *SICStus Prolog* required eight procedures (predicates), against 10 classes and 1 *XML* configuration file for the *OptaPlanner* implementation. The difference in modelling complexity possibly causes an additional overhead. Another important remark is that, given the experience of implementing the problem and playing with the solvers options, two contrasts can be highlighted: (1) *SICStus Prolog* is very intuitive at the problem modelling phase, on the other hand, *OptaPlanner* required more effort, both in implementing an perceiving the methodology; (2) tuning the solvers, for example the time out feature that allows to stop the solver in the desired time, it is more intuitive in the *OptaPlanner* approach.

Regarding the optimization presented, the solution quality suffers with the constraint proposed in Equation (11). This decrease in quality of the solution is due to the fact that buffers involved cannot be equal. Despite achieving a worse variance, in cases were it is possible to achieve the ideal solution of zero variance, this implementation will find it faster, as shown in Figure 5. In this case, there exists a trade-off between better sub-optimal solutions (the non optimized version) and better chance to find optimal solutions (optimized version).

Considering all pros and cons, *SICStus Prolog* most probably will be chosen to integrate the Smart Node in future work. These experiments were made off-line, as future work, the Smart Component can embed the optimization code and adopt a strategy to optimize the variance in idle CPU time until an optimal solution is found on-line. In this extended version can be verified that, when the problem is too big, the complexity outperforms a reasonable time for a solution. As future work, an idea to split the DAG in sub-graphs, arrange individual solutions, and later join them using intermediary buffers.

Acknowledgment

SelSus EU Project (FoF.NMP.2013-8) Health Monitoring and Life-Long Capability Management for SELf-SUStaining Manufacturing Systems funded by the European Commission under the Seventh Framework Programme for Research and Technological Development.

References

[1] L. Neto, H. L. Cardoso, C. Soares, and G. Gonçalves, "Optimizing network calls by minimizing variance in data availability times," in Proceedings of INTELLI 2016 : The Fifth International Conference on Intelligent Systems and Applications (includes InManEnt 2016). IARIA, 2016, pp. 142–147.

[2] M. Peschl, N. Link, M. Hoffmeister, G. Gonçalves, and F. L. Almeida, "Designing and implementation of an intelligent manufacturing system," Journal of Industrial Engineering and Management, vol. 4, no. 4, 2011, pp. 718–745.

[3] G. Gonçalves, J. Reis, R. Pinto, M. Alves, and J. Correia, "A step forward on intelligent factories: A smart sensor-oriented approach," in Proceedings of the 2014 IEEE Emerging Technology and Factory Automation (ETFA). IEEE, 2014, pp. 1–8.

[4] R. Fomseca, S. Aguiar, M. Peschl, and G. Gonçalves, "The reborn marketplace: an application store for industrial smart components," in INTELLI 2016 : The Fifth International Conference on Intelligent Systems and Applications (includes InManEnt 2016). IARIA, Nov. 2016, pp. 136–141.

[5] L. Neto, J. Reis, D. Guimaraes, and G. Goncalves, "Sensor cloud: Smartcomponent framework for reconfigurable diagnostics in intelligent manufacturing environments," in Industrial Informatics (INDIN), 2015 IEEE 13th International Conference on. IEEE, 2015, pp. 1706–1711.

[6] K.-K. Lau and Z. Wang, "Software component models," IEEE Transactions on software engineering, vol. 33, no. 10, 2007, pp. 709–724.

[7] C. Maga, N. Jazdi, and P. Göhner, "Reusable models in industrial automation: experiences in defining appropriate levels of granularity," IFAC Proceedings Volumes, vol. 44, no. 1, 2011, pp. 9145–9150.

[8] F. Fouquet, B. Morin, F. Fleurey, O. Barais, N. Plouzeau, and J.-M. Jezequel, "A dynamic component model for cyber physical systems," in Proceedings of the 15th ACM SIGSOFT symposium on Component Based Software Engineering. ACM, 2012, pp. 135–144.

[9] I. Ioachim, J. Desrosiers, F. Soumis, and N. Bélanger, "Fleet assignment and routing with schedule synchronization constraints," European Journal of Operational Research, vol. 119, no. 1, 1999, pp. 75–90.

[10] K. Avrachenkov, U. Ayesta, E. Altman, P. Nain, and C. Barakat, "The effect of router buffer size on the tcp performance," in In Proceedings of the LONIIS Workshop on Telecommunication Networks and Teletraffic Theory. Citeseer, 2001.

[11] K. Avrachenkov, U. Ayesta, and A. Piunovskiy, "Optimal choice of the buffer size in the internet routers," in Decision and Control, 2005 and 2005 European Control Conference. CDC-ECC'05. 44th IEEE Conference on. IEEE, 2005, pp. 1143–1148.

[12] A. Gogu, D. Nace, A. Dilo, and N. Meratnia, Review of optimization problems in wireless sensor networks. InTech, 2012.

[13] M. Jadliwala, Q. Duan, S. Upadhyaya, and J. Xu, "On the hardness of eliminating cheating behavior in time synchronization protocols for sensor networks," Technical Report 2008-08, State University of New York at Buffalo, Tech. Rep., 2008.

[14] J. Błazewicz, W. Kubiak, and S. Martello, "Algorithms for minimizing maximum lateness with unit length tasks and resource constraints," Discrete applied mathematics, vol. 42, no. 2, 1993, pp. 123–138.

[15] B. Gacias, C. Artigues, and P. Lopez, "Parallel machine scheduling with precedence constraints and setup times," Computers & Operations Research, vol. 37, no. 12, 2010, pp. 2141–2151.

[16] K. Rustogi et al., "Machine scheduling with changing processing times and rate-modifying activities," Ph.D. dissertation, University of Greenwich, 2013.

[17] A. Malapert, C. Guéret, and L.-M. Rousseau, "A constraint programming approach for a batch processing problem with non-identical job sizes," European Journal of Operational Research, vol. 221, no. 3, 2012, pp. 533–545.

[18] J. H. Patterson and J. J. Albracht, "Technical noteassembly-line balancing: Zero-one programming with fibonacci search," Operations Research, vol. 23, no. 1, 1975, pp. 166–172.

[19] O. Team, OptaPlanne - Constraint Satisfaction Solver, Red Hat, (Last accessed 09-May-2017). [Online]. Available: http://www.optaplanner.org/

[20] ——, OptaPlanner User Guide, Red Hat, (Last accessed 09-May-2017). [Online]. Available: http://docs.jboss.org/optaplanner/release/6.3.0.Final/optaplanner-docs/pdf/optaplanner-docs.pdf

[21] M. Carlsson, J. Widen, J. Andersson, S. Andersson, K. Boortz, H. Nilsson, and T. Sjöland, SICStus Prolog user's manual. Swedish Institute of Computer Science Kista, Sweden, 1988, vol. 3, no. 1.

[22] M. Carlsson, G. Ottosson, and B. Carlson, "An open-ended finite domain constraint solver," in Programming Languages: Implementations, Logics, and Programs. Springer, 1997, pp. 191–206.

[23] I. P. Gent, K. E. Petrie, and J.-F. Puget, "Symmetry in constraint programming," Foundations of Artificial Intelligence, vol. 2, 2006, pp. 329–376.

Microarea Selection Method for Broadband Infrastructure Installation Based on Service Diffusion Process

Motoi Iwashita, Akiya Inoue
Dept. of Management Information Science
Chiba Institute of Technology
Chiba, Japan
email:{iwashita.motoi, akiya.inoue}@it-chiba.ac.jp

Takeshi Kurosawa
Dept. of Mathematical Information Science
Tokyo University of Science
Tokyo, Japan
email: tkuro@rs.kagu.tus.ac.jp

Ken Nishimatu
Network Technology Laboratories
NTT
Tokyo, Japan
email: nishimatsu.ken@lab.ntt.co.jp

***Abstract*—Wired/wireless information communication networks have been expanded to meet the demand of broadband services as part of information and communication technology (ICT) infrastructure. As the installation and expansion of ICT infrastructure requires a large amount of time and money, the decision on how to select the installation area is a key issue. Low-usage facilities can cause problems for businesses in terms of investment efficiency. Moreover, it takes time to select areas because of the need to estimate the potential demand and to manage the installation of the infrastructure for thousands of municipal areas across a nation. In this paper, we propose an efficient microarea selection method for use during the life cycle of broadband services, i.e., from early to late stage. This method is developed considering consumer segmentation, the broadband service diffusion model by consumer behaviour, and area characteristics based on employee fluidity. The proposed method is evaluated on worldwide interoperability for microwave access (WiMAX) and its applicability is ascertained on the basis of the infrastructure's area penetration rate and area characteristics.**

Keywords-broadband services; infrastructure installation; data mining; area marketing; area characteristics; demand forecast; decision support system; algorithm.

I. INTRODUCTION

Broadband access services can be rapidly deployed by asymmetric digital subscriber line (ADSL) penetration. This has enabled consumer-generated media (CGM) such as social networking service (SNS) and YouTube to be widely used on a broadband access infrastructure. These multimedia services have dramatically changed the modern lifestyle and made it possible for individuals to obtain and share information with ease. The research of broadband infrastructure installation has been done [1] for providing these services. Some local governments are trying to utilize ICT infrastructure for healthcare and nursing among other applications in their respective regions [2]. Many companies have also introduced ICT elements such as mobile gadgets for sales, maintenance, operation, and production to improve the efficiency of corporate functions.

Wired broadband access infrastructure has propagated rapidly first by the use of ADSL and then optical fibres in the fibre-to-the-home (FTTH) infrastructure. FTTH is an ultra-high-speed broadband access infrastructure, which is being provided in Japan since 2002. Such an ICT infrastructure provides a variety of technologies and benefits for corporate activity. Although the coverage rate of FTTH as a percentage of the total number of households nationwide in 2014 was approximately 98% [3], the customer rate (percentage of customers using FTTH) in the coverage area was merely 43%. With respect to wireless broadband access, long-term evolution (LTE) for high-speed wireless access is being provided in Japan since December 2010. The coverage rate of LTE was more than 90%, while the customer rate was approximately 42% in 2014 [4]. The other high-speed wireless access worldwide interoperability for microwave access (WiMAX), which is being provided since 2009, had a coverage rate of greater than 90%, and 7 million users in 2014.

Because installation of infrastructure is capital intensive, business profitability is significantly impacted if the facility usage is low. It is difficult to identify low-usage areas when we focus on the average data. This demonstrates the importance of considering not only macro areas but also micro areas when installing the infrastructure. Therefore, strategic and economic considerations are necessary for the installation of ICT infrastructure, such as broadband and wireless access facilities. Such installations greatly depend on the potential demand in different microareas. Further, the existence of more than a thousand microareas, such as municipal areas, necessitates using an efficient estimation method.

The goal of providing an area with ICT services is to determine the investment order of microareas, where the ICT infrastructure is installed several months prior to the installation. ICT infrastructure installation per area is more effective and less expensive than on-demand installation in which a facility is installed on a case-to-case basis. Furthermore, a method to efficiently select a microarea will have a positive impact on the operations and financial efficiency of an enterprise.

In this paper, we propose a microarea selection method that is simpler to use than trade analysis [5]. Our target is ICT infrastructure installation during the life cycle, which covers different stages of ICT infrastructure installation for broadband services. The proposed method is based on consumer segmentation based on different consumer behaviours in the broadband service propagation model and area characteristics based on employee fluidity. We verified the proposed model with the penetration of WiMAX services. The remainder of the paper is organized as follows: Section II introduces related works. Section III describes the trend of WiMAX demand in Japan. Section IV discusses the hypothesis of service diffusion and its model. Section V describes the proposed method for the selection of microareas. Section VI presents the simulation results and evaluates the method. Section VII clarifies the applications of the proposed method based on area characteristics. Section VIII concludes this paper.

II. Related Works

The determination of the target area for marketing, such as areas to focus on for sales activities and areas to install the facility in, is based on trade analysis. Trade analysis is a well-known method for the investigation of geographical areas for business deals and involves demographic data and field surveys. For instance, the setting up of a convenience store is decided on the basis of demographic data and field surveys. Geographic information system (GIS) [6] is an effective tool for area-related decision making. An empirical study using GIS for trade analysis has been previously [7] reported and many companies uses this method with map data. These approaches are effective for deciding whether a store should be set up in a given area.

Application of these methods to ICT infrastructure installation requires spending a large amount of time on selecting areas. This is because installation in only one target area has little effect from the viewpoint of network externality [8], which makes it more convenient to have more users, if it is carried out in one area rather than in several areas simultaneously and nationwide. The idea of modelling spatial data that represent a geographical location has been proposed earlier [9], [10]. This approach is now being practically used to understand geographical features.

To select the areas, we need to first consider potential demand. Previous research [11]-[13] has focused on macro demand forecast to provide facility installation principles and to not select installation areas. There has been one study on microarea forecasting [14]. It describes only the guidelines for microarea forecasting by using multiple regression analysis.

To proceed with microarea marketing, we focused on the expansion of ICT infrastructure in accordance with service reputation in areas where ICT infrastructure has been provided as a trial. In such cases, individuals tend to exhibit a "go type behaviour" where individuals tend to go to issues/people when forming preferences [15], [16]. Therefore, who pushes service forward is an important question. An innovative early adopter in the technology lifecycle is characterized as an information source affecting acquaintances from the viewpoint of innovative diffusion [17]. The innovative early adopter is generally reckoned as a person who gets stimulated with many contacts through his/her mobility. It is difficult to characterise each person in an area from the viewpoint of the technology lifecycle (e.g., who is an early adopter). Recently, a city planning study that uses mobile phones (life log data) to obtain mobility data by area has been initiated [18]. The researchers expect to analyse human behaviour by utilizing the life log data, and if it yields successful results, it can be applied to various fields. However, currently, there is no such information available.

Concerning the diffusion of the broadband infrastructure facilities at the moment, the framework of microarea marketing is based on commuting flows in terms of considering human behaviour [19]. Such a flow-based microarea selection method has been developed and been compared to the population-based method, which is a simple application of the population order in some regions as the case study [20]. Although these studies show the efficiency of selecting microareas, the results obtained are not stable; i.e., setting up the conditions in advance is difficult. The condition for the application of flow-based microarea selection method is decided empirically and analytically [21]. However, the application of this method is limited to only the early stage of providing broadband services, which means that the area penetration is low. Therefore, a mixed algorithm that consists of both the flow-based and population-based microarea selection methods is proposed that is applicable throughout the life cycle (from early to late stage) of broadband services [1]. However, the obtained results are not stable, i.e., the cause that the mixed algorithm gives the optimal order of microareas depends on the area itself. Therefore, conditions considering not only consumer behaviour but also area characteristics are needed.

III. WiMAX Services and Trend in Japan

WiMAX is a wireless broadband access service that has been in place in Japan since 2009. It is defined in IEEE 802.16-2004 as an international standard with a maximum transmission distance of 50 km and maximum transmission rate of 70 Mbps. WiMAX network is explained in Fig. 1. Mobile gadgets such as smartphones and ultra-mobile PCs can access the nearest base station by air in each region. The base station transmits signals to the providers' server through the carrier's network. The user can then make use of wireless high-speed internet access services. Table I shows in chronological order the events that are related to WiMAX service diffusion. In seven months after WiMAX started to be commercially available, 5,000 base stations were installed nationwide. The pace of base station installation slowed until April 2012 when providers achieved 20,000 base station installations. The number of customers grew steeply from 2009 to 2013, and it took only five months for the growth from 2 to 3 million customers. In October 2013, the new WiMAX service, which could achieve a much higher high-speed transmission rate, was introduced. It was simultaneously provided by mobile virtual network operators (MVNOs). An MVNO is defined as a network service operator that does not have a network facility itself, but rather borrows the facility from a real network operator. Therefore, new MVNOs provide low-priced services and value-added services, such as character brand gadgets and rich video content. Customers have many options for network operators through SIM-free terminals. As for the base station installation for new WiMAX service, the installation pace is shorter than that of WiMAX.

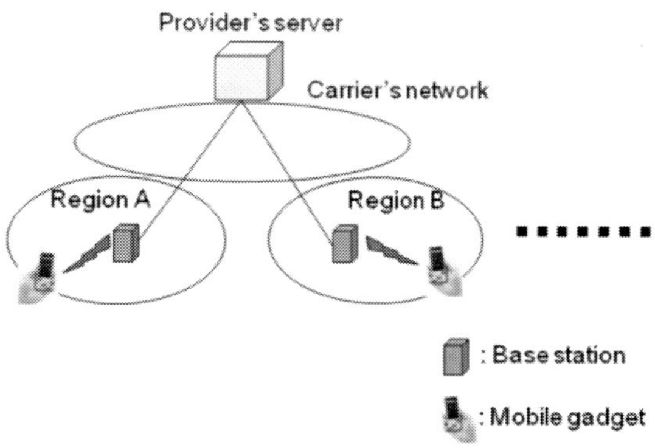

Figure 1. WiMAX network.

TABLE I. EVENTS IN CHRONOLOGICAL ORDER

Date	Event
Feb/2009	WiMAX trial (cost-free) service started
Jul/2009	WiMAX commercial service started
Jan/2010	5,000 base stations installed
Aug/2010	10,000 base stations installed
May/2011	15,000 base stations installed
Jun/2011	1,000,000 customers
Feb/2012	2,000,000 customers
Apr/2012	20,000 base stations installed
Jul/2012	3,000,000 customers
Feb/2013	4,000,000 customers
Oct/2013	New WiMAX service (ultra-high speed) started/ MVNO started
Feb/2015	20,000 base stations installed for new WiMAX service

The total demand for WiMAX has been increasing, with about 20 billion customers in 2015 as shown in Fig. 2. The demand increased at a consistent rate until 2014, and then increased sharply from 2014 to 2015. This is because MVNOs were introduced in mid-2013. MVNO*1 represents the demand excluding real mobile network operators, while MVNO*2 represents the demand including the results from real mobile network operators as MVNOs. These results show that the effect of MVNO*1 on the total demand is smaller, while the total demand is almost the same with MVNO*2. Considering these results, customers who have already been WiMAX users do not change their service to MVNO, this is because the total demand is almost the same as that of MVNO*2. Therefore, newer customers tend to choose their MVNO in terms of pricing compared to 2013.

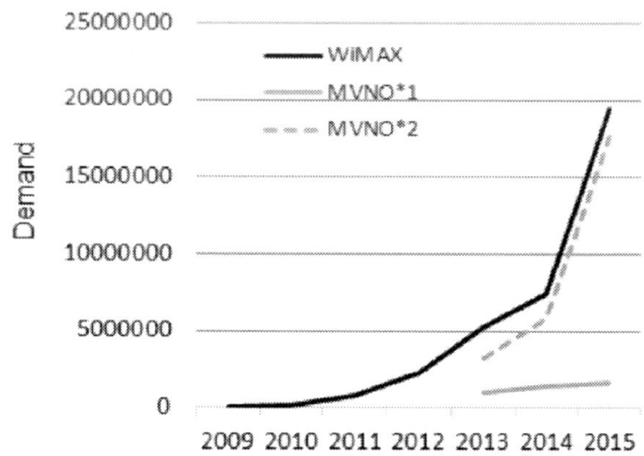

Figure 2. Demand for WiMAX in Japan.

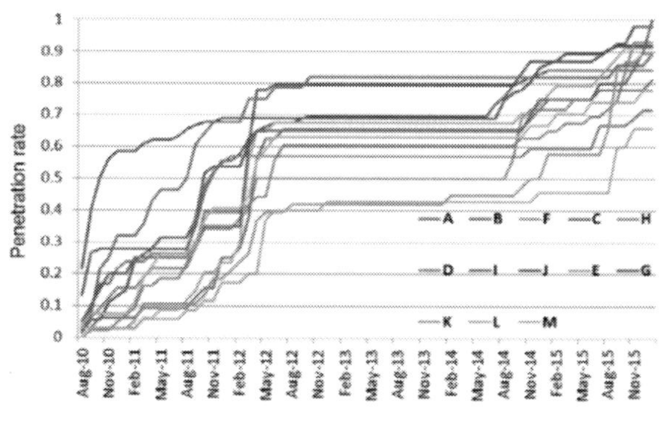

Figure 3. Trend for number of microareas for WiMAX.

Fig. 3 shows the trend of penetration of microareas for WiMAX from August 2010 to November 2015. A microarea is defined as the municipal area in this study. The vertical axis is the penetration rate of WiMAX services, which means the ratio of the number of microareas for a WiMAX facility installed against the total number of microareas in the prefecture. Thirteen prefectures were considered and defined as A to M. The graph shows that many microareas were selected and that the facilities were installed from August 2010 to April 2012. This time interval corresponds to the early stage of WiMAX diffusion. The demand grew inside the areas from 2012 to 2014 since the number of installed microareas did not change. In late 2014, the number of installed microareas began to increase. This situation corresponds to the introduction of MVNO and this means that the customers who are interested in the price of services are major factors for demand increase.

IV. Hypothesis of Service Diffusion and Its Model

In this section, the assumption of how broadband services are propagated is explained. Many ICT services are already being provided. Therefore, we investigated the features of the propagation of such services. For example, analysis of the mechanism of word of mouth has been studied [22]-[24]. Let us first consider the terminal equipment. The diffusion of audio-visual (AV) and digital equipment depends on the users' experiences through their use and the sharing of their experience with their friends and families by word of mouth. Since many people refer to the site of collecting word-of-mouth information, consumers tend to be affected by a person who has similar preferences.

Broadband services based on the ICT infrastructure become more widespread owing to the sharing of information among users of the AV and digital equipment such as smartphones and tablet PCs. CGM depends significantly on network externality; for example, the ratio of users who choose internet video sites on the basis of recommendations of friends/acquaintances was found to be about 38% [25]. Network externality is defined as the phenomenon in which the benefit of the customers is greater with a greater increase in the number of customers, particularly in terms of networked services.

If an individual has to pay for a new software application or a service upgrade, he/she tends to decide on the basis of face-to-face information from friends/acquaintances [26]. Since the wired/wireless broadband access infrastructure is not a free service, we expect customers to respond to it in the same way they respond to software and service upgrade purchases.

There are five types of consumers, namely the innovator, early adopter, early majority, late majority, and the laggard. An early adopter is a trend-conscious person who collects information, makes decisions by himself/herself, and plays an important role for service diffusion. It is widely known that an early adopter has a considerable influence on general consumers as an opinion leader. This implies that he/she sends interesting information to his/her acquaintances. We made a hypothesis of service diffusion in early stage on the basis of personal behaviour [21]. As face-to-face communication with friends/acquaintances is the key of broadband service diffusion, it is necessary to introduce the concept of innovation diffusion [17]. If an individual (especially early majority) has many contacts with early adopters, the possibility that he/she will demand the service is high [27], as shown in Fig. 4 (a).

Early majority is commonly a person who is easily affected by not only the early adopter but also the affected majority [28]. This implies that each early majority changes his/her mind based on the advice from friend/family/acquaintance. Therefore, face-to-face communication in neighbourhood influences the increase in early majority, as shown in Fig. 4 (b).

The late majority tends to be sceptical of the services, price-oriented and follow the maturity of the early majority after the service has sufficiently penetrated the field. Therefore, the late majority is not affected by contact with the early majority through face-to-face communication, but rather by resonance [29] with early majority, as show in Fig. 4 (c).

Next, we explain the mechanism of potential demand diffusion physically, i.e., what kind of microareas have quick service diffusion. Basically, there are two kinds of service propagation conditions. One is population in a microarea. Higher the population in an area, higher the possibility of increased contacts (face-to-face communication). The other is the in-/out-flow such as human fluidity of microarea. Higher the flows in an area, higher is the possibility of contacts.

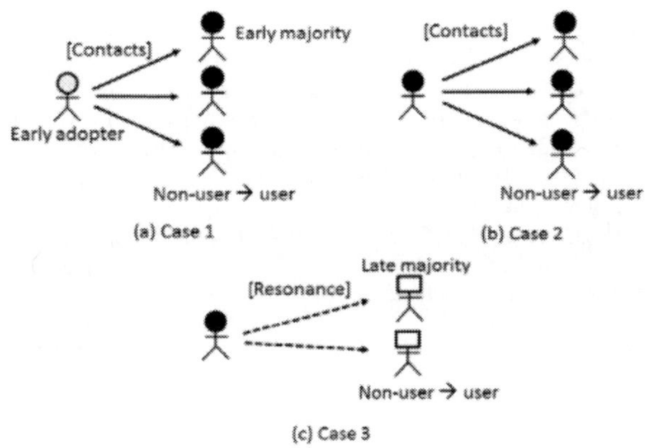

Figure 4. Relationship between service diffusion and customer segmentation.

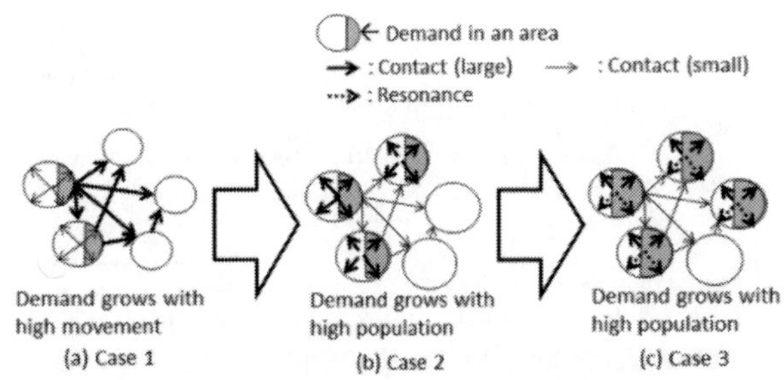

Figure 5. Mechanism of potential demand diffusion.

As face-to-face communication is important in the diffusion of wired/wireless broadband services, the mobility of an early adopter may influence broadband service diffusion through contacts with many individuals in Case 1 (see Fig. 5). Therefore, our hypothesis of Case 1 is that demand grows faster in case of high movement among microareas compared to the case of high population in a microarea, as shown in Fig. 5 (a).

Although face-to-face communication is still effective in Case 2, the contacts among early majority are dominant. Therefore, the service is diffused by friends/acquaintances/families nearby location. Our hypothesis of Case 2 is that the demand grows with high population as shown in Fig. 5 (b). If the differences of population among microareas are small, high movement still results in service diffusion.

In Case 3, resonance leads to the increase in late majority. This means that diffusion does not depend on face-to-face communication. The deeds of early majority decide the deeds of late majority. Therefore, the effect of population in microareas becomes great when compared to that of movement among microareas as shown in Fig. 5 (c). If the differences of population among microareas are small, the same situation occurs in Case 2.

Next, the movement between microareas is defined. Since the diffusion of ICT infrastructure strongly depends on the application (SNS, Net-Game, etc.), it would be desirable to identify commuting flow on the basis of attributes (employee, student, etc.). In addition, if we could access life log data, we could perform an even more detailed analysis. For the frequency of collecting commuting flow information, we assume that an average commuting flow per day or yearly can be used. This is because the interval of ICT infrastructure installation is not frequent (no real-time installation). Therefore, movement between microareas as shown in Fig. 6 (a) is assumed to be modelled applying commuting flow between microareas (Fig. 6 (b)).

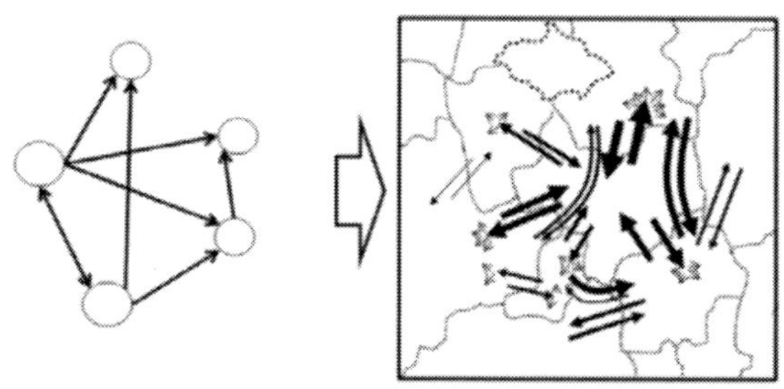

(a) Movement between microareas (b) Commuting flow

Figure 6. Definition of movement between microareas.

Now we discuss the relationship between our three cases and WiMAX service diffusion. The early stage of service diffusion corresponds to the time interval between 2010 and 2012 according to the results in Figs. 2 and 3. The penetration rate grew with a steep slope and the number of microareas increased sharply. In this stage, the early majority was affected by early adopters as Case 1. The middle stage of service diffusion corresponds to the time interval between 2012 and 2014. In this stage, there was no increase in the number of installed microareas. This means that the early majority who were affected by early adopters contacted others in the early majority in the same microarea. Thus, the demand increased inside a microarea as seen in Case 2. The penetration rate increased in all areas during the late stage of service diffusion after 2014. The new type of services provided by MVNO started in this stage, where there was potential demand from the late majority. The demand grows inside a microarea and this results in addition of new microareas, therefore, the number of micoareas increases. This stage corresponds to Case 3.

V. Microarea Selection Algorithms

Let us introduce three algorithms to select microareas in this section.

A. *Flow-based algorithm*

To select microareas on the basis of the movement, we created a table of the inflows and outflows to and from microareas based on commuting flows among microareas, as shown in the table presented in Fig. 7.

Table of in- and outflows among microareas

Out \ In	Area 1	Area 2	Area 3	...
Area 1	f_{11}	f_{12}	f_{13}	
Area 2	f_{21}	f_{22}	f_{23}	
Area 3	f_{31}	f_{32}	f_{33}	
⋮				

Area selection policy:
- Sort $\{f_{ij}\}$ in the descending order
- Select areas having larger flows

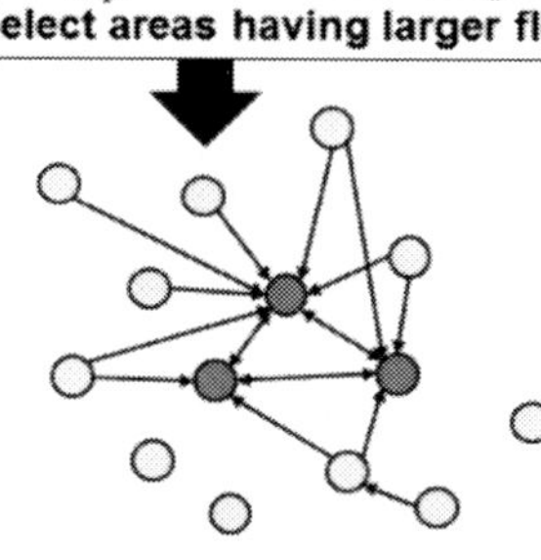

Figure 7. Concept of flow-based algorithm.

Let these flows be sorted in the descending order to estimate the area selection efficiently. Furthermore, we built a graph model in which a microarea is denoted as a node and a commuting flow among the microareas is denoted as a link. Each link has an arrow to indicate the direction of the commuting flow. A link was added among the specified areas if the in/outflow was greater than or equal to the given threshold, α, penetration rate. In other words, we selected links that contained a high average number of commuters as shown in the lower part of Fig. 7.

Thus, a microarea selection method using a flow-based algorithm was constructed according to the above procedure, as shown in Fig. 8. Its definition and notation are as follows:

Let $G = (N, L)$ be a graph, where N denotes a finite set of nodes i ($i \in N$), and L represents a set of links l_{ij} ($l_{ij} \in L$, $i, j \in N$).

Let f be a function such that $f(l_{ij}) = z_{ij}$ in N_0 (non-negative integer) for $l_{ij} \in L$.

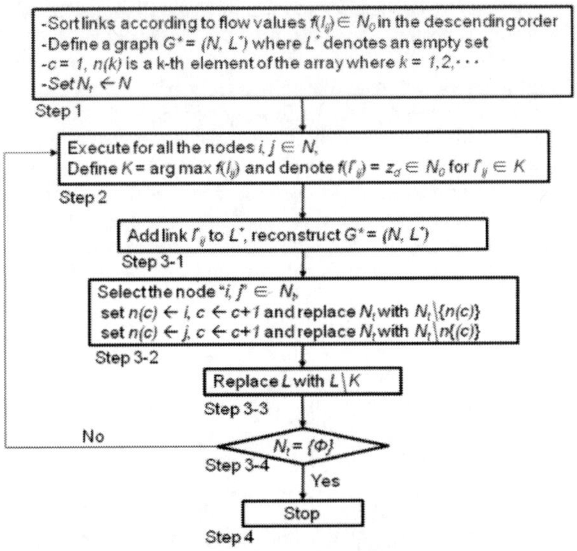

Figure 8. Flow-based algorithm.

B. Population-based algorithm

To select microareas on the basis of population, we created a table of the population of each microarea, as shown in the table presented in Fig. 9.

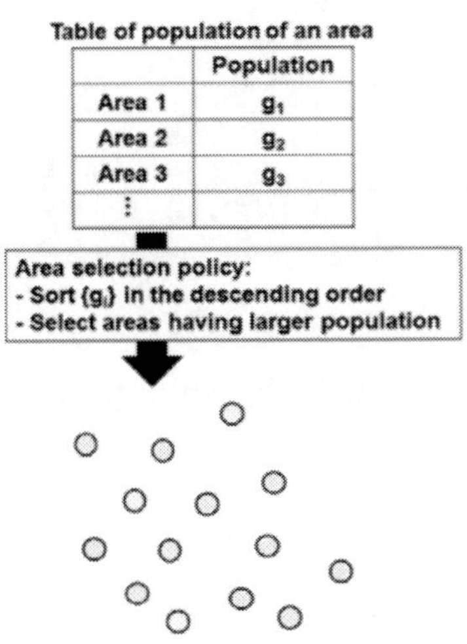

Figure 9. Concept of population-based algorithm.

Let these values be sorted in the descending order to select the node with larger values as shown in the lower part of Fig. 9.

Thus, microarea selection method using population-based algorithm was constructed according to the below procedure, as shown in Fig. 10. Its definition and notation are as follows:

Let $G = (N, L)$ be a graph, where N denotes a finite set of nodes i ($i \in N$).

Let g be a function such that $g(n_i) = u_i$ in N_0 (non-negative integer) for $n_i \in N$.

Therefore, g gives population in each microarea.

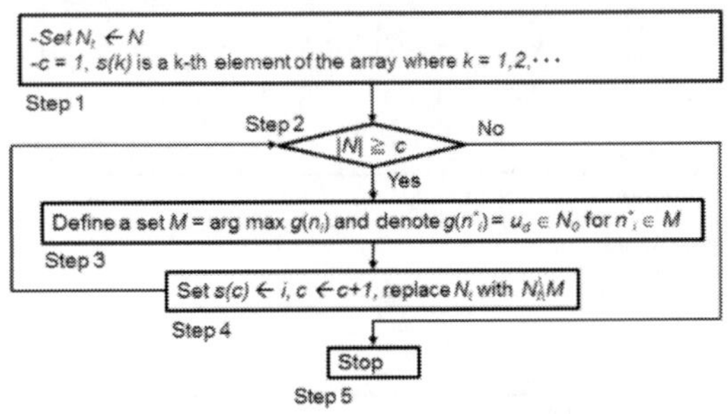

Figure 10. Population-based algorithm.

C. Mixed algorithm

The population-based algorithm is defined as the method that selects areas by the application of the population order; therefore, areas with a large population tend to be selected. The flow-based algorithm is defined as a method that selects areas on the basis of the inflows and outflows among areas. According to the mechanism described in the previous subsections, the mixed algorithm is constructed so that the flow-based algorithm is used in the early stage while the population-based algorithm is used in the middle and late stages as shown in Fig. 11.

Let $G = (N, L)$ be a graph, where N denotes a finite set of nodes ($i \in N$) and L represents a set of links ($l_{ij} \in L$).

There exists a function f: $L \rightarrow N_0$ (non-negative integer) such that $f(l_{ij}) = z_{ij}$ for any $l_{ij} \in L$, and a function g: $N \rightarrow N_0$ (non-negative integer) such that $g(n_i) = u_i$ for $n_i \in N$.

The procedure to construct the mixed algorithm is as follows;

- Step 1: Let c be a counter with an initial value '1', and $n(k)$ be the k-th element of the array where $k = 1, 2, \ldots$ Let "p" denote the number of selected areas by WiMAX evolution under the penetration rate (α%), Set $N_t \leftarrow N$.
  Sort links according to flow values $f(l_{ij})$ in the descending order.
  Sort nodes according to population values $g(n_i)$ in the descending order.

- Step 2: While $p \geq c$, then the following steps are performed (flow-based algorithm):
    - Step 2-1: Define a set K ($\subset L$) = arg max $f(l_{ij})$, and denote $f(l^*_{ij}) = z_d \in N_0$ for $l^*_{ij} \in K$.
    - Step 2-2: Select nodes 'i, j' $\in N_t$, then set $n(c) \leftarrow i$, $c \leftarrow c+1$ and replace N_t with $N_t \backslash \{n(c)\}$, and set $n(c) \leftarrow j$, $c \leftarrow c+1$ and replace N_t with $N_t \backslash \{n(c)\}$.
    - Step 2-3: Replace L with $L \backslash K$.
- Step 3: $c \leftarrow p + 1$.
- Step 4: While $|N| \geq c$, then the following steps are performed (population-based algorithm):
    - Step 4-1: Define a set M ($\subset N_t$) = arg max $g(n_i)$, and denote $g(n^*_i) = u_d \in N_0$ for $n^*_i \in M$.
    - Step 4-2: Select node 'i', and set $n(c) \leftarrow i$, $c \leftarrow c+1$, and replace N_t with $N_t \backslash M$.

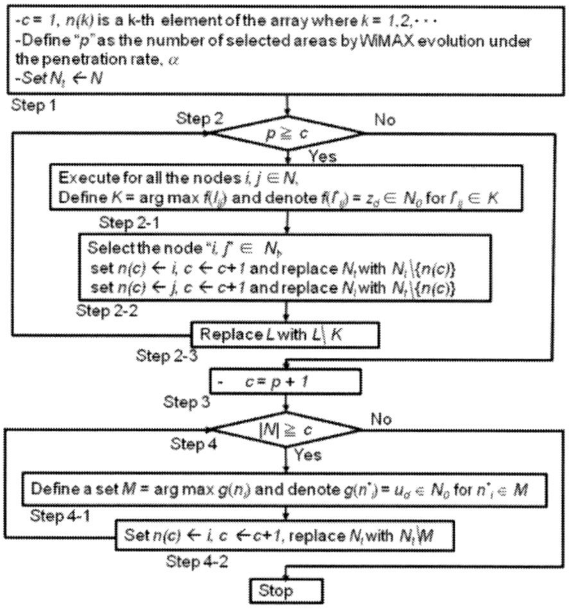

Figure 11. Mixed algorithm.

VI. Evaluation of Algorithms

Firstly, microareas are classified according to employee fluidity, then three algorithms are compared. Moreover, the relationship between algorithms and area characteristics are described.

A. *Classification of prefectures*

As a microarea usually belongs to a prefecture, it is better to target microareas in a specified prefecture. Forty-one prefectures are considered to be representative of all the prefectures in Japan in terms of the population size. However, the following two types of prefectures are considered to be exceptions and are excluded from this study:

- Prefectures with a very large population, such as Tokyo, Osaka, Kyoto, and Kanagawa, which have high fluidity and a high diffusion speed in their own region
- Prefectures such as Hokkaido and Okinawa, which are islands with low fluidity as compared to the other prefectures.

As employee fluidity (as commuting flows) depends on the area selected especially in the early stage [20], the attributes of prefectures are considered to be 'number of employees in own microarea', 'inflow of employees among microareas', and 'outflow of employees among microareas'. We classified the prefectures into the following five categories in terms of employee fluidity according to the correspondence analysis shown in Fig. 12. The vertical axis represents the occurrence ratio of the in- or outflow among the microareas in the prefecture. The horizontal axis represents the staying ratio of employees in their own microareas.

- Group 1: areas with large inflow; Aichi (A)
- Group 2: areas with large in- and outflows; Ibaraki (B) and Shiga (F)
- Group 3: areas with large outflow; Saitama (C) and Nara (H)
- Group 4: areas with staying in own area as little movement; Niigata (D), Okayama (I) and Hiroshima (J)
- Group 5: balanced areas of average in- and out-flow; Kagawa (E), Ishikawa (G), Yamagata (K), Tokushima (L) and Fukui (M)

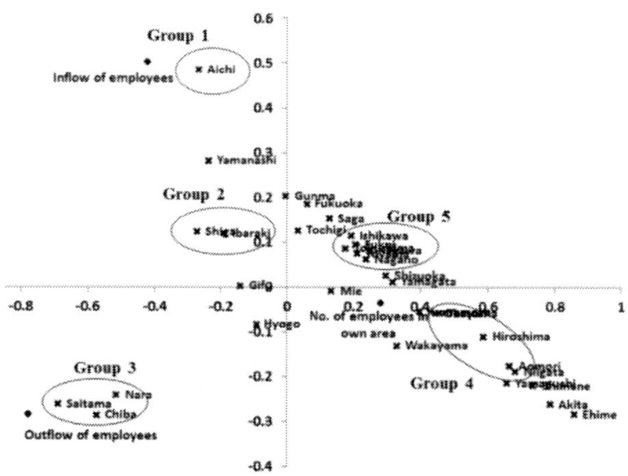

Figure 12. Correspondence analysis of employee fluidity.

B. *Comparison with algorithms*

In this section, we compare and evaluate the population-based, flow-based and mixed algorithms. To determine the difference in results depending on region, thirteen prefectures were considered among five groups (A to M).

Since infrastructure installation takes a large amount of time, a yearly plan of the area installation order is necessary. The penetration rate is calculated as the ratio of the number of areas, where WiMAX has been introduced by the provider (WiMAX evolution), to the number for all areas in the given prefecture. We take two conditions as penetration rate: 40% and 80% corresponding to low and high stage, respectively.

Table II shows the concordance ratio (CR) comparison among flow-based and population-based algorithms when the penetration rate is 40%. The CR of the number of selected areas between WiMAX evolution and each algorithm is defined by the following equation.

TABLE II. COMPARATIVE RESULTS AT LOW PENETRATION

Prefecture (Area no.)	Group	Population-based algorithm	Flow-based algorithm
A (83)	1	0.62	0.72
B (54)	2	0.6	0.65
F (32)	2	0.77	0.85
C (87)	3	0.69	0.69
H (42)	3	0.81	0.81
D (43)	4	0.53	0.71
I (32)	4	0.58	0.67
J (28)	4	0.71	0.71
E (34)	5	0.79	0.79
G (20)	5	0.57	0.86
K (38)	5	0.73	0.87
L (35)	5	0.79	0.79
M (27)	5	0.73	0.82

CR = (Number of selected areas matching WiMAX evolution areas /Number of WiMAX evolution areas). (1)

The underlined values (in Table II) indicate the highest CR at each prefecture. Although the CR by population-based algorithm is sometimes the highest, the CR by flow-based algorithm is always the highest for all Groups. Therefore, flow-based algorithm is suitable in the early stage.

Table III shows the concordance ratio comparison among the three algorithms. Table III results are for the penetration rate of 80% in each prefecture. The mixed algorithm works such that flow-based algorithm is used when the penetration rate reaches 40%, population-based algorithm is used beyond 40%.

Although the CR by flow-based algorithm is sometimes the highest, the CR by population-based algorithm is always the highest for Groups 1 to 4. Employee fluidity explains well, the behaviour in the early stage by applying the flow-based algorithm, while the resonant effect well explains the demand increase by population in the late stage by applying the population-based algorithm. Therefore, the mixed algorithm is for use in accordance with the penetration rate for Groups 1, 2, 3 and 4 during the life cycle of the services. However, the CR by flow-based algorithm is always superior to that by population-based algorithm for Group 5. It is better to use the flow-based algorithm for the whole penetration rate.

TABLE III. COMPARATIVE RESULTS AT HIGH PENETRATION

Prefecture (Area no.)	Group	Population -based algorithm	Flow-based algorithm	Mixed algorithm
A (83)	1	0.94	0.92	0.94
B (54)	2	0.79	0.79	0.79
F (32)	2	0.80	0.80	0.80
C (87)	3	0.93	0.91	0.93
H (42)	3	0.97	0.93	0.97
D (43)	4	0.82	0.82	0.82
I (32)	4	0.92	0.88	0.92
J (28)	4	0.91	0.86	0.91
E (34)	5	0.81	0.89	0.81
G (20)	5	0.81	0.81	0.81
K (38)	5	0.81	0.87	0.81
L (35)	5	0.87	0.91	0.87
M (27)	5	0.86	0.90	0.86

C. *Consideration for microarea characteristics*

In this subsection, we consider the differences between Group 5 and the other groups to apply the proposed algorithm. The differences of population between areas are focused and analysed. Figs. 13, 14, 15, 16, and 17 show the relationship between the population in a microarea, and ranking of microareas for prefectures. The target microareas excluded the microareas that were selected by WiMAX evolution when the penetration rate was lower than α (α = 40% in this study) in each prefecture.

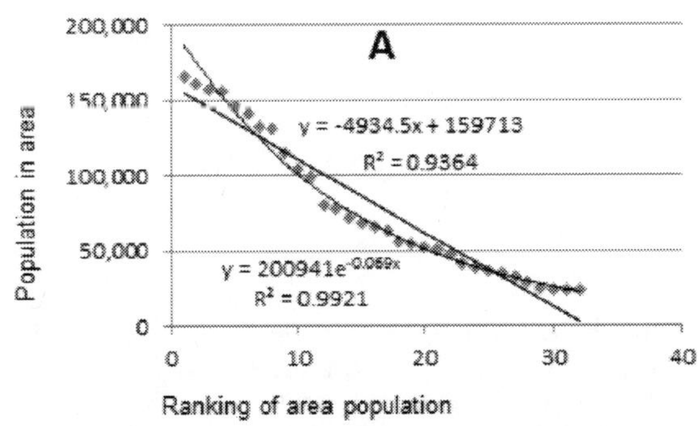

Figure 13. Relationship between population in the area and its ranking (Group 1).

Three approximation curves and their R-square (R^2) values are calculated as exponential, logarithmic, and linear regressions. The result showed that the approximation by exponential regression fits into the scatter diagram at the highest R^2 (R^2 = 0.9921) in A (Group 1), while the approximation by linear regression has R^2 = 0.9364 as shown in Fig. 13. There are many microareas and their population is considered to be linearly decreasing according to the regression line, since R^2 difference of two regressions is small within the given microareas. Therefore, the effect by population difference is large because of linearity. Thus, the population-based algorithm works well in the late stage.

Next, the scatter diagrams in C and H (Group 3) are shown in Fig. 14. The results showed that the approximation by exponential regression also fits into them at the highest R^2 = 0.9834, 0.9493 in C and H, respectively. Their population is considered to be linearly decreasing according to the regression line, since the R^2 difference of two regressions is small with the given microareas. Therefore, the effect by population difference is large because of linearity. Thus, the population-based algorithm works well in the late stage.

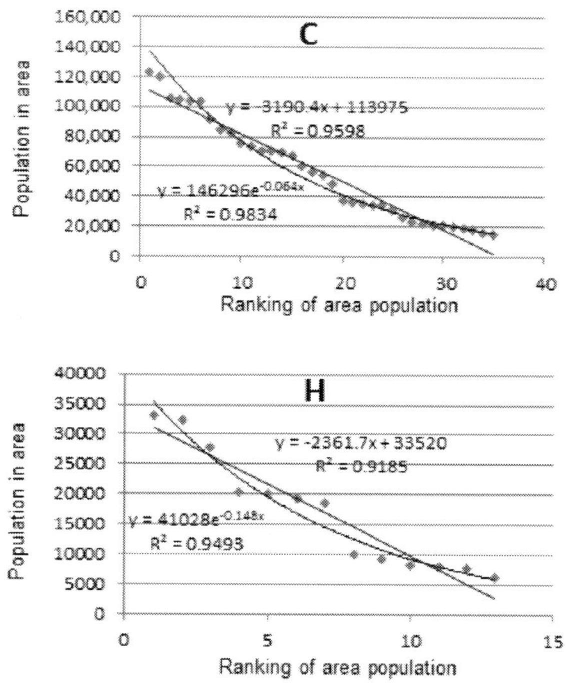

Figure 14. Relationship between population in the area and its ranking (Group 3).

The scatter diagrams in D, I, and J (Group 4) are shown in Fig. 15. The result showed that the approximation by exponential regression also fits into it at the highest R^2 = 0.9753 in D, while those by logarithmic regression fit into them at the highest R^2 = 0.9097, 0.9834 in I and J, respectively. Their population is considered to be linearly decreasing according to the regression line, since the R^2 difference of two regressions is small with the given microareas. Therefore, the effect by population difference is large because of linearity. Thus, the population-based algorithm works well in the late stage.

The scatter diagrams in B and F (Group 2) are shown in Fig. 16. The results showed that the approximation by logarithmic regression fits into them at the highest R^2 = 0.9424, 0.8435 in B and F, respectively. However, the difference of two regressions is large, linear regression does not fit in B or F. It is understandable that the population difference is small for low-ranking microareas in B and F according to logarithmic regression, so the effect of fluidity is greater than that of population.

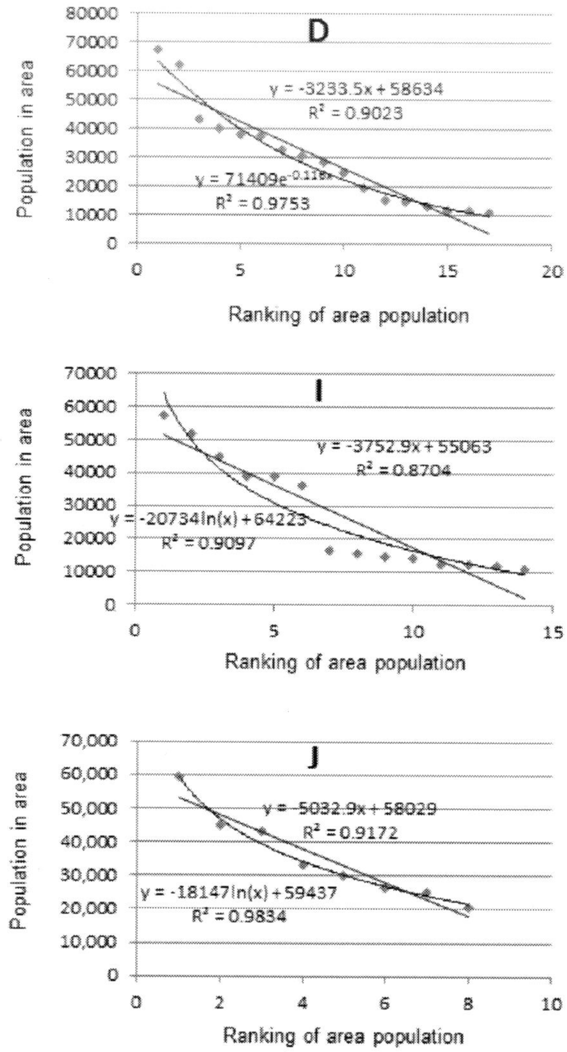

Figure 15. Relationship between population in the area and its ranking (Group 4).

The scatter diagrams in K, L, and M (Group 5) are shown in Fig. 17. The results showed that the approximation by logarithmic regression fit into them at the highest R^2 = 0.9645, 0.9513, 0.955, in K, L and M, respectively. However, the difference of two regressions is large, linear regression does not fit in K, L, or M. It is understandable that the population difference is small for low-ranking microareas in

K, L, and M according to logarithmic regression, so the effect of fluidity is greater than that of population.

The results with effect by fluidity are significant for Group 5, while the same results are obtained for Group 2. Note that the effect by fluidity and that by population are almost the same in Group 2 because of obtaining the same CR by the three algorithms.

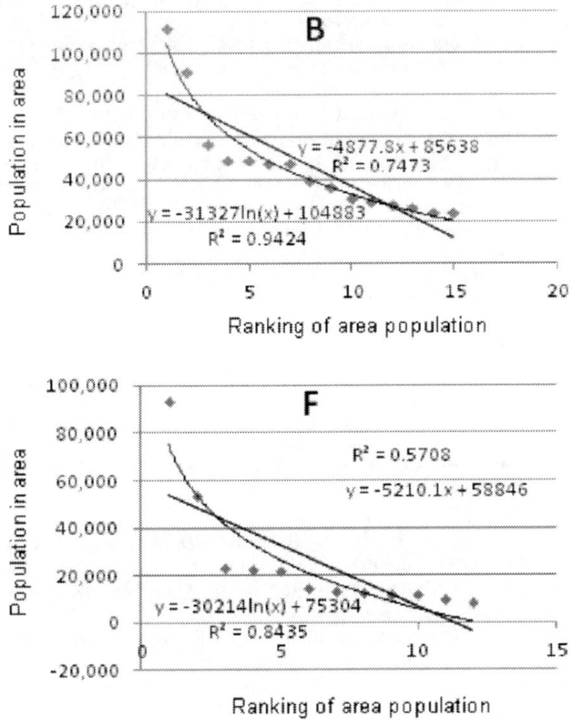

Figure 16. Relationship between population in the area and its ranking (Group 2).

The R^2 difference ratio (DR) is calculated using the following equation.

$$\text{DR} = 100 * \{(R^2 \text{ of optimal regression}) - (R^2 \text{ of linear regression})\} / (R^2 \text{ of linear regression}). \quad (2)$$

The calculated results are shown in Table IV. DRs in Group 1, 3 and 4 are small, less than 10%. It means that the population with low-ranking microareas has linearity. Therefore, population difference has a large effect for microarea selection. Group 1 shows feature with large inflow. Group 3 shows features with large outflow. In addition, Group 4 has the feature of staying in its microarea as there is little movement. These groups are affected by population in the late stage.

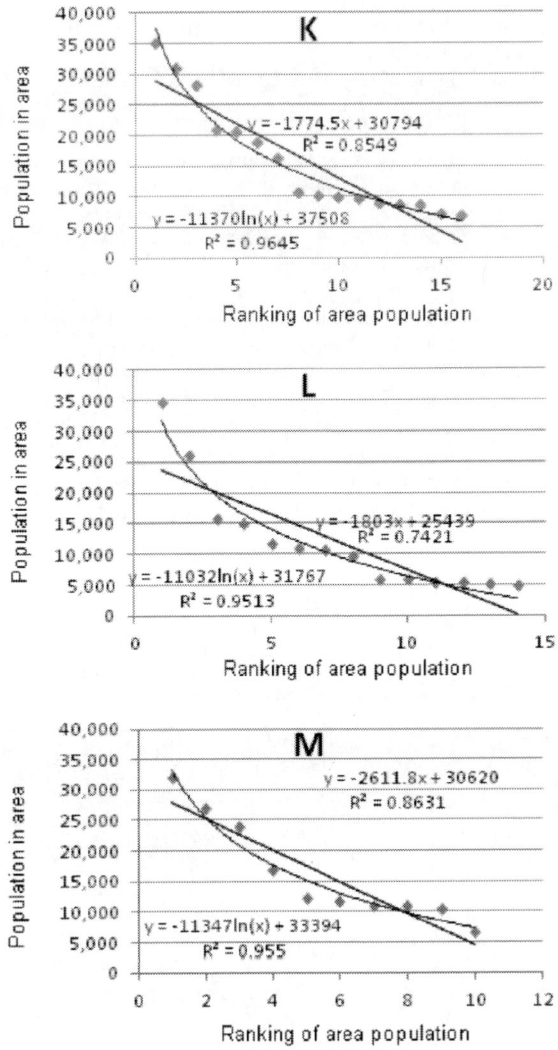

Figure 17. Relationship between population in the area and its ranking (Group 5).

DRs in Group 2 and 5 are large, greater than 10%. It means that the population with low-ranking microareas does not have linearity. Therefore, population difference has little effect for microarea selection. Group 2 has the feature with large in- and outflows as balanced movement, while Group 5 has the feature with small in- and outflows as balanced movement. These groups are affected by the fluidity even in the late stage.

VII. MICROAREA SELECTION METHOD BASED ON AREA CHARACTERISTICS

Summing up the results obtained in the previous section, the characteristics of each prefecture is an important factor.

These characteristics obtained by correspondence analysis are grouped into two types.

Char-1: Prefecture with biased in-/out-flow, or immobilization

Char-2: Prefecture with balanced in and outflows

The framework of the mixed algorithm considering area characteristics is constructed as follows.

- Step 1: Let areas be grouped by the correspondence analysis as 'number of employees in own microarea', 'inflow of employees among microareas', and 'outflow of employees among microareas' for inputs.
- Step 2: If the given area belongs to Char-1, then mixed algorithm is used at the given threshold value, α, i.e., flow-based algorithm is applied when the penetration rate is equal to or smaller than α, and population-based algorithm is applied when the penetration rate is greater than α.
- Step 3: If the given area belongs to Char-2, then the mixed algorithm is used under $\alpha = 100\%$, i.e., flow-based algorithm is applied during the life cycle.

TABLE IV. R^2-DIFFERENCE BETWEEN OPTIMAL AND LINEAR REGRESSIONS

Prefecture (Area no.)	Group	R^2 value of optimal regression	R^2 value of linear regression	Difference ratio: DR (%)
A (83)	1	0.9921	0.9364	6
B (54)	2	0.9424	0.7473	26
F (32)	2	0.8435	0.5708	48
C (87)	3	0.9834	0.9598	2
H (42)	3	0.9493	0.9185	3
D (43)	4	0.9753	0.9023	8
I (32)	4	0.9097	0.8704	5
J (28)	4	0.9834	0.9172	7
K (38)	5	0.9645	0.8549	13
L (35)	5	0.9513	0.7421	28
M (27)	5	0.955	0.8631	11

VIII. CONCLUSIONS

It is significantly important to select an area in which an ICT infrastructure should be introduced so as to ensure quick and economic development of an advanced information society. Area selection strongly depends on the potential demand, and one of the main features of the ICT infrastructure is network externality; therefore, a great amount of time and labour is required to select specified areas from among a large number of candidate areas.

In this paper, we proposed an efficient area selection method based on a service diffusion model. We evaluated the method using real field data from 13 prefectures, and we obtained the application of flow-based and population-based algorithms during the life cycle of the services. It is also advised that the areas are classified into two types in terms of employee fluidity and the application of mixed algorithm deeply depends on the microarea characteristics for population differences.

We intend to apply the method to other information network infrastructures, such as FTTH, LTE, and energy management services for future works.

REFERENCES

[1] M. Iwashita, A. Inoue, T. Kurosawa, and K. Nishimatsu, "Microarea selection method based on services diffusion process for broadband services," Proc. of The Eleventh International Multi-Conference on Computing in the Global Information Technology (ICCGI 2016), pp. 30-35, 2016.

[2] The Ministry of Information and Communications, White Paper Information and Communications in Japan, 2009.

[3] The Ministry of International Affairs and Communications of Japan, "Broadband Service Coverage Rate With Respect to the Total Number of Households," [Online]. Available from: http://www.soumu.go.jp/soutsu/tohoku/hodo/h2501-03/images/0110b1006.pdf (accessed 24 May 2017).

[4] The Ministry of International Affairs and Communications of Japan, "Information and Communications in Japan," White Paper, p. 174, 2014.

[5] K. Yonetaka, Fact of area marketing, Tokyo: Nikkei Pub. Inc., 2008.

[6] Y. Murayama and R. Shibazaki, GIS theory, Tokyo: Asakura Pub. Co. Ltd., 2008.

[7] T. Sakai et al., "Use of Web-GIS area marketing and its application to the local region," Bulletin of Global Environment Research, Rissho Univ., vol. 6, pp. 125-130, 2004.

[8] T. Ida, Broadband economics, Tokyo: Nikkei Pub. Inc., 2007.

[9] H. Seya and M. Tsutsumi, Spatial Statistics, Tokyo: Asakura Pub. Co. Ltd., 2014.

[10] S. Mase and M. Tsutsumi, Spatial Data Modeling, Tokyo: Kyoritsu Pub., 2001.

[11] R. L. Goodrich, Applied statistical forecasting, Belmont: Business Forecast Systems Inc., 1992.

[12] T. Abe and T. Ueda, "Telephone revenue forecasting using state space model," Trans. on IEICE, vol. J68-A, no. 5, pp. 437-443, 1985.

[13] H. Kawano, T. Takanaka, Y. Hiruta, and S. Shinomiya, "Study on teletraffic method for macro analysis and its evaluation," Trans. on IEICE, vol. J82-B, no. 6, pp. 1107-1114, 1999.

[14] M. Iwashita, K. Nishimatsu, T. Kurosawa, and S. Shimogawa, "Broadband analysis for network building," Rev. Socionetwork Strat., vol. 4, pp. 17-28, 2010.

[15] M. J. Benner and M. L. Tushman, "Exploitation, Exploration, and Process Management: The Productivity Dilemma Revisited," The Academy of Management Review, vol. 28, no. 2, pp. 238-256, 2003.

[16] R. W. White, "Motivation Reconsidered: The concept of competence," Psychol. Rev., vol. 66, pp. 297-333, 1959.

[17] E. Rogers, "Diffusion of innovation," 5th ed. New York: Free Press, 2003.

[18] S. Nakamichi, "NTT Docomo and The Univ. of Tokyo Have Just Started Analysis of Population Movement Using Location Information Obtained by Wireless Base Station," [Online]. Available from: http://techon.nikkeibp.co.jp/article/NEWS/20100915/185680/ (accesses 24 May 2017).

[19] M. Iwashita, "A consideration of an area classification method for ICT service diffusion," Knowl. Intell. Inf. Eng. Syst., LNAI, 6883, pp. 256-264, 2011.

[20] M. Iwashita, A. Inoue, T. Kurosawa, and K. Nishimatsu, "Micro area selection framework for ICT infrastructure diffusion based on commuting flow," Int. J. Comp. Inf. Sci., vol. 13, no. 2, pp. 10-19, 2012.

[21] M. Iwashita, A. Inoue, T. Kurosawa, and K. Nishimatsu, "Efficient microarea selection algorithm for infrastructure installation of broadband services," Int. J. Comput. Intell. Stud., Inderscience publishers, Vol. 5, Nos 3/4, pp. 29-236, 2017.

[22] K. Ikeda, "The Diffusion of Innovation Through Word-Of-Mouth and Social Networks: A social Psychological Study Combining Snowball Surveys and Multi-Agent Simulation," Tokyo: Univ. of Tokyo Press, 2010.

[23] S. P. A. T. Dentsu, "How to Create an Atmosphere to Make You Feel Buying," Tokyo: Diamond Inc., 2007.

[24] H. Katahira, "New theory AIDEES like big tidal stream," Diamond Visionary, vol. 42, no. 7, pp. 34-37, 2006.

[25] Macromill, "Field Survey of Using Internet Video Site". [Online]. Available from: http://monitor.macromill.com/researchdata/20070701movie/index.html (accessed 24 May 2017).

[26] "The Institute for Information and Communications Policy, Research Study of Determinative Factors for Internet Usage and Reality of Use" Tokyo: The Institute for Information and Communications Policy, 2009.

[27] S. Shimogawa and M. Iwashita, "Method for analyzing sociodynamics of telecommunication-based services," Proc. of 9th IEEE/ACIS International Conference on Computer and Information Science, pp. 99-104, 2010.

[28] G. A. Moor, "Crossing the chasm: Marketing and selling high-tech goods to mainstream customers," New York: Harper Business, 1991.

[29] Y. Ohsawa, M. Matsumura, and K. Takahashi, "Resonance without Response: The Way of Topic Growth in Communication," Chance Discov. Real World Decis. Making, Stud. Comput. Intell., Vol. 30, pp. 155-165, 2006.

International Journal on Advances in Telecommunications, vol 10 no 1 & 2, year 2017, http://www.iariajournals.org/telecommunications/

An Improved Preamble Aided Preamble Structure Independent Coarse Timing Estimation Method for OFDM Signals

Soumitra Bhowmick, Kasturi Vasudevan

Department of Electrical Engineering
Indian Institute of Technology
Kanpur, India 208016
Email: {soumitb, vasu}@iitk.ac.in

***Abstract*—Timing estimation has been one of the major research issue in orthogonal frequency division multiplexing (OFDM) systems. In the literature there are mainly two types of preamble (data) aided timing estimation methods have been proposed. One type of timing estimation methods that depend on the specific structure of the preamble and the other type of timing estimation methods that work independent of the structure of the preamble. Performance of most of the timing estimation methods, which work independent of the structure of the preamble is severely affected in the presence of carrier frequency offset (CFO). The challenge is to design a preamble structure independent timing metric that should be robust to CFO. In this paper, a data aided coarse (initial) timing estimation scheme for OFDM system is proposed. Proposed timing estimation method is independent of the structure of the preamble and it works better than the other existing methods in the presence of CFO. The algorithm is also capable of using multiple preambles for coarse timing estimation. The performance is compared in terms of probability of erasure, probability of correct estimation and mean square error (MSE) with the existing timing synchronization methods for OFDM systems.**

Keywords*—*Timing synchronization; OFDM; Preamble; carrier frequency offset; Timing metric; MSE; Probability of erasure; Probability of correct estimation.

I. INTRODUCTION

A part of this work was presented at ICWMC 2016 conference [1]. The main impairments in a wireless communication system are multipath fading and noise [2]. Multipath fading introduces inter symbol interference (ISI). The major requirements of a digital communication system is to maximize the bit rate, minimize bit error rate, minimize transmit power and minimize transmission bandwidth [2] [3]. Orthogonal frequency division multiplexing (OFDM) has emerged as a powerful technique which meets the above requirements in multipath fading channels [4]. However, OFDM is known to be very sensitive to timing and carrier frequency synchronization errors [5].

Timing and frequency synchronization in OFDM systems can be achieved by either data aided (DA) or non data aided (NDA) method. In data aided method preamble or pilot is transmitted along with data through multipath fading channel for synchronization. It is assumed that preamble or pilot is known to the receiver. Preamble is transmitted separately along with the data in the time domain whereas pilots are inserted within OFDM data in frequency domain. Preamble is used for both timing and frequency synchronization as well as channel estimation, whereas pilots are mainly used for carrier frequency synchronization and channel estimation. In non data aided method [6] [7], cyclic prefix is used for synchronization, it is bandwidth efficient because there is no need of additional information (preamble). The drawback of this method is that it is less accurate because CP is the part of OFDM data and it (CP) is distorted by multipath fading (ISI) [8]. On the other hand, DA method requires additional preambles for synchronization; hence, it is less bandwidth efficient than the NDA method but accuracy is better than the NDA method. In this paper, we focus on the data aided (DA) timing estimation methods. Data aided timing estimation methods proposed in the literature can be broadly classified into two categories:

1) Approaches that depend on the special structure of the preamble [5] [9] [10] [11] [12] [13] [14] [15] [16] [17] [18] [19] [20] [21] [22] [23] [24] [25] [26] [27].
2) Approaches that work independent of the structure of the preamble [28] [29] [30] [31] [32] [33] [34].

Approaches that depend on the special structure of the preamble can be categorized as

1) Approaches that utilize repeated structure of the preamble [5] [9] [10] [12] [15] [18] [20] [22] [26].
2) Approaches that utilize symmetrical correlation of the preamble [11] [13] [16] [17] [21].
3) Approaches that utilize weighted structure of the preamble [14] [23] [24] [25].
4) Approaches that utilize both symmetrical correlation as well as the weighted structure of the preamble [19] [27].

The first data aided timing estimation technique is proposed in the literature by *Schmidl et al.* [5]. In [5], a preamble with two identical halves is used for timing estimation. However, the variance of the timing estimation is large due to timing metric plateau. To reduce the variance of timing estimate a modified preamble structure and new timing metric are proposed by *Minn et al.* [9] [10]. In [9] [10], a preamble with four identical halves with specific sign pattern is used to improve the performance. However, the variance of *Minn's* method is still high in ISI channel. The performance is further improved by *Shi et al.* [12]. Unlike *Minn's* method a preamble with four identical halves with specific sign pattern is used in [12]. In *Minn's* method correlations between the adjacent blocks of the preamble are utilized, whereas *Shi's* method is capable of utilizing correlations between the adjacent blocks as well as correlations between the non adjacent blocks of the preamble.

Differential cross correlation is used in the methods proposed by *Awoseyila et al.* [18] [22], to estimate the timing offset. A preamble with two identical halves is utilized in the methods proposed in [18] [22]. The methods proposed in [5] [9] [10] [12] [15] [18] [22] utilize time domain repeated preamble to estimate the timing offset. The method proposed by *Pushpa et al.* [20] utilize frequency domain repeated preamble to estimate the timing offset. *Park et al.* [11] propose the idea of utilizing symmetrical correlation of the preamble for timing synchronization. Later, the methods proposed by *Kim et al.* [13], *Seung et al.* [16], *Guo et al.* [17], utilize symmetrical correlation with their own preamble structure to estimate the timing offset. Timing metrics proposed in [11] [13] [16] [17] have impulsive shape at the correct timing point, so they give better performance in multipath Rayleigh fading scenario but the drawback of these metrics is they have sub peaks apart from the correct timing point. In order to solve this problem a new timing metric is proposed by *Sajadi et al.* [21]. *Ren et al.* [14] propose the technique of utilizing weighted structure of the preamble for timing synchronization. Later, the methods proposed by *Wang et al.* [23], *Fang et al.* [24], *Silva et al.* [25] utilize different weighted structure of the preamble to estimate the timing offset. *Zhou et al.* [19] propose the idea of utilizing both symmetrical correlation as well as weighted structure of the preamble to estimate the timing offset. Later, a similar type of technique is used in the method proposed by *Shao et al.* [27].

All these methods are dependent on the special structure of the preamble; hence, they cannot work with other preambles and moreover the variance of the timing estimation of these methods is high in multipath fading scenario. *Kang et al.* [28] propose a technique to estimate timing offset that work independent of the preamble structure. In [28], a delayed correlation of the preamble is used for timing synchronization. The performance is further improved by *Hamed et al.* [29] [30]. In [29] [30], all correlation points are utilized without repetition. In [32] [33] [34], a new timing estimation method using a matched filter is proposed, which gives better performance than [28] [29]. All these methods proposed in the literature [28] [29] [30] [32] [33] [34], which work independent of the structure of the preamble, utilize only one preamble for timing synchronization. *Hamed et al.* [31] propose a timing estimation method by utilizing more than one preamble. The main drawback of these methods [28] [29] [30] [31] [32] [33] is that the coarse timing estimation is severely degraded in the presence of carrier frequency offset (CFO). CFO arises due to two reasons, first one is due to frequency mismatch between the local oscillators used in the transmitter and receiver and the another one is due to Doppler shift. CFO causes phase rotation in the samples of the received signal. The phase rotation affects timing synchronization. Here, we propose a new timing estimation method using multiple preambles and we also propose a modified timing estimation method, which is robust to CFO.

This paper is organized as follows. The system model is presented in Section II. The existing timing estimation methods are discussed in Section III. The proposed method is presented in Section IV. The simulation results are given in Section V and finally, the conclusions in Section VI.

II. SYSTEM MODEL

Fig. 1 shows the typical structure of a OFDM frame in the time domain. An OFDM frame contains preamble, cyclic prefix (CP) and data. The preamble is used for synchronization.

$\mathbf{x}_0$	$\mathbf{x}_1$	....	$\mathbf{x}_{M-1}$	$\mathbf{x}_{cp}$	$\mathbf{x}_d$

Figure 1. OFDM frame structure in the time domain

The mth preamble in the frequency domain can be represented in vector form as follows.

$$\mathbf{X}_m = [X_m(0)\ X_m(1)\ ...\ X_m(N-1)] \tag{1}$$

where $0 \le m \le M-1$. The IFFT of the mth preamble is given by

$$x_m(n) = \frac{1}{N}\sum_{k=0}^{N-1} X_m(k)\, e^{j2\pi nk/N}. \tag{2}$$

The mth preamble in the time domain can be represented in vector form as follows

$$\mathbf{x}_m = [x_m(0)\ x_m(1)\ ...\ x_m(N-1)] \tag{3}$$

where $0 \le k, n \le N-1$. Let $\mathbf{X}_d$ denotes the frequency domain data of the OFDM frame. $\mathbf{X}_d$ can be represented in vector form as follows:

$$\mathbf{X}_d = [X_d(0)\ X_d(1)\ ...\ X_d(N_d-1)]. \tag{4}$$

The IFFT of the frequency domain data $\mathbf{X}_d$ is given by

$$x_d(n) = \frac{1}{N_d}\sum_{k=0}^{N_d-1} X_d(k)\, e^{j2\pi nk/N_d}. \tag{5}$$

The time domain data $\mathbf{x}_d$ (see Fig. 1) of the OFDM frame can be represented in vector form as follows

$$\mathbf{x}_d = [x_d(0)\ x_d(1)\ ...\ x_d(N_d-1)] \tag{6}$$

where $0 \le k, n \le N_d - 1$. A cyclic prefix $\mathbf{x}_{cp}$ of length N_g is introduced in front of time domain data $\mathbf{x}_d$. The value of the N_g is $L-1$, where L is the number of channel taps. $\mathbf{x}_{cp}$ is given by

$$\mathbf{x}_{cp} = [x_d(N_d - N_g)\ ...\ x_d(N_d-1)]. \tag{7}$$

Let $\mathbf{x}_0$ to $\mathbf{x}_{M-1}$ are the preambles of the frame in the time domain. Let the transmitted frame is given by (see Fig. 1)

$$\begin{aligned}\mathbf{x} &= [\mathbf{x}_0 \ ..\ \mathbf{x}_{M-1}\ \mathbf{x}_{cp}\ \mathbf{x}_d] \\ &= [x(0)\ x(1)\ ...\ x(MN + N_d + N_g - 1)]. \end{aligned} \tag{8}$$

Now, $\mathbf{x}$ is transmitted through the frequency selective channel. The channel is assumed to be quasi static and it is fixed for one frame and varies independently from frame to frame. Its impulse response for a given frame can be expressed as:

$$\mathbf{h} = [h(0)\ h(1)\ h(2)\ .....\ h(L-1)] \tag{9}$$

where L is the number of channel taps. The received signal $\mathbf{r}$ in the time domain is given by:

$$r(n) = y(n)\, e^{j2\pi n\epsilon/N} + w(n) \tag{10}$$

where

$$y(n) = h(n) \star x(n) = \sum_{l=0}^{L-1} h(l)\, x(n-l) \quad (11)$$

where $0 \leq n \leq MN + N_g + N_d + L - 2$ and $w(n)$ is zero mean Gaussian noise sample and ϵ is the normalized frequency offset. Vector form representation of $\mathbf{r}$ is given by

$$\mathbf{r} = [r(0)\, r(1) \,...\, r(MN + N_d + N_g + L - 2)]. \quad (12)$$

III. EXISTING TIMING SYNCHRONIZATION METHODS

In this section we describe some of the existing data (preamble) aided timing synchronization methods. In general, the timing metric, which is used for OFDM timing synchronization, is given by

$$G(d) = \frac{|T(d)|^2}{R^2(d)}. \quad (13)$$

Some authors use another timing metric given by

$$G(d) = \frac{T(d)}{R(d)} \quad (14)$$

where $T(d)$ is the correlation function, $R(d)$ is the energy of the received signal used for normalization, d is the index of the correlation, where $0 \leq d \leq N-1$. The start of the frame can be estimated by finding the peak of the timing metric (13) or (14).

A. Schmidl et al. method

The time domain preamble proposed by *Schmidl et al.* [5] is given by

$$\mathbf{x}_{0sch} = \left[\mathbf{A}_{N/2}\, \mathbf{A}_{N/2}\right] \quad (15)$$

where $\mathbf{A}_{N/2}$ is the sample of length $N/2$. $T(d)$ and $R(d)$ are given by

$$T(d) = \sum_{n=0}^{N/2-1} r^{\star}(d+n) . r(d+n+N/2) \quad (16)$$

$$R(d) = \sum_{n=0}^{N/2-1} |r(d+n+N/2)|^2 \quad (17)$$

where N is the FFT size. $\mathbf{r}$ is the received signal given by (12) and the timing metric can be calculated using (13).

B. Minn et al. method

The time domain preamble proposed by *Minn et al.* [9] is given by

$$\mathbf{x}_{0minn} = \left[\mathbf{A}_{N/4}\, \mathbf{A}_{N/4}\; -\mathbf{A}_{N/4}\; -\mathbf{A}_{N/4}\right] \quad (18)$$

where $\mathbf{A}_{N/4}$ is the sample of length $N/4$. $T(d)$ and $R(d)$ are given by

$$T(d) = \sum_{k=0}^{1} \sum_{n=0}^{N/4-1} r^{\star}(d+n+kN/2) . r(d+n+kN/2+N/4) \quad (19)$$

$$R(d) = \sum_{k=0}^{1} \sum_{n=0}^{N/4-1} |r(d+n+kN/2+N/4)|^2 \quad (20)$$

where N is the FFT size. $\mathbf{r}$ is the received signal given by (12) and the timing metric can be calculated using (13).

C. Park et al. method

The time domain preamble proposed by *Park et al.* [11] is given by

$$\mathbf{x}_{0park} = \left[\mathbf{A}_{N/4}\, \mathbf{B}_{N/4}\, \mathbf{A}^{\star}_{N/4}\, \mathbf{B}^{\star}_{N/4}\right] \quad (21)$$

where $\mathbf{A}_{N/4}$ is the sample of length $N/4$. $\mathbf{A}^{\star}_{N/4}$ is the conjugate of $\mathbf{A}_{N/4}$. $\mathbf{B}_{N/4}$ is designed to be symmetric with $\mathbf{A}_{N/4}$. $\mathbf{B}^{\star}_{N/4}$ is the conjugate of $\mathbf{B}_{N/4}$. $T(d)$ and $R(d)$ are given by

$$T(d) = \sum_{n=0}^{N/2-1} r(d-n) . r(d+n) \quad (22)$$

$$R(d) = \sum_{n=0}^{N/2-1} |r(d+n)|^2 \quad (23)$$

where N is the FFT size. $\mathbf{r}$ is the received signal given by (12) and the timing metric can be calculated using (13).

D. Ren et al. method

The time domain preamble proposed by *Ren et al.* [14] is given by

$$\mathbf{x}_{0ren} = \left[\mathbf{A}_{N/2}\, \mathbf{A}_{N/2}\right] \circ \mathbf{S} \quad (24)$$

where $\circ$ is the Hadamard product and $\mathbf{S}$ is the pseudo noise sequence with values +1 or -1. $T(d)$ and $R(d)$ are given by

$$T(d) = \sum_{n=0}^{N/2-1} s(n).s(n+N/2).r^{\star}(d+n) . r(d+n+N/2) \quad (25)$$

$$R(d) = \frac{1}{2} \sum_{n=0}^{N-1} |r(d+n)|^2. \quad (26)$$

The timing metric can be calculated using (13).

E. Sajadi et al. method

The time domain preamble proposed by *Sajadi et al.* [21] is given by

$$\mathbf{x}_{0sajadi} = \left[\mathbf{A}_{N/8}\, \mathbf{A}_{N/8}\, \mathbf{A}^{\star}_{N/8}\, \mathbf{A}^{\star}_{N/8}\, \mathbf{A}_{N/8}\, \mathbf{B}_{N/8}\, \mathbf{A}^{\star}_{N/8}\, \mathbf{B}^{\star}_{N/8}\right] \quad (27)$$

where $\mathbf{A}_{N/8}$ is the sample of length $N/8$. $\mathbf{A}^{\star}_{N/8}$ is the conjugate of $\mathbf{A}_{N/8}$. $\mathbf{B}_{N/8}$ is designed to be symmetric with $\mathbf{A}_{N/8}$. $\mathbf{B}^{\star}_{N/8}$ is the conjugate of $\mathbf{B}_{N/8}$. Two correlation functions $T_1(d)$, $T_2(d)$ and two normalization functions $R_1(d)$, $R_2(d)$ are used in [21]. $T_1(d)$, $R_1(d)$ are given by

$$T_1(d) = \sum_{k=0}^{1} \sum_{n=0}^{N/8-1} r^{\star}(d+n+kN/4) . r(d+n+kN/4+N/8) \quad (28)$$

$$R_1(d) = \sum_{k=0}^{1} \sum_{n=0}^{N/4-1} |r(d+n+kN/4+N/8)|^2. \quad (29)$$

$T_2(d)$, $R_2(d)$ are given by

$$T_2(d) = \sum_{n=0}^{N/4-1} r(d-n).r(d+n) \quad (30)$$

$$R_2(d) = \sum_{n=0}^{N/4-1} |r(d+n)|^2. \quad (31)$$

The timing metric proposed in [21] given by

$$G(d) = G_1(d).G_2(d) \quad (32)$$

where $G_1(d)$ and $G_2(d)$ are same as (13) can be calculated using $T_1(d)$, $R_1(d)$ and $T_2(d)$, $R_2(d)$.

F. Kang et al. method

Kang et al. [28] propose a preamble pattern independent technique. In [28], a correlation sequence of preamble $\mathbf{C}$ (CSP) is derived as $\mathbf{C} = \mathbf{x}_0^\star \circ \mathbf{x}_0^n$, where $\circ$ represents the Hadamard product. $\mathbf{x}_0$ is the preamble of length N. $\mathbf{x}_0^\star$ is the conjugate of $\mathbf{x}_0$. $\mathbf{x}_0^n$ is the circular shift of $\mathbf{x}_0$ by an amount equal to n. The length of the vector $\mathbf{C}$ is N. Autocorrelation of $\mathbf{C}$ has an impulsive characteristics at the optimum value of n. Let $\mathbf{r}_0^d$ be the vector of length N obtained from the received signal $\mathbf{r}$ starting from index d. $\mathbf{r}_0^d$ is given by

$$\begin{aligned} \mathbf{r}_0^d &= \left[r_0^d(0)\, r_0^d(1) \, ... \, r_0^d(N-1)\right] \\ &= \left[r(d)\, r(d+1) \, ... \, r(d+N-1)\right]. \end{aligned} \quad (33)$$

$T(d)$ is given by

$$T(d) = \text{Re}\left[\left(\mathbf{r}_0^d\right)^\star \circ \mathbf{r}_0^{d,n}\right] \mathbf{p}^T + \text{Im}\left[\left(\mathbf{r}_0^d\right)^\star \circ \mathbf{r}_0^{d,n}\right] \mathbf{q}^T \quad (34)$$

and $R(d)$ is given by

$$R(d) = \left\|\text{Re}\left[\left(\mathbf{r}_0^d\right)^\star \circ \mathbf{r}_0^{d,n}\right]\right\| + \left\|\text{Im}\left[\left(\mathbf{r}_0^d\right)^\star \circ \mathbf{r}_0^{d,n}\right]\right\| \quad (35)$$

where $\left(\mathbf{r}_0^d\right)^\star$ is the conjugate of $\mathbf{r}_0^d$ and $\mathbf{r}_0^{d,n}$ is the circular shift of $\mathbf{r}_0^d$ by an amount equal to n and $0 \leq d \leq N-1$ and $0 \leq n \leq N-1$. The vectors $\mathbf{p}$ and $\mathbf{q}$ represent the sign vectors of $\mathbf{C}$ (CSP). The timing metric can be calculated using (14).

G. Hamed et al. method (M=1)

Hamed et al. [29] [30] extend *Kang's* work for timing synchronization. In this works, *Hamed et al.* extend the correlation length upto $N(N-1)/2$, where N is the FFT size. An adjustable correlation sequence of preamble $\mathbf{C}$ (ACSP) is derived without repetition. $\mathbf{C}$ is given by

$$\begin{aligned} \mathbf{C} = \{&x_0^\star(0)\, x_0(1), x_0^\star(0)\, x_0(2), ..., x_0^\star(0)\, x_0(N-1), \\ &x_0^\star(1)\, x_0(2), x_0^\star(1)\, x_0(3), .., x_0^\star(1)\, x_0(N-1), \\ &..., x_0^\star(N-2)\, x_0(N-1)\} \end{aligned} \quad (36)$$

where $\mathbf{x}_0$ is the preamble of length N. The length of the vector $\mathbf{C}$ (ACSP) is upto $N(N-1)/2$. Let $\mathbf{r}_0^d$ be the vector of length N obtained from the received signal $\mathbf{r}$ starting from index d. $\mathbf{r}_0^d$ is given by (33). A sequence $\mathbf{V}^d$ is derived from $\mathbf{r}_0^d$. $\mathbf{V}^d$ is given by

$$\begin{aligned} \mathbf{V}^d = \Big\{&\left(r_0^d(0)\right)^\star r_0^d(1), \left(r_0^d(0)\right)^\star r_0^d(2), \\ &..., \left(r_0^d(0)\right)^\star r_0^d(N-1), \left(r_0^d(1)\right)^\star r_0^d(2), \\ &\left(r_0^d(1)\right)^\star r_0^d(3), ..., \left(r_0^d(1)\right)^\star r_0^d(N-1), \\ &..., \left(r_0^d(N-2)\right)^\star r_0^d(N-1)\Big\}. \end{aligned} \quad (37)$$

Length of the vector $\mathbf{V}^d$ is upto $N(N-1)/2$. $T(d)$ is given by [29]

$$T(d) = \text{Re}\left[\mathbf{V}^d\right] \mathbf{p}^T + \text{Im}\left[\mathbf{V}^d\right] \mathbf{q}^T \quad (38)$$

or $T(d)$ is given by [30]

$$T(d) = \mid \mathbf{V}^d \mathbf{C}^H \mid^2. \quad (39)$$

$R(d)$ is given by

$$R(d) = \left\|\text{Re}\left[\mathbf{V}^d\right]\right\| + \left\|\text{Im}\left[\mathbf{V}^d\right]\right\|. \quad (40)$$

The vectors $\mathbf{p}$ and $\mathbf{q}$ represent the sign vectors of $\mathbf{C}$ (ACSP). The timing metric can be calculated using (14). Timing estimation using (39) gives better performance than (38).

H. Matched filter method

In matched filtering approach [32] [33] the received signal is correlated with a known preamble. $T(d)$ and R are given by

$$T(d) = \sum_{n=0}^{N-1} r^\star(d+n).x_0(n) \quad (41)$$

$$R = \sum_{n=0}^{N-1} \mid x_0(n) \mid^2. \quad (42)$$

Timing metric $G(d)$ is given by

$$G(d) = \frac{\mid T(d) \mid^2}{R}. \quad (43)$$

I. Hamed et al. method (M=2)

In this work, *Hamed et al.* [31] extend the correlation length upto N^2, by utilizing two preambles, where N is the FFT size. In this work, the correlation sequence $\mathbf{C}$ is derived by using two preambles $\mathbf{x}_0$ and $\mathbf{x}_1$. $\mathbf{x}_0$ and $\mathbf{x}_1$ are the preambles of length N. Correlation sequence $\mathbf{C}$ is given by

$$\mathbf{C} = \left[\mathbf{C}^0\, \mathbf{C}^1 \, ... \, \mathbf{C}^{N-1}\right]. \quad (44)$$

The nth sub vector of vector $\mathbf{C}$ is given by

$$\mathbf{C}^n = \mathbf{x}_0^\star \circ \mathbf{x}_1^n \quad (45)$$

where $\mathbf{x}_0^\star$ is the conjugate of $\mathbf{x}_0$ and $\mathbf{x}_1^n$ is the circular shift of $\mathbf{x}_1$ by an amount equal to n and $0 \leq n \leq N-1$. Let $\mathbf{r}_0^d$ be the vector of length N obtained from the received signal $\mathbf{r}$ starting from index d. $\mathbf{r}_0^d$ is given by

$$\begin{aligned} \mathbf{r}_0^d &= \left[r_0^d(0)\, r_0^d(1) \, ... \, r_0^d(N-1)\right] \\ &= \left[r(d)\, r(d+1) \, ... \, r(d+N-1)\right]. \end{aligned} \quad (46)$$

Let $\mathbf{r}_1^d$ be the vector of length N obtained from the received signal $\mathbf{r}$ starting from index $d+N$. $\mathbf{r}_1^d$ is given by

$$\begin{aligned}\mathbf{r}_1^d &= \left[r_1^d(0)\, r_1^d(1) \ldots .\, r_1^d(N-1)\right] \\ &= \left[r(d+N)\, r(d+N+1) \ldots .\, r(d+2N-1)\right] \quad (47)\end{aligned}$$

A sequence $\mathbf{Q}^d$ generated from $\mathbf{r}_0^d$ and $\mathbf{r}_1^d$ is given by

$$\mathbf{Q}^d = \left[\mathbf{Q}^{d,0}\, \mathbf{Q}^{d,1} \ldots .\, \mathbf{Q}^{d,N-1}\right]. \quad (48)$$

The nth sub vector of vector $\mathbf{Q}^d$ is given by

$$\mathbf{Q}^{d,n} = \left(\mathbf{r}_0^d\right)^* \circ \mathbf{r}_1^{d,n} \quad (49)$$

where $\left(\mathbf{r}_0^d\right)^*$ is the conjugate of $\mathbf{r}_0^d$ and $\mathbf{r}_1^{d,n}$ is the circular shift of $\mathbf{r}_1^d$ by an amount equal to n and $0 \le d \le N-1$ and $0 \le n \le N-1$. $T(d)$ is given by

$$T(d) = \left| \sum_{j=0}^{\lambda N-1} Q^d(j) . C^*(j) \right| \quad (50)$$

and $R(d)$ is given by

$$R(d) = \sum_{j=0}^{\lambda N-1} \mid Q^d(j) \mid^2 \quad (51)$$

where $0 \le \lambda \le N-1$. The timing metric can be calculated using (14).

Methods (A) to (H) use one preamble ($M = 1$) for timing estimation. Method (I) use two preambles ($M = 2$) for timing estimation. Methods (A) to (E) depend on the special structure of the preamble, whereas methods (F) to (I) work independent of the structure of the preamble.

The preamble structure dependent timing metrics proposed in [5] [9] [11] [14] [21] utilize received signal for correlation, whereas the preamble structure independent timing metrics proposed in [28] [29] [30] [31] [32] utilize the correlation between received signal and locally generated reference signal. Timing metrics proposed in [5] [9] [11] [14] [21] are not affected by the CFO because the correlation functions given by (16), (19), (22), (25), (28), (30) are not affected by the CFO [26]. Correlation functions given by (34), (38), (39), (41), (50) are affected due to phase rotation caused by the CFO in the received signal. As a result the correlation peak is destroyed in the presence of CFO. So the timing metrics proposed in [28] [29] [30] [31] [32] are severely affected by the CFO.

IV. PROPOSED MODEL

The received signal $r(n)$ is used to estimate the start of the frame $\hat{\theta}_t$. It is assumed that the preambles $\mathbf{x}_0, \mathbf{x}_1, \ldots, \mathbf{x}_{M-1}$ are known to the receiver. We define the correlation function given by

$$T(d) = \sum_{n=0}^{N-1} \sum_{m=0}^{M-1} r^*(d+n+mN)\, x_m(n) \quad (52)$$

$$R = \sum_{n=0}^{N-1} \sum_{m=0}^{M-1} \mid x_m(n) \mid^2 \quad (53)$$

$$G(d) = \frac{\mid T(d) \mid^2}{M.R} \quad (54)$$

The estimated start of the frame is given by

$$\hat{\theta}_t = \max_d \left[G(d)\right]. \quad (55)$$

Note that in the special case of $M = 1$ in (52), $T(d)$ reduces to

$$T(d) = \sum_{n=0}^{N-1} r^*(d+n)\, x_0(n). \quad (56)$$

It is equivalent to the method proposed in [32], which is a matched filtering approach using one preamble. The performance of the proposed timing metric (54) is severely degraded in the presence of CFO. Hence, we propose a modified timing metric which performs better than (54) in the presence of CFO. Let the frequency offset ϵ lie within $[-I, I]$. We divide the interval $[-I, I]$ into B sub intervals. The length of the each sub interval is 0.1. The modified correlation function $T_{CFO}(d)$ is given by

$$T_{CFO}(d) = \sum_{p=1}^{p=P} \left\{ \left| \sum_{n=0}^{N-1} \sum_{m=0}^{M-1} r^*(d+n+mN)\, x_m(n)\, e^{(j2\pi(i(p))(n+mN)/N)} \right|^2 \right\} \quad (57)$$

where $i(p)$ takes equally spaced points within the interval $[-I, I]$. The spacing between two successive points is 0.1. $i(p)$ is defined as

$$i(p) = -I + (p-1)\, 0.1 \quad (58)$$

$$i(P) = I \quad (59)$$

where $1 \le p \le P$ and $P = B + 1$. The estimated start of the frame is given by

$$\hat{\theta}_t = \max_d \left[T_{CFO}(d)\right]. \quad (60)$$

From (58) and (59) we have

$$\begin{aligned} i(P) &= -I + (P-1)\, 0.1 \\ &= I \\ \Rightarrow \frac{2I}{0.1} &= P - 1 \\ \Rightarrow 20I + 1 &= P. \quad (61)\end{aligned}$$

From (61), it is clear that in the proposed method the computational complexity is high as the range of CFO increases because as the value of I increases, the value of P is also increases. Note that in the special case of $M = 1$ in (57) $T_{CFO}(d)$ becomes

$$T_{CFO}(d) = \sum_{p=1}^{p=P} \left| \sum_{n=0}^{N-1} r^*(d+n)\, x_0(n)\, e^{(j2\pi(i(p))n/N)} \right|^2. \quad (62)$$

Now, (62) is the proposed timing estimation method using one preamble, which is independent of the structure of the preamble. Note that (62) gives better performance than (56) in the presence of CFO.

The advantages of the proposed method in (62) using one preamble ($M = 1$) over the matched filtering approach in (56) are:

1) Use of exponential term in (62) to compensate the phase rotation caused by CFO. The phase rotation caused by CFO destroys the correlation peak in match filtering operation given in (56).
2) Averaging the cross correlation over the interval $[-I, I]$ improves the performance of the proposed timing metric (62) in the presence of CFO.

A. Probability of erasure

If the estimated start of the frame $\hat{\theta}_t$ satisfies the condition $1 \le \hat{\theta}_t \le L$ then the frame is processed further, otherwise frame is discarded and considered as an erasure. Let $F1$ be the total number of frames that is considered as erasure and $F2$ be the total number of frames that is transmitted. The Probability of erasure (PE) is given by

$$PE = \frac{F1}{F2}. \quad (63)$$

B. Mean square error

Let the number of detected frames be given by

$$F = F2 - F1. \quad (64)$$

The mean squared error (MSE) of the detected frames is given by

$$MSE = \frac{\sum_{f=0}^{F-1}\left(\theta_{tf} - \hat{\theta}_{tf}\right)^2}{F} \quad (65)$$

where θ_{tf} is the time index corresponding to the maximum absolute value of the channel impulse response for the fth detected frame given by

$$\theta_{tf} = \arg\max\left(\text{abs}\left(\mathbf{h}_f\right)\right) \quad (66)$$

where $\mathbf{h}_f$ is the channel impulse response for the fth detected frame and $\hat{\theta}_{tf}$ is the estimated start of the fth detected frame.

C. Probability of correct estimation

Let $F3$ be the total number of frames for which $\hat{\theta}_t = \theta_t$, then the probability of correct estimation $P(\hat{\theta}_t = \theta_t)$ is given by

$$P(\hat{\theta}_t = \theta_t) = \frac{F3}{F2} \quad (67)$$

where θ_t is the time index corresponding to the maximum absolute value of the channel impulse response for a given frame, given by

$$\theta_t = \arg\max\left(\text{abs}\left(\mathbf{h}\right)\right) \quad (68)$$

where $\mathbf{h}$ is the channel impulse response for a given frame and $\hat{\theta}_t$ is the estimated start of that frame.

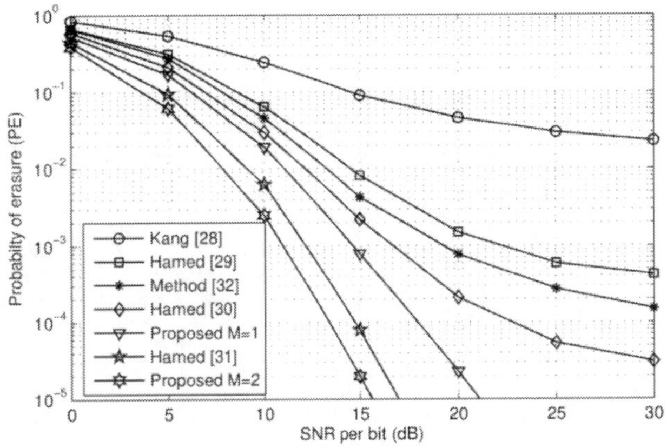

Figure 2. Probability of erasure of different estimators using randomly generated preamble in the presence of CFO [(M=1,2), I=0.5]

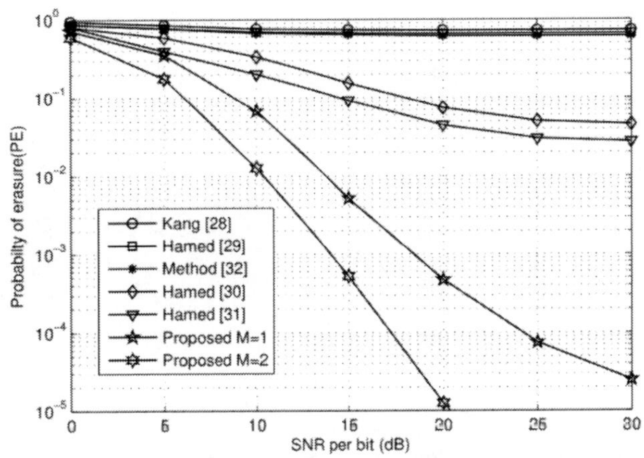

Figure 3. Probability of erasure of different estimators using randomly generated preamble in the presence of CFO [(M=1,2), I=32]

V. SIMULATION RESULTS AND DISCUSSION

In this section, the performance of the proposed method is compared with the major existing timing synchronization methods [28] [29] [30] [31] [32], which work independent of the structure of the preamble. Matlab simulation is performed for performance comparison. We have assumed N=64 and performed the simulations over 5×10^5 frames. QPSK signaling is assumed. A frequency selective Rayleigh fading channel is assumed with $L = 5$ path taps and path delays $\mu_l = l$ for $l = 0, 1, ..., 4$. The channel has an exponential power delay profile (PDP) with an average power of $\exp\left(-\mu_l/L\right)$. The CFO takes random value within the range $[-I, I]$ and it varies independently from frame to frame. For the methods presented in [29] [30], we have considered all the available correlation points without repetition, i.e., $N(N-1)/2$=2016 and for the method presented in [31], we have considered all the available

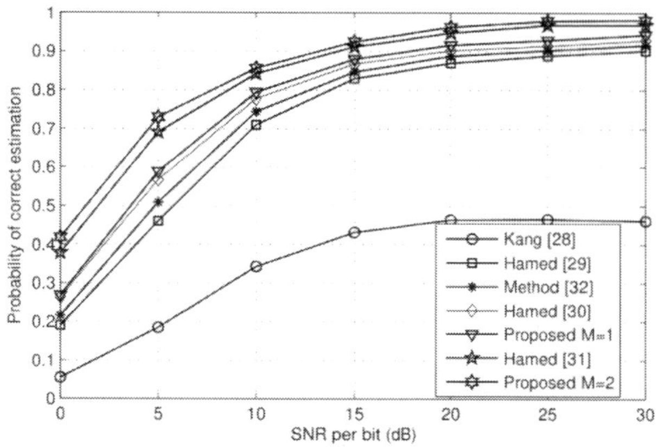

Figure 4. Probability of correct estimation of different estimators using randomly generated preamble in the presence of CFO [(M=1,2), I=0.5]

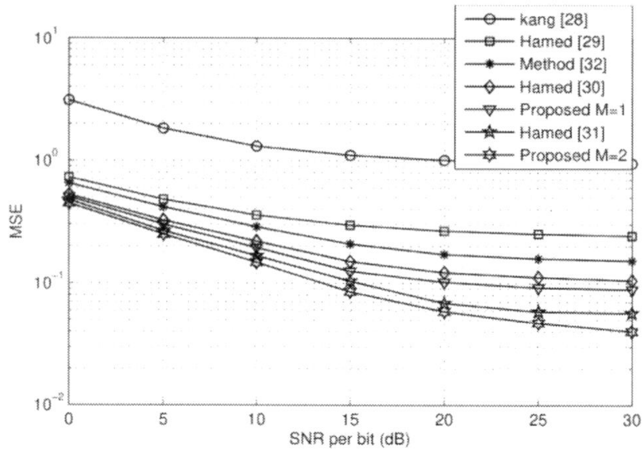

Figure 6. Timing MSE of different estimators using randomly generated preamble in the presence of CFO [(M=1,2), I=0.5]

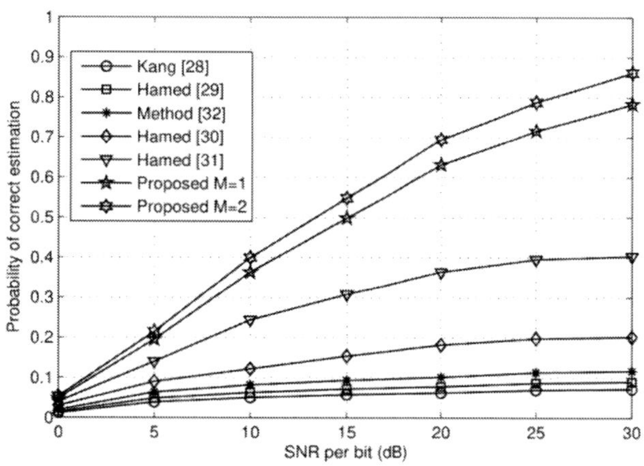

Figure 5. Probability of correct estimation of different estimators using randomly generated preamble in the presence of CFO [(M=1,2), I=32]

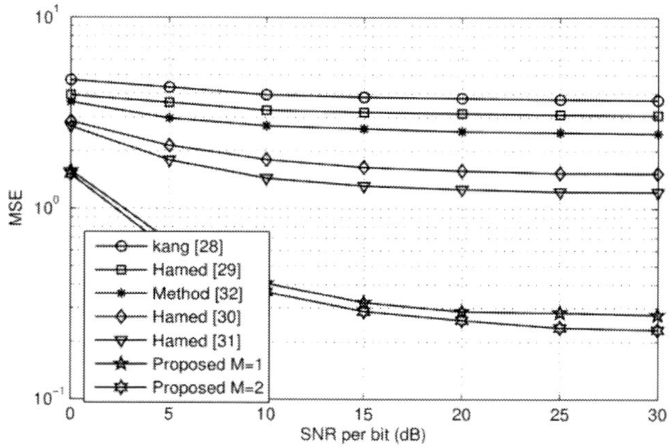

Figure 7. Timing MSE of different estimators using randomly generated preamble in the presence of CFO [(M=1,2), I=32]

correlation points utilized by two preambles, i.e., N^2=4096. In order to compare with [28] [29] [30] [32], we consider M=1 and to compare with [31], we consider M=2. Methods proposed in [28] [29] [30] [31] [32] give satisfactory results when the range of CFO is within ± 0.5, i.e., $I = 0.5$, beyond that the performance starts degrading. So, for performance comparison, we consider the value of I is 0.5 another value of I is considered as 32 for simulation because the whole range of CFO of the OFDM system is within $\pm N/2$, i.e., $I = N/2 = 32$.

The SNR per bit is defined as [34]

$$\begin{aligned} \text{SNR per bit} &= \frac{E\left[\mid H(k) X_m(k) \mid^2\right]}{E\left[\mid W(k) \mid^2\right]} \\ &= \frac{E\left[\mid H(k) \mid^2\right] E\left[\mid X_m(k) \mid^2\right]}{E\left[\mid W(k) \mid^2\right]} \end{aligned} \tag{69}$$

where $X_m(k)$ is the mth preamble in the frequency domain, $H(k)$ is the frequency response of the channel and $W(k)$ is the FFT of the noise. In the case of uniform power delay profile of the channel [34]

$$\begin{aligned} E\left[\mid H(k) \mid^2\right] &= E\left[H(k) H^{\star}(k)\right] \\ &= 2L\sigma_f^2 \end{aligned} \tag{70}$$

Hence, the SNR per bit in decibels becomes

$$\text{SNR per bit } (dB) = 10 \log_{10}\left(\frac{2L\sigma_f^2}{N\sigma_w^2}\right) \tag{71}$$

In the case of exponential power delay profile of the channel

$$\begin{aligned} E\left[\mid H(k) \mid^2\right] &= E\left[H(k) H^{\star}(k)\right] \\ &= 2\sigma_f^2 \sum_{l=0}^{L-1} \exp\left(-\mu_l / L\right) \end{aligned} \tag{72}$$

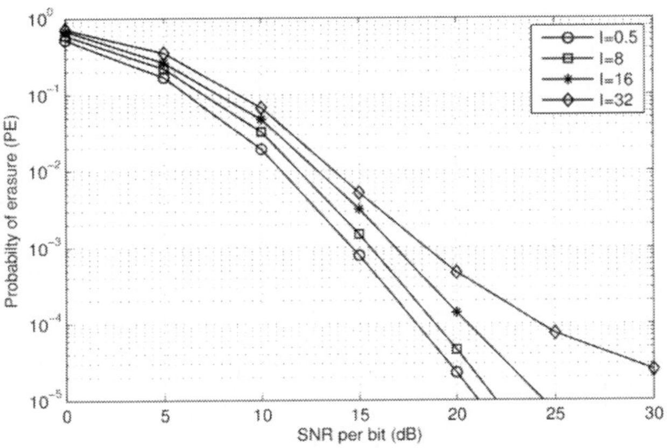

Figure 8. Probability of erasure of proposed estimator using randomly generated preamble for different values of I [(M=1)]

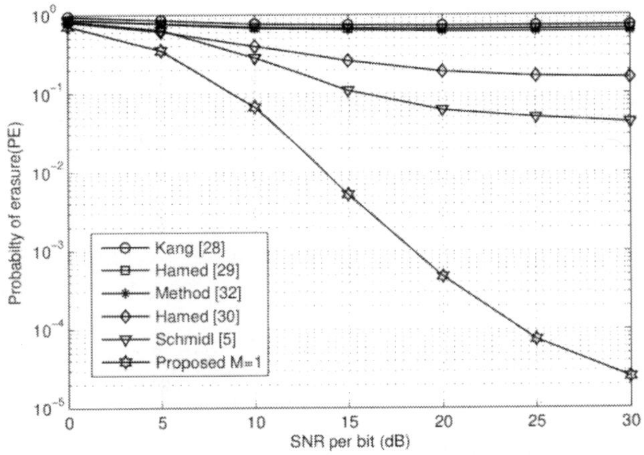

Figure 10. Probability of erasure of different estimators using Schmidl's preamble in the presence of CFO [M=1, I=32]

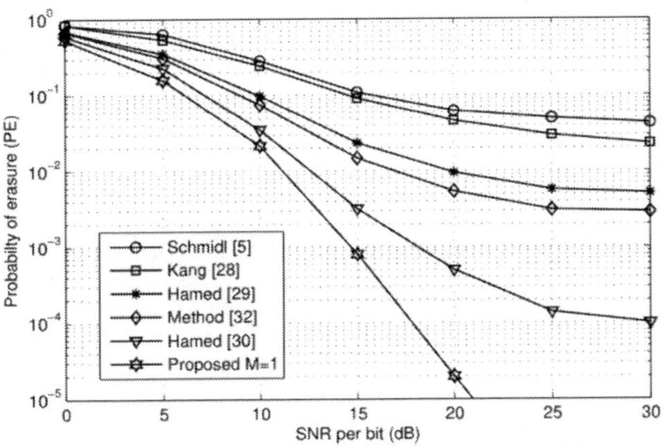

Figure 9. Probability of erasure of different estimators using Schmidl's preamble in the presence of CFO [M=1, I=0.5]

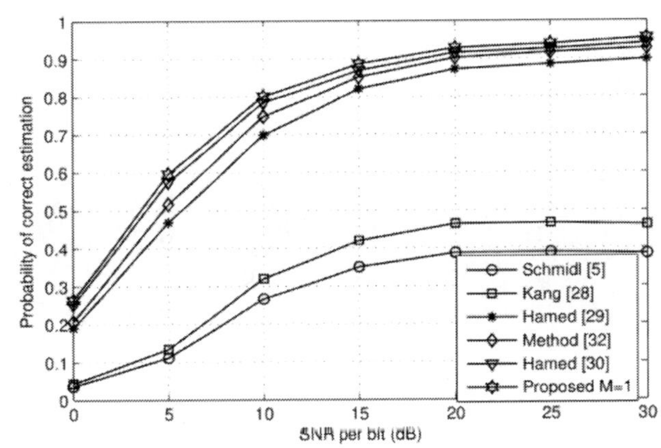

Figure 11. Probability of correct estimation of different estimators using Schmidl's preamble in the presence of CFO [M=1, I=0.5]

Hence, the SNR per bit in decibels becomes

$$\text{SNR per bit } (dB) = 10\ \log_{10}\left(\frac{2\sigma_f^2\sum_{l=0}^{L-1}\exp\left(-\mu_l/L\right)}{N\sigma_w^2}\right) \tag{73}$$

where σ_f^2 and σ_w^2 are the fade and noise variance. In Matlab simulation, probability of erasure (63), probability of correct estimation (67), timing MSE (65) performance of the existing methods as well as of the proposed method are shown for different values of SNR per bit. Random preamble and preambles proposed in [5] [9] [11] [14] [21] are considered for simulation.

In Figs. 2 to 7, probability of erasure, probability of correct estimation and timing MSE of the proposed method are compared with major existing timing synchronization methods in the presence of CFO using a randomly generated preamble. Random preamble means preamble with no repetition. One randomly generated preamble (M=1) is used for the methods in [28] [29] [30] [32] and the proposed method and two randomly generated preambles (M=2) are used for the method in [31] and the proposed method. Figs. 2, 4 and 6 show the performance comparison considering $I = 0.5$. Figs. 3, 5 and 7 show the performance comparison considering $I = N/2 = 32$. It is observed that there is a major performance degradation of the methods proposed in [28] [29] [30] [31] [32] using random preamble when the CFO increases (large value of I). It is also observed that the proposed method performs better than the existing methods in the presence of large range of CFO. Note that in the presence of CFO ($I \neq 0$) with $M = 1$ in the proposed method, there is a significant improvement in the performance as compared to method presented in [32]. It is also observed that the proposed method performs better especially in high SNR per bit. Fig. 8 shows the probability of erasure of the proposed estimator considering different values of I (different range of CFO). It is observed that the proposed

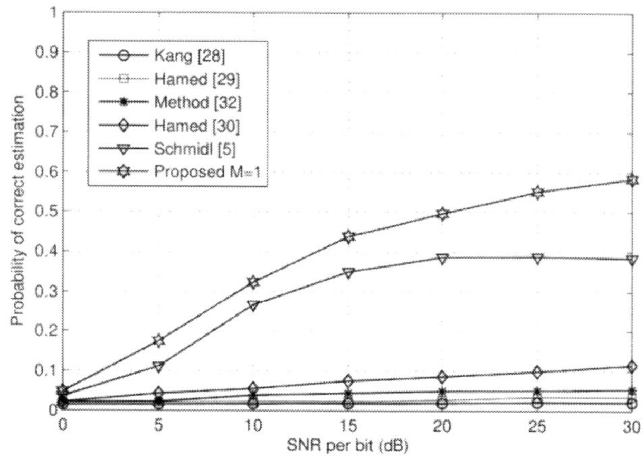

Figure 12. Probability of correct estimation of different estimators using Schmidl's preamble in the presence of CFO [M=1, I=32]

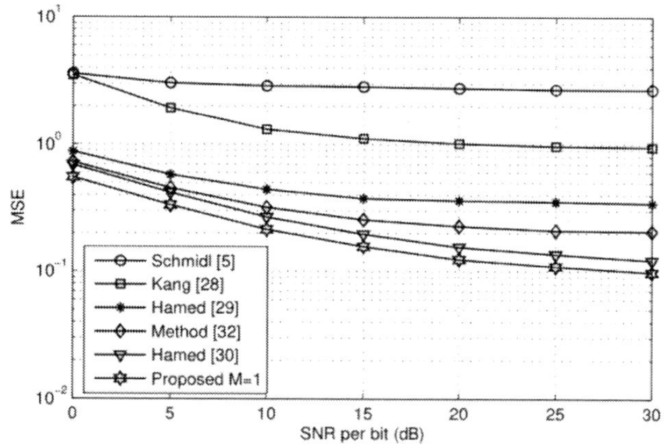

Figure 13. Timing MSE of different estimators using Schmidl's preamble in the presence of CFO [M=1, I=0.5]

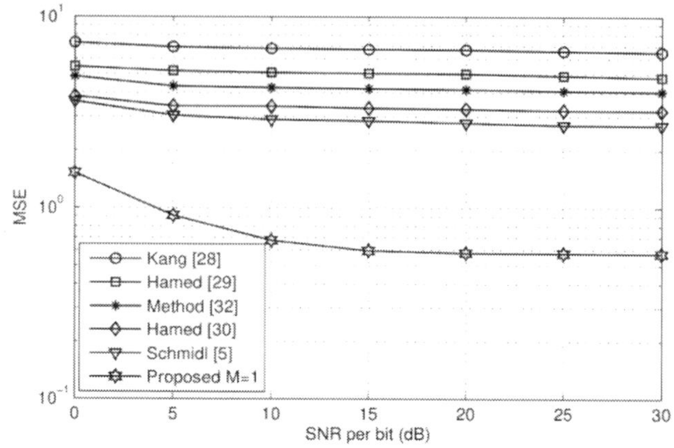

Figure 14. Timing MSE of different estimators using Schmidl's preamble in the presence of CFO [M=1, I=32]

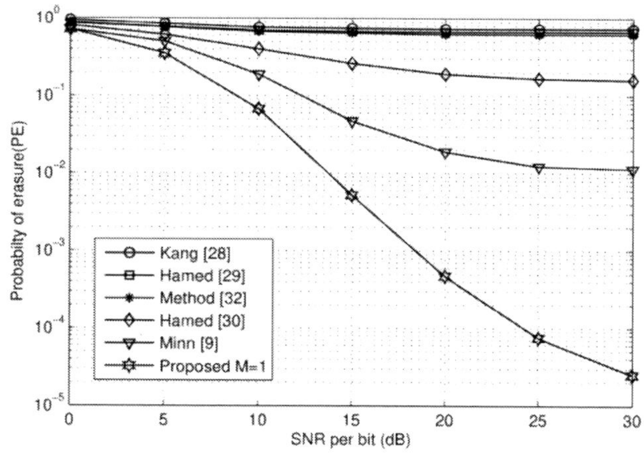

Figure 15. Probability of erasure of different estimators using Minn's preamble in the presence of CFO [M=1, I=32]

method gives satisfactory result even when the range of CFO increases.

In order to compare with the timing estimation methods that depend on the specific structure of the preamble, *Schmidl's* preamble [5] is considered. In Figs. 9 to 14, probability of erasure, probability of correct estimation and timing MSE of the proposed method are compared with the major existing timing synchronization methods using *Schmidl's* preamble [5] considering $M = 1$. Figs. 9, 11 and 13 show the performance comparison with $I = 0.5$. Figs. 10, 12 and 14 show the performance comparison with $I = N/2 = 32$. Like random preamble case, it is also observed that there is a major performance degradation of the methods proposed in [28] [29] [30] [32] using Schmidl's preamble when the CFO increases (large value of I). Hence, from the simulation results (as shown in Figs. 9 to 14), it is clear that the timing metrics proposed in [28] [29] [30] [32] are affected by the CFO whereas the timing metric propsed in [5] is not affected by the CFO. It is again concluded that the proposed timing metric is more robust to CFO as compared to methods in [28] [29] [30] [32].

In Figs. 15 to 22, probability of erasure and timing MSE of the proposed method are compared with the major existing timing synchronization methods using other preambles. In Figs. 15 to 16, *Minn's* preamble [9] is used with $M = 1$. In Figs. 17 to 18, *Park's* preamble [11] is used with $M = 1$. In Figs. 19 to 20, *Ren's* preamble [14] is used with $M = 1$. In Figs. 21 to 22, *Sajadi's* preamble [21] is used with $M = 1$. We assume $I = 32$. From simulation results it is observed that the proposed method gives better performance using other preambles. Figs. 23 to 24 show the performance comparison by using both *Schmidl's* and *Minn's* preamble with $M = 2$. Figs. 25 to 26 show the performance comparison by using both *Park's* and *Ren's* preamble with $M = 2$. We assume $I = 32$. From Figs. 23 to 26, we find that the proposed method gives the best performance. In Table 1, computational complexity of the proposed estimator along with existing estimators are given. Computational complexity mainly consists of complex calculations and real calculations. Most of the preamble structure independent methods require both complex and real calculations while the proposed method only require complex calculations, which is high as compared to other methods but the proposed method gives better performance.

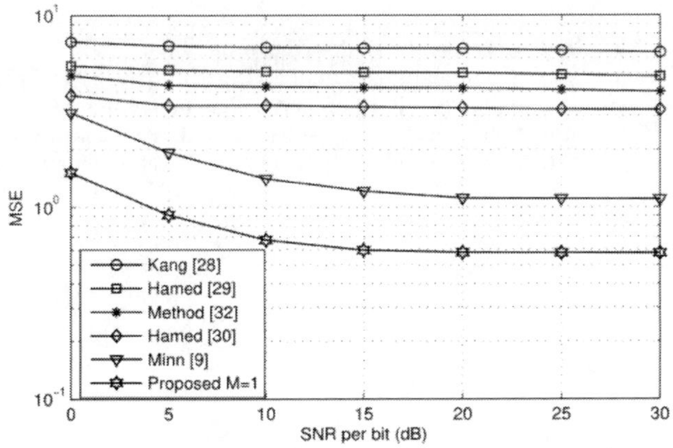

Figure 16. Timing MSE of different estimators using Minn's preamble in the presence of CFO [M=1, I=32]

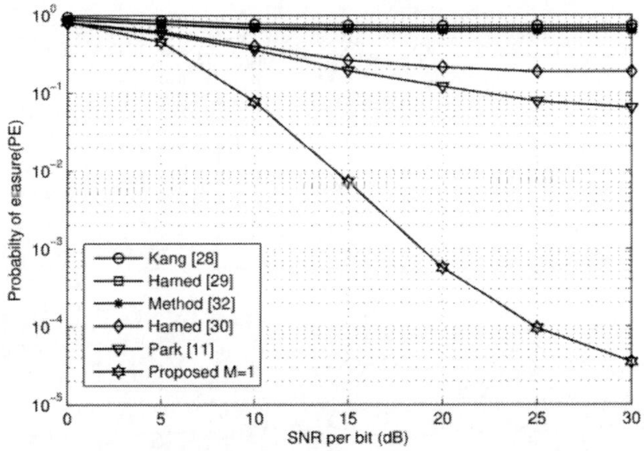

Figure 17. Probability of erasure of different estimators using Park's preamble in the presence of CFO [M=1, I=32]

VI. CONCLUSION

In this paper, different data aided timing estimation methods are explained and compared. Both preamble structure dependent as well as preamble structure independent timing estimation methods are discussed. It is concluded that preamble structure dependent timing estimation methods perform better than preamble structure independent methods in the

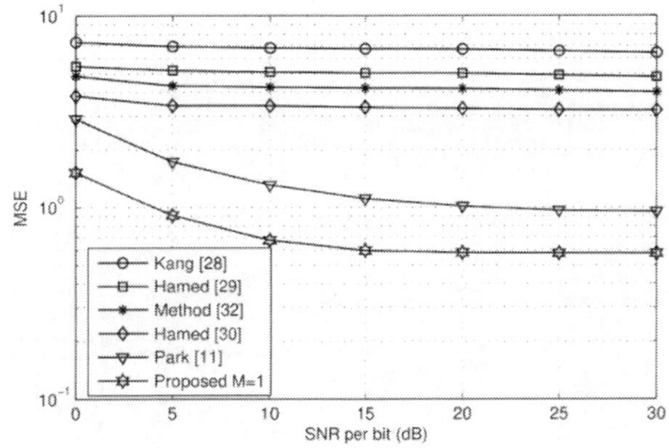

Figure 18. Timing MSE of different estimators using Park's preamble in the presence of CFO [M=1, I=32]

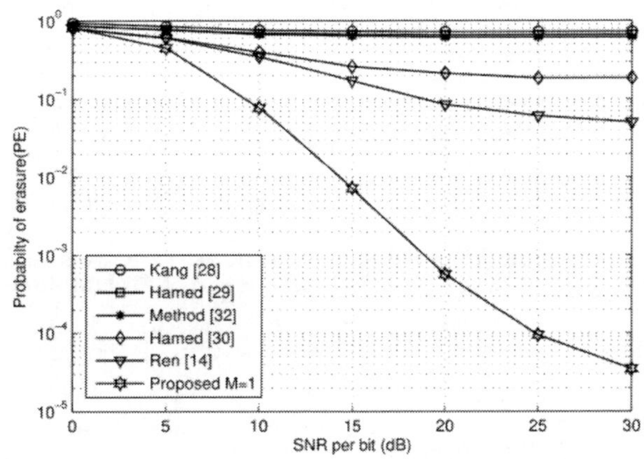

Figure 19. Probability of erasure of different estimators using Ren's preamble in the presence of CFO [M=1, I=32]

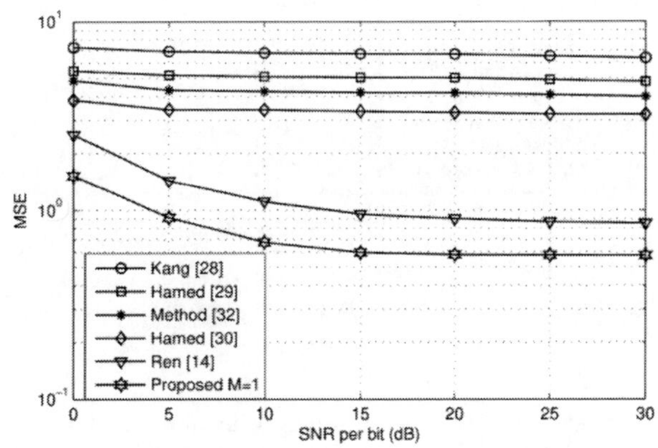

Figure 20. Timing MSE of different estimators using Ren's preamble in the presence of CFO [M=1, I=32]

TABLE I: COMPUTATIONAL COMPLEXITY

Sl. No.	Method	Complex multiplications	Complex additions	Complex divisions	Real multiplications	Real additions	Real divisions
I	Schmidl [5]	$N(N+2)$	$N(N-2)$	N	0	0	0
II	Minn [9]	$N(N+2)$	$N(N-2)$	N	0	0	0
III	Kang [28]	N^2	0	0	$2N^2$	$N(3N-1)$	N
IV	Hamed [29]	$0.5N^2(N-1)$	0	0	$N^2(N-1)$	$(1.5N^2-1.5N-1)N$	N
V	Hamed [30]	$N(N^2-N+1)$	$N(0.5N^2-0.5N-1)$	0	0	$0.5N^2(N-1)$	N
VI	Method [32]	N^2	$N(N-1)$	N	0	0	0
VII	Hamed [31]	$3N^3$	$N(2N^2-2)$	0	0	0	N
VIII	Proposed M=1	$PN(2N+1)$	$N(NP-1)$	0	0	0	0
IX	Proposed M=2	$PN(4N+1)$	$N(2NP-1)$	0	0	0	0

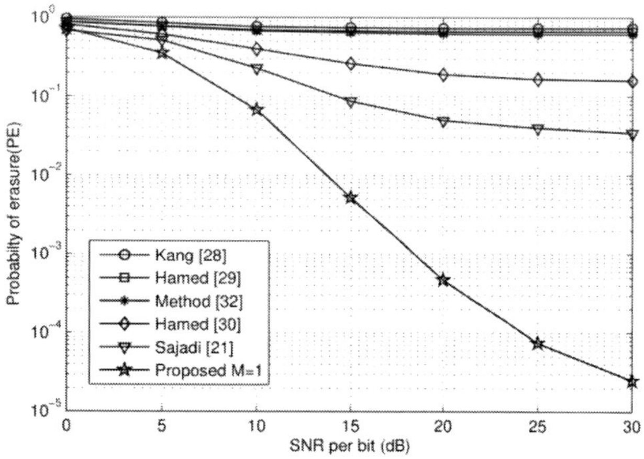

Figure 21. Probability of erasure of different estimators using Sajadi's preamble in the presence of CFO [M=1, I=32]

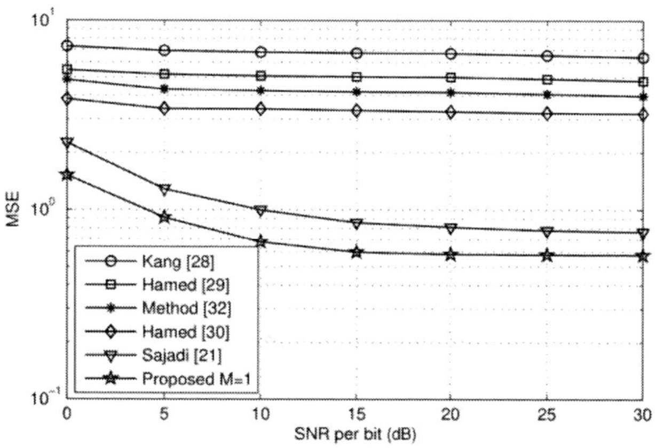

Figure 22. Timing MSE of different estimators using Sajadi's preamble in the presence of CFO [M=1, I=32]

presence of CFO. A new timing estimation method, which is independent of the structure of the preamble, is proposed. A timing estimation method using multiple preambles is also proposed. The performance of the proposed method along with existing methods are investigated in the presence of CFO. Performance is investigated in the presence of different range of CFO. It is observed that the proposed method is robust to CFO. Computational complexity of different estimators are also explained. It is observed that the proposed method performs better than the existing methods in the presence of CFO at the cost of increased computational complexity.

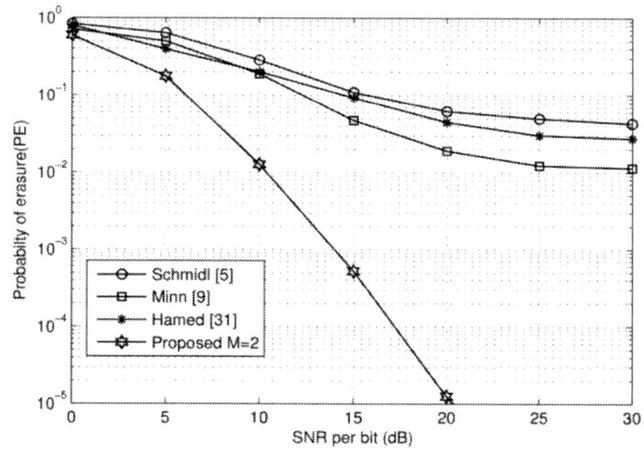

Figure 23. Probability of erasure of proposed estimator using Schmidl's and Minn's preamble in the presence of CFO [M=2, I=32]

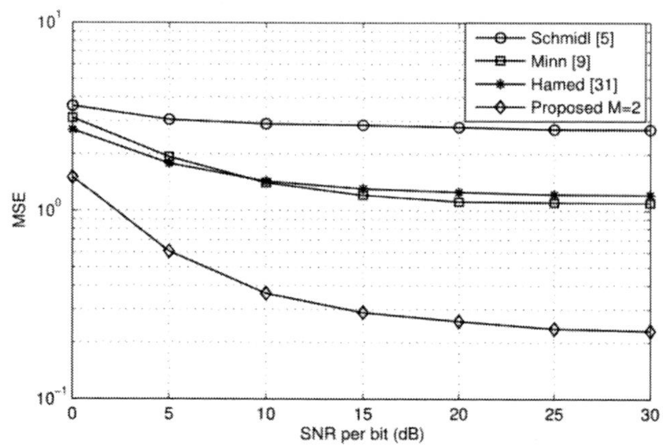

Figure 24. Timing MSE of proposed estimator using Schmidl's and Minn's preamble in the presence of CFO [M=2, I=32]

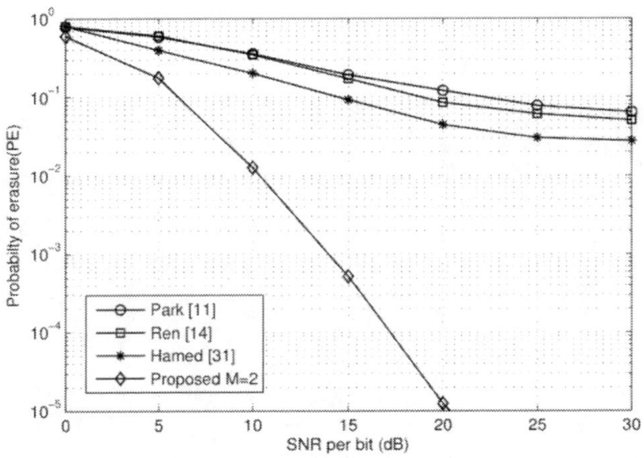

Figure 25. Probability of erasure of proposed estimator using Park's and Ren's preamble in the presence of CFO [M=2, I=32]

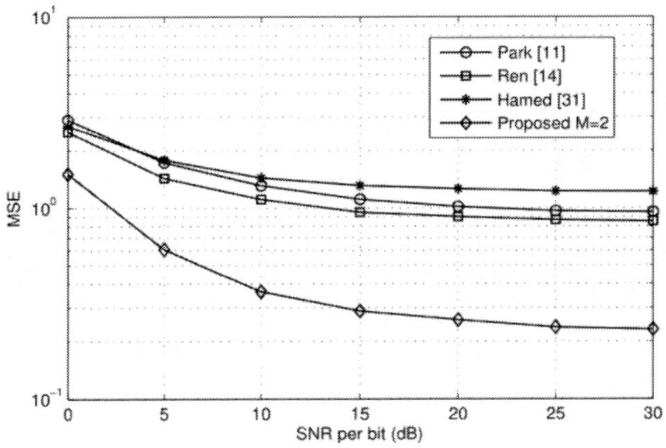

Figure 26. Timing MSE of proposed estimator using Park's and Ren's preamble in the presence of CFO [M=2, I=32]

REFERENCES

[1] S. Bhowmick and K. Vasudevan, "A new coarse timing estimation method for OFDM signals," *The Twelfth International Conference on Wireless and Mobile Communications (ICWMC 2016)*, pp. 80–85, Barcelona, Spain, November, 2016.

[2] K. Vasudevan, "Coherent detection of turbo-coded OFDM signals transmitted through frequency selective rayleigh fading channels with receiver diversity and increased throughput," *Wireless Personal Communications*, vol. 82, no. 3, pp. 1623–1642, 2015.

[3] K. Vasudevan, "Coherent turbo coded MIMO OFDM," *ICWMC 2016*, pp. 91–99, 2016.

[4] K. Vasudevan, *Digital communications and signal processing*. Universities Press, 2007.

[5] T. M. Schmidl and D. C. Cox, "Robust frequency and timing synchronization for OFDM," *IEEE Transactions on Communications*, vol. 45, no. 12, pp. 1613–1621, 1997.

[6] J.-J. Van de Beek, M. Sandell, P. O. Borjesson *et al.*, "Ml estimation of time and frequency offset in OFDM systems," *IEEE Transactions on signal processing*, vol. 45, no. 7, pp. 1800–1805, 1997.

[7] W.-L. Chin, "Ml estimation of timing and frequency offsets using distinctive correlation characteristics of OFDM signals over dispersive fading channels," *IEEE Transactions on Vehicular Technology*, vol. 60, no. 2, pp. 444–456, 2011.

[8] B. Ai, Z.-x. Yang, C.-y. Pan, J.-h. Ge, Y. Wang, and Z. Lu, "On the synchronization techniques for wireless OFDM systems," *IEEE Transactions on Broadcasting*, vol. 52, no. 2, pp. 236–244, 2006.

[9] H. Minn, M. Zeng, and V. K. Bhargava, "On timing offset estimation for OFDM systems," *IEEE Communications Letters*, vol. 4, no. 7, pp. 242–244, 2000.

[10] H. Minn, V. K. Bhargava, and K. B. Letaief, "A robust timing and frequency synchronization for OFDM systems," *IEEE Transactions on Wireless Communications*, vol. 2, no. 4, pp. 822–839, 2003.

[11] B. Park, H. Cheon, C. Kang, and D. Hong, "A novel timing estimation method for OFDM systems," *IEEE Communications Letters*, vol. 7, no. 5, pp. 239–241, 2003.

[12] K. Shi and E. Serpedin, "Coarse frame and carrier synchronization of OFDM systems: a new metric and comparison," *IEEE Transactions on Wireless Communications*, vol. 3, no. 4, pp. 1271–1284, 2004.

[13] J. Kim, J. Noh, and K. Chang, "Robust timing & frequency synchronization techniques for OFDM-FDMA systems," *IEEE Workshop on Signal Processing Systems Design and Implementation*, pp. 716–719, 2005.

[14] G. Ren, Y. Chang, H. Zhang, and H. Zhang, "Synchronization method based on a new constant envelop preamble for OFDM systems," *IEEE Transactions on Broadcasting*, vol. 51, no. 1, pp. 139–143, 2005.

[15] M. Wu and W.-P. Zhu, "A preamble-aided symbol and frequency synchronization scheme for OFDM systems," *IEEE International Symposium on Circuits and Systems*, pp. 2627–2630, 2005.

[16] S. D. Choi, J. M. Choi, and J. H. Lee, "An initial timing offset estimation method for OFDM systems in rayleigh fading channel," *IEEE 64th Vehicular Technology Conference*, pp. 1–5, 2006.

[17] G. Yi, L. Gang, and G. Jianhua, "A novel time and frequency synchronization scheme for OFDM systems," *IEEE Transactions on Consumer Electronics*, vol. 54, no. 2, pp. 321–325, 2008.

[18] A. B. Awoseyila, C. Kasparis, and B. G. Evans, "Improved preamble-aided timing estimation for OFDM systems," *IEEE Communications Letters*, vol. 12, no. 11, pp. 825–827, 2008.

[19] E. Zhou, X. Hou, Z. Zhang, and H. Kayama, "A preamble structure and synchronization method based on central-symmetric sequence for OFDM systems," *IEEE Vehicular Technology Conference*, pp. 1478–1482, 2008.

[20] K. Pushpa, C. N. Kishore, and Y. Yoganandam, "A new technique for frame synchronization of OFDM systems," *Annual IEEE India Conference*, pp. 1–5, 2009.

[21] A. H. Sajadi, H. Bakhshi, M. Manaffar, and M. Naderi, "A new joint time and frequency offset estimation method for OFDM systems," *IEEE International Conference on Wireless Communications & Signal Processing (WCSP)*, pp. 1–4, 2009.

[22] A. B. Awoseyila, C. Kasparis, and B. G. Evans, "Robust time-domain timing and frequency synchronization for OFDM systems," *IEEE Transactions on Consumer Electronics*, vol. 55, no. 2, pp. 391–399, 2009.

[23] H. Wang, L.-j. Zhu, Y.-s. Shi, T. Xing, and Y. Wang, "A novel synchronization algorithm for OFDM systems with weighted cazac sequence," *Journal of Computational Information Systems*, vol. 8, no. 6, pp. 2275–2283, 2012.

[24] Y. Fang, Z. Zhang, and G. Liu, "A novel synchronization algorithm based on cazac sequence for OFDM systems," *IEEE International Conference on Wireless Communications, Networking and Mobile Computing (WiCOM)*, pp. 1–4, 2012.

[25] F. J. Harris, G. J. Dolecek *et al.*, "On preamble design for timing and frequency synchronization of OFDM systems over rayleigh fading channels," *IEEE International Conference on Digital Signal Processing (DSP)*, pp. 1–6, 2013.

[26] H. Abdzadeh-Ziabari and M. G. Shayesteh, "Sufficient statistics, classification, and a novel approach for frame detection in OFDM systems," *IEEE Transactions on vehicular technology*, vol. 62, no. 6, pp. 2481–2495, 2013.

[27] H. Shao, Y. Li, J. Tan, Y. Xu, and G. Liu, "Robust timing and frequency synchronization based on constant amplitude zero autocor-

relation sequence for OFDM systems," *IEEE International Conference on Communication Problem-Solving (ICCP)*, pp. 14–17, 2014.

[28] Y. Kang, S. Kim, D. Ahn, and H. Lee, "Timing estimation for OFDM systems by using a correlation sequence of preamble," *IEEE Transactions on Consumer Electronics*, vol. 54, no. 4, pp. 1600–1608, 2008.

[29] H. Abdzadeh-Ziabari, M. G. Shayesteh, and M. Manaffar, "An improved timing estimation method for OFDM systems," *IEEE Transactions on Consumer Electronics*, vol. 56, no. 4, pp. 2098–2105, 2010.

[30] H. Abdzadeh-Ziabari and M. G. Shayesteh, "Robust timing and frequency synchronization for OFDM systems," *IEEE Transactions on Vehicular Technology*, vol. 60, no. 8, pp. 3646–3656, 2011.

[31] H. Abdzadeh-Ziabari and M. G. Shayesteh, "A novel preamble-based frame timing estimator for OFDM systems," *IEEE Communications Letters*, vol. 16, no. 7, pp. 1121–1124, 2012.

[32] U. Samal and K. Vasudevan, "Preamble-based timing synchronization for OFDM systems," *IEEE 3rd International Advance Computing Conference (IACC)*, pp. 313–318, 2013.

[33] A. Saadat, M. Salman, and H. Saadat, "Matched filter based timing synchronization for orthogonal frequency division multiplexing systems," *IEEE 8th Conference on Industrial Electronics and Applications (ICIEA)*, pp. 1156–1161, 2013.

[34] K. Vasudevan, "Coherent detection of turbo coded OFDM signals transmitted through frequency selective rayleigh fading channels," *IEEE International Conference on Signal Processing, Computing and Control (ISPCC)*, pp. 1–6, 2013.

iaria journals

www.iariajournals.org

International Journal On Advances in Intelligent Systems
issn: 1942-2679

International Journal On Advances in Internet Technology
issn: 1942-2652

International Journal On Advances in Life Sciences
issn: 1942-2660

International Journal On Advances in Networks and Services
issn: 1942-2644

International Journal On Advances in Security
issn: 1942-2636

International Journal On Advances in Software
issn: 1942-2628

International Journal On Advances in Systems and Measurements
issn: 1942-261x

International Journal On Advances in Telecommunications
issn: 1942-2601

International Academy, Research,
and Industry Association (IARIA)
412 Derby Way
Wilmington, DE 19810

ISBN 978-1-5108-5644-8
9 781510 856448

CURRAN ASSOCIATES INC.
proceedings
.com